Be Your Own Financial Adviser

About the author

Jonquil Lowe is a freelance journalist and former head of the
Money Group at *Which?* magazine. She is author of several other
books on personal finance including *The Which? Guide to Pensions*,
The Which? Guide to Giving and Inheriting and *The Which? Guide to
Shares*, all *Which?* books.

Be Your Own Financial Adviser

Jonquil Lowe

CONSUMERS' ASSOCIATION

Which? Books are commissioned and researched by
Consumers' Association and published by
Which? Ltd, 2 Marylebone Road, London NW1 4DF
Email address: books@which.net

Distributed by The Penguin Group:
Penguin Books Ltd, 27 Wrights Lane, London W8 5TZ

First edition March 1996
Reprinted February 1997, September 1997
This edition March 1998

British Library Cataloguing-in-Publication Data
A catalogue record for this book is available from the British Library

ISBN 0 85202 673 0

For a full list of *Which?* books, please write to Which? Books, Castlemead, Gascoyne Way,
Hertford X, SG14 1LH, or access our web site at http://www.which.net

Cover and text design by Kyzen Creative Consultants

Typeset by Saxon Graphics Ltd, Derby
Printed and bound by in Great Britain by Clays Ltd, Bungay, Suffolk

Contents

Addresses, telephone numbers and, where applicable, Internet sites for those organisations marked with an asterisk (*) can be found in the address section starting on page 337.

Introduction

This is a book about financial planning. No, financial plans are not just for the well-heeled or seriously enthusiastic. If you set out to drive from Land's End to John o' Groats, you could pick a lane at random and hope that eventually you get there. More likely, you would get out your road atlas and spend some time planning your route. You might get diverted on the way, but you'd take the maps with you and review your progress, making adjustments to your course as need arose. Managing your finances is very similar. You can take a haphazard approach and hope that, by chance, you'll own your own home one day, have enough to live on in retirement and perhaps even manage to educate the children. Alternatively, you can decide on your aims and plan a route to achieving them. Financial planning makes financial success more likely.

Since the first edition of this book was published in 1996, personal finance has moved into an era of unprecedented change: the regulatory system to protect investors is being replaced; capital taxes that affect the return you may get from many investments are under review; the sword of Damocles hangs over two great favourites, Tax-Exempt Special Savings Accounts (TESSAs) and personal equity plans (PEPs), which are to make way for Individual Savings Accounts (ISAs) from 1999; building society conversions have transformed us into a nation of small shareholders; the Stock Exchange has embraced new technological wizardry with far-reaching consequences for professional and private investors alike; the government's 'stakeholder pensions' wait in the wings; and future provision of long-term care has become the focus of a Royal Commission. Meanwhile, normal life in the financial world goes on, which means constant innovation bringing to market new products, such as flexible mortgages, bank accounts from supermarkets and the comically named 'OEICs'. All of which underlines an important reason for having your own well-thought-out, soundly based financial plan: it gives you the power to cope with change. You can see quickly how you will be affected by alterations to the financial system and you can assess rapidly whether new products have anything to offer you.

However, rather than a trip along the length of Britain, financial planning can seem more akin to a trek across the world. Uncharted territory and numerous pitfalls strew the way, as evidenced by the catalogue of financial scandals in recent years. Thousands of people have been sold endowment mortgages when other options would have served them better; elderly people have faced the loss of their homes through dubious home income schemes; pensioners have seen life savings at risk after investing through the seemingly highly respectable retirement specialist, Knight Williams; miners, nurses and thousands more were persuaded to leave excellent company pension schemes in favour of more costly and less secure personal pension plans; bondholders saw their blue chip investments founder as a single derivatives trader brought about the collapse of Barings Bank; and a regular parade of smaller, less prominent financial advisers have been struck off week by week for breaking the rules of ethical business practice.

In any walk of life, there will inevitably be some rotten apples. No system of regulation can stop a determined fraudster. But the financial services industry seems to have more than fraud to contend with. Too often, investors appear to lose, not because of some elaborate Maxwell-type machination, but because of simple incompetence or, worse still, a blurring of the line between acceptable competitive practice and outright greed. Too often, it seems that financial advisers have not even been aware of having strayed across the boundary until, years later, the rules have been clarified. And the lumbering financial regulators have often been slow in setting the record straight. A staggering six years after the worries arose about pension plans being mis-sold, anxious consumers are still awaiting redress. Pension providers are fined daily for their delays in sorting out the mess but progress remains unbelievably slow. At one stage, financial companies anxious to avoid a bill for putting matters right even took their own regulators (unsuccessfully) to court. This hardly shows a concern for the investor.

This is a black picture of an industry which is trying very hard to re-create its image and show its worth. And there really should be no doubt that financial advice is valuable. Surveys show regularly that people give very high priority to their financial health, find personal finance complex and would like professional help. But the next step is the problem: who can be trusted to provide that help? In reality, there is no lack of good, even excellent, financial advisers, but if you are starting from scratch you may find it something of a lottery: your local financial firms may be good or bad, highly skilled or barely up to the job, ethical or self-interested. This leaves you with three options:

- take a chance and hope you stumble on a good adviser (quite a gamble, this course, because you might not find out whether the adviser was good or bad until many years later)
- do your homework so that you have enough knowledge of your own financial affairs and personal finance generally to make an informed judgement about the quality of advice you are given
- go the whole hog and learn enough about personal finance to be able to handle your own affairs without professional help.

Notwithstanding the title of this book, the last option is realistic for only a minority of people. Personal finance is a large and ever-changing field. Keeping abreast of insurance, mortgages, pensions, investments, tax and other financial matters is feasible only if you have both time and a genuine interest in the subject.

However, the middle option – to learn enough and then to seek help, in essence being your own front-line financial adviser – should be most people's choice. While there is no excuse for an adviser to behave unethically or negligently or incompetently, you make yourself an easy target if you abdicate from your financial responsibility to yourself. Most financial advice is given in private, behind closed doors, in a personal exchange between you and the adviser. Checks and rules try to prevent the worst abuses, but ultimately you are the regulator in the front line. If you can evaluate the advice you are given, you both protect yourself and help to raise standards in the industry as a whole. You also help the good advisers to do their job properly, because financial advice is not about a professional telling you what you should do. It is a partnership between you and the adviser, where you pool your knowledge – on your side, knowledge about yourself, your aspirations and your circumstances, on the adviser's side, a knowledge of the ins and outs of the financial system and its products – to find jointly the best solution to your financial problems.

Your role in this need not be daunting. Many people go some way down the road anyway, reading the weekend financial press, looking at the money articles in *Which?*, glancing at some – at least – of the copious leaflets and brochures which drop through the letterbox. But this is a piecemeal approach which cannot, on its own, help you to make the best decisions. Being your own financial adviser means taking a systematic look at your own resources and circumstances, identifying your financial aims and building a holistic strategy for achieving those aims. Having done that, you will be in a position to relate the multitude of financial products to your personal financial plan. You can then see readily whether an investment, insurance policy or whatever would help you to achieve your particular goals, and you have a framework within which to assess any advice you are being given.

The aim of this book is to show you how to draw up your own financial plan and to form a first view of the financial tools which you can use to make your plan work. If you want to develop your expertise further than this and do without the professionals altogether, this book is a first step on which you can build. The sections on where to get further information should help you to take the subsequent steps.

Chapter 1

Why be your own financial adviser?

A glance at your local telephone directory or high street will tell you quickly that there is no shortage of firms and individuals eager to help you organise your finances. So why should people choose to be their own financial adviser? Since you would not be reading this book if you had not already been tempted to handle your financial affairs yourself, one or more of the following reasons for choosing the d-i-y route has probably occurred to you. Some are good reasons, others less so.

Reason 1: I can't afford financial advice

In fact, most financial advice is, on the face of it, free. What happens is this: most advisers get paid only if they sell you something. Then they get commission from the company whose product you have bought or invested in. The commission is financed out of the payments you make for the product. This means that you *do* pay for the advice really. In fact, payment can be very hefty and, because of the structure of the charges, with most products all customers pay even if they do not all take financial advice. Just a few companies offer products (usually low-charging ones) which do not have commission payments built in. These products are either offered by companies dealing direct with the public and selling on a no-advice basis or aimed at advisers who charge fees instead of relying on commission.

The commission system can lead to problems (see page 13), but does have the advantage that everyone can afford financial advice.

Reason 2: I'm not wealthy enough to have an adviser

However large or small your savings are, you need to invest them wisely. Often, the smaller the amount you have, the more important it is to take the right financial decisions, since you can ill afford to make mistakes. Some financial advisers are willing to give time and attention to even the smallest of clients, but most are not because, if you have only small savings, the most suitable investments for you are likely to be schemes like building society accounts and National Savings. Advisers generally receive little or no commission if they recommend this type of investment. You are also unlikely to take up many of the health and other insurance products which are important sources of income for many advisers.

An adviser who charges you fees, rather than relying on commission income, does not suffer these drawbacks, but the fees charged will often outweigh the benefits of the advice given to a client with only small means.

Reason 3: Financial advisers cannot be trusted

Barlow Clowes, Roger Levitt, Knight Williams, home income plans, pension transfers, endowment mortgages – all are familiar from newspaper headlines and have fuelled the public's general mistrust of financial advisers in recent times. But it would be a mistake to tar all advisers with the same brush: there are many skilled, knowledgeable, conscientious and trustworthy advisers the length and breadth of the UK. The problem is to spot and avoid their less honourable colleagues. Certainly, the more you find out about handling your finances, the less likely you are to fall prey to a fraudulent or incompetent adviser.

Reason 4: It's hard to find a reliable adviser

Outright fraud is thankfully rare but, sadly, there are other ways in which an adviser can let you down. The commission system described on page 11 is a less than ideal way of paying an adviser who is supposed to have your best interests at heart. It means there is a built-in incentive for advisers to recommend:

- products or courses of action which produce a commission rather than those which do not: for example, a personal pension

plan rather than membership of a company pension scheme, or unnecessary switching from one company to another
- products which pay higher commission than others: for example, endowment mortgages rather than repayment mortgages, investment-type life insurance policies rather than personal equity plans (PEPs)
- the product of a company paying higher commission than other companies (this applies only where the adviser is independent; see page 17)
- that you invest more, or buy more insurance cover, than might really be ideal for you.

A good adviser will not be swayed by the lure of commission – not only would it be unethical, but it could be bad business if the adviser wants to build up a base of satisfied customers who will generate a steady stream of further business over the years. Unfortunately, not all advisers fit this mould. *Which?* keeps a check on the standard of advice being offered to consumers. In one such test in December 1995, a third of advisers failed to give best advice to an actor posing as a prospective client (see the box on page 15). In September 1996, a third to a half of advisers gave a poor service to *Which?* recruits seeking help with their real pension problems (see pages 15–16). However, both these tests found that independent financial advisers gave good advice more often than other types of adviser.

To help you guard against commission bias, since 1 January 1995, whenever you ask for details about life-insurance-based investments or pensions, you must automatically be given details about the commission your adviser – if you are using one – will receive. This information must be given to you, in writing, before you sign any proposal or application form. The rules broadly work like this:

- if you use an independent adviser (see page 17), the adviser must tell you the total commission the firm stands to get
- if the adviser is a company representative or tied agent (see page 17), the provider whose product you are interested in must tell you how much the representative or agent stands to get both as a cash commission and including the rough value of any non-cash benefits, assistance and support which the provider gives and which are attributable to the proposed deal.

Information about charges must also be provided and is instantly useful, helping you to compare different companies' products and weeding out those which are overly expensive. Information about commissions is less easy to use. In theory, you can query any recommendations which would seem to earn an adviser an unexpectedly large fee. In practice, few people at present have much of a feel for what would be a reasonable level of commission for a particular contract. But the financial press is tending to publish commission surveys more regularly, so this information is likely to become more useful over time.

You can avoid the problem of possible commission bias alto-

Financial advisers on test

Which? periodically tests financial advice by sending actors, briefed as potential investors, or volunteers with genuine problems, to visit a range of advisers. The advice given is assessed by a panel of experts.

- A researcher posed as a 44-year-old who had just been made redundant and given a £15,000 redundancy cheque. He said he lived alone and had no dependants. He had a repayment mortgage, which cost him around £500 a month, and no savings or investments. However, he had been a member of his employer's pension scheme. He was hopeful of finding a new job soon, but he had no idea how long this would take. He visited 24 financial advisers to find out what he should do with his redundancy money. Best advice would have been for him to keep the £15,000 in bank or building society accounts – he hadn't found a new job, so he needed easy access to his money with no risk to his capital until he could be more certain of his circumstances. Two-thirds of the advisers tested gave this advice. However, three advisers told him to take out a personal equity plan (PEP) with £6,000; the experts thought this tied up too much of his money. Another five advisers recommkgended that the researcher put all or most of his cash into medium- to long-term investments, such as PEPs and investment bonds. This was appalling advice.

Which? December 1995

---

gether if you use an adviser paid by fees. Typically, the products you invest in will still pay the adviser commission (a few do not) but the commission received can be set against the fees, reducing the amount you pay or used to enhance the benefits you get from the products. You can get a list of local independent financial advisers who are paid by fees from the Money Management National Register of Independent Fee-Based Advisers.* Non-investment professionals, such as solicitors, accountants and actuaries, are also fee-based. Fees vary widely. *Which?* suggests you will typically pay £60–£100 for each hour the adviser works on your case, so always check out the charges before choosing a particular adviser.

The results of a second test were as follows:

- Ten volunteers with genuine pension problems visited 34 advisers (16 tied and 18 independent). Half of the advisers did not gather enough information at the first meeting, typically failing to obtain a valuation of earlier pensions or to take account of any state pension entitlement. Only half the advisers managed competently to assess how much pension income the volunteers would need. Two-thirds of tied advisers and a third of the independents did not provide a written report of the interview or follow up with a second meeting, as required by law. In general, advice to employees was sound, but the self-employed volunteers were generally poorly advised. Peter Tyler's experience was typical. Self-employed Peter wanted to top up his pension savings but, owing to health problems, was anxious not to overcommit himself financially. Despite this, the two tied advisers he visited recommended a regular-premium pension plan, and neither of them confirmed in writing their reasons why they thought Peter should take out that sort of plan. Advice from two independent advisers was better. One suggested a series of single-premium plans rather than a regular commitment. The other advised that Peter did not need extra pension savings and should instead invest his money in a personal equity plan (PEP).

Which? September 1996

Reason 5: The need for financial advice is overrated

There is no reason at all why you should not make an excellent job of handling your own financial affairs. But do not make the mistake of assuming that this is a trivial task. Superficially, your finances may seem simple, but you could be unaware of, or underestimate, the importance of certain aspects. If your circumstances genuinely are straightforward and your resources modest, it might not take long to sort out your finances – this time. But financial planning is not a one-off exercise: as your circumstances change, and as the economic and political climate alters, you will need to revise your affairs, which might become more or less complex. If you have substantial wealth or, for example, your family circumstances are complicated, understanding and organising your finances will already be a challenging task. Whatever your situation, proper financial planning requires adequate time, thought and care. If you are unable or disinclined to give the job the attention it demands, you should seriously consider consulting a professional financial adviser instead.

Reason 6: Handling my own finances would be fun

This is the best reason for being your own financial adviser. If you would not find it a satisfying and enjoyable experience, you would do better to concentrate your energies on finding a professional adviser whom you trust.

What you can expect from a financial adviser

Before deciding how far down the d-i-y financial planning road to go, you should have a clear understanding of the services that a professional can offer. You will then be in a position to assess which of those services you can provide for yourself. The factors you will need to look at include the following:

- Do you have the right temperament to undertake those activities for yourself? Financial planning could be stressful, for example, if you find figurework dull, are not reasonably decisive or find it hard to be objective about risks
- Have you, or can you obtain, the skills needed to undertake those activities? This book will introduce you to basic financial planning. You can build on this to develop more sophisticated skills and understanding, if you decide to go further down the d-i-y road

- Do you have access to the information you will need to make investment decisions? For example, living or working near a good reference library with a reasonable range of statistical and business sources, or having access to the Internet, could make all the difference. Throughout this book, we indicate what source materials are useful and where you can obtain them
- Can you successfully complete those activities within an acceptable time-scale? This does not simply mean having enough spare time *per se*. You should also consider whether d-i-y financial planning is an enjoyable way for you to spend your leisure hours, given that it may mean cutting back on other activities.

Types of financial adviser

Since the implementation of the Financial Services Act 1986, there are just two types of advisers who deal with the public giving advice about investments, such as insurance savings plans, pensions and unit trusts:

- **independent** An independent financial adviser (IFA)★ can recommend to you products from the whole range of companies on the market. In practice, this does not necessarily mean that the advisers check out every company every time you want to invest. Instead, they can conduct regular surveys and identify the best few companies for certain types of customers and situations
- **company representative or tied agent** This type of adviser can advise on and sell the products of only one company.

The position is less clear-cut with financial products which do not count as investments: for example, term insurance and many types of health insurance. Company representatives sell only their own company's products, but other advisers might be looking at the whole market or acting as agents for a handful of companies.

What an investment adviser must do

With the Financial Services Act have come weighty rule books imposing numerous duties and obligations on financial advisers, but two rules are paramount. Whether independent or tied, advisers must:

- **'know their customer'**, that is, find out all relevant information about the customer's circumstances and objectives

- **give 'best advice'**, that is, give advice or sell products that are suitable for the client.

As far as knowing the customer goes, an adviser is initially at a disadvantage to you. You know your circumstances intimately and you are in the best position to identify your financial aims. However, you could fail to recognise aims which you should be weaving into your financial structure, unless you take a dispassionate and systematic look at your finances. Chapter 2 will help you to do this.

When it comes to giving best advice, be aware that there is seldom any one solution which is definitely 'the best'. Usually, there is a range of options of broadly equal merit. Even so, recognising those options as the suitable ones for you does require:

- a good knowledge of the financial system
- a good knowledge of the broad financial tools available
- an understanding of how these tools can be matched to your financial situation
- good information about the specific products on the market.

Chapters 4–17 will introduce you to tools, techniques and information sources, but a knowledgeable, experienced and well-equipped financial adviser will inevitably be able to undertake the task more easily than you.

To sum up, good financial advice is the successful marrying of financial tools to personal details. At one extreme, you can simply hand your personal details to an adviser and leave him or her to do the rest. But, besides being rash, this is unlikely to be the preferred option with a good adviser, who (unless offering a discretionary service) really will see his or her role as one of advising and helping *you* to reach decisions rather than taking decisions on your behalf. At the other extreme, you can take on the role of finding the financial tools by becoming, in effect, your own adviser.

There is a halfway house which has a lot to recommend itself. You can learn the broad principles of financial planning and block in your own 'financial skeleton' before you seek advice. Your adviser and you will then be able to work together efficiently in partnership to choose the appropriate financial cladding. This will save both of you time – and save you money, if you are using a fee-based adviser. You will also be well armed to spot rogue advisers or careless advice.

In practice, you are likely to find that, some of the time, your own counsel is adequate. But in new or complex areas, such as pension planning or inheritance tax, it is well worth supplementing your own research with the opinion of advisers. In some provinces of financial planning, you should be especially wary of doing without professional advice: for example, if you have a farm or run your own business, are involved in family trusts or have investments abroad. Bear in mind that the more specialist your financial affairs are, the more specialist the advice you will require. Check carefully to ensure that the advisers you select have the expertise you need.

Commission refunds

Many advisers are willing to forgo part of their commission in order to attract your custom. The amount forgone – called the 'commission refund' – can be paid to you as a cash rebate or be used to increase the amount invested in the product you are buying or enhance in some other way the benefits you'll get from the product. Some advisers specialise in discount business and offer commission refunds as standard. With others, it's a matter for negotiation.

Do not be shy to ask about commission refunds. Nowadays most providers offer a 'commission menu' so that the adviser has a choice between, say, a high commission or a lower one coupled with enhanced benefits for the client. There is often also a choice about the extent to which commission is paid 'upfront' (called 'initial commission') or spread over part or all of the lifetime of the policy (called 'renewal commission'). Moreover, the market for financial advice is very competitive, and you have a lot of consumer power – so use it. Just as haggling over the discount on a new car or the price of a jacket in your local market square is perfectly acceptable, so is negotiating a commission refund. You should consider this course especially if you think that the commission the adviser stands to receive looks higher than the norm – though, in that case, you should be alert to the possibility that the advice might have been biased by the high commission and might not be the most suitable for you.

To negotiate a refund, follow these steps:

- ask what commission the adviser stands to get if you invest in or buy the recommended product
- decide whether you would prefer to have a cash rebate or enhanced product terms
- if you have seen the commission payable on similar products and know this commission looks high, or if you know the deal which

a discount business could get for you, use this information as a basis for deciding on the rough amount of commission refund you are seeking

- ask what rebate the adviser is willing to consider or what enhanced terms he or she can get for you
- be prepared to haggle
- if you cannot get the commission refund you think is reasonable, be prepared to take your custom elsewhere.

How much commission?

Now that commissions have to be disclosed, many changes are being made to the way advisers are paid: for example, spreading commission over a longer period instead of concentrating on lump sums at the time a plan or policy is first arranged. This means there is no 'typical' amount of commission, but here are a few examples as reported in a leading trade journal:

Type of product	Commission rate	Example
Personal pension plan	Up to 8% initial (reduced on a one-for-one basis to enhance investor's deal), and optional 0.5% of the fund each year met by increased charges to you	If you invested £5,000, normally 95% of your investment – i.e. £4,750 – (for simplicity, ignoring other charges) would be 'allocated' to your plan and the adviser would receive £400. If the adviser gave up 2% commission, he would receive £300 and your allocation would rise to 97% – i.e. £4,850
Unit trust personal equity plan (PEP)	3% initial plus 0.5% (of fund) renewal or 4.2% initial	If you invest £5,000 over the year, the adviser gets £150 immediately plus additional commission for each year you keep the investment, or £210 upfront with no further payments
Low-cost private medical insurance plan	25% of the first annual premium plus 5% renewal	If your premium is £26 a month, the adviser receives £78 in the first year and £15.60 each year in which you renew your plan

Chapter 2

Your financial skeleton

It is very easy to respond to *ad hoc* needs and opportunities as they arise without thinking about how they contribute to your overall financial situation: for example, buying newly issued shares on a whim, or finding yourself unexpectedly shelling out for school fees. Such impulsive decisions might turn out to be good ones, but, equally, with hindsight they might look like white elephants or could prove to be unnecessarily heavy burdens. The key to financial planning is to have a comprehensive overview of your circumstances, your needs, your wants and the priority which you attach to each of your financial objectives. This gives a framework, or a skeleton, on which to base your decisions.

To draw out your skeleton, you need to work through the following stages:

- identify and prioritise your financial targets
- assess what resources you have available to commit towards meeting those targets
- if necessary, revise your targets in the light of available resources
- consider the personal factors which will influence how you meet your targets.

This will give you a strong, coherent structure on which to build. You can then go on to identify the appropriate financial tools for meeting your targets, given your priorities, resources and personal factors. The final step – deciding which particular companies' products to choose – is perhaps the hardest for the d-i-y financial planner. You need to keep a close eye on the various financial markets, being aware of new product launches, changes to existing products, special promotions, and the impact of external events, such as changes in the law or economic crises, on the various types of product. Unless you have a lot of time and a very keen interest in financial affairs, it will usually make sense to seek professional advice to help you choose the specific insurances and investments you need.

Finally, be aware that your financial skeleton and the choice of products to meet your needs should be reviewed regularly. Certain events in life – such as marriage, separation or divorce, having children, promotion at work, receiving an inheritance, being made redundant, reaching retirement – clearly signal that it is time for a review. Even apart from these events, there are changes over time to the economic and social climate and to the opportunities available, so it makes sense to review your financial skeleton every year or so. The review is also a time to assess how well on track you are for your longer-term objectives and to decide whether you need to make any adjustments, such as increasing the amount you are saving.

The whole process of drawing up your financial skeleton and fitting a financial plan around it is summarised in the chart opposite.

Identifying and prioritising your targets

Just as the body's skeleton grows and alters as you grow up, so your financial skeleton should adapt to the changing phases of your life. To some extent, these phases vary from person to person, but it is possible to map out a typical sequence – see the chart on page 24. You personally might not pass through all these phases, but some will certainly apply.

Each phase is characterised by a different set of opportunities and demands which will tend to determine the financial priorities you choose. Possible priorities are outlined in the descriptions that follow. These are not set in stone, and what is right for one person may be quite wrong for another. Their aim is to set you thinking about your own phase of life and your own financial aims.

To the targets dictated by the life phase you need to add your own personal hopes and ambitions: for example, maybe you want to retire when you are 50, in which case pension planning will need to be a much higher priority in the early phases of life than shown in the outlines below; or you might want to take a year off work to sail around the world, which would probably influence your savings targets.

How to build your financial plan

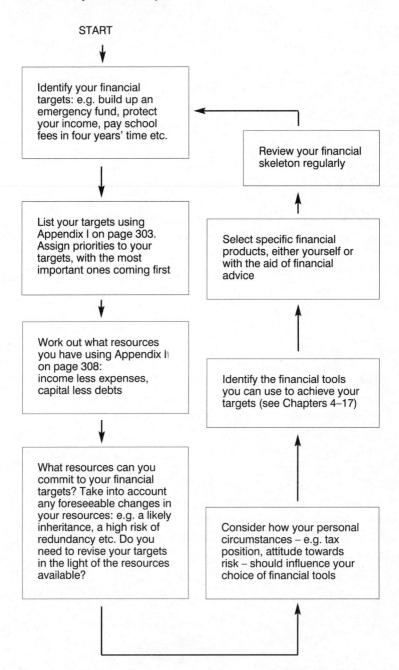

START

Identify your financial targets: e.g. build up an emergency fund, protect your income, pay school fees in four years' time etc.

Review your financial skeleton regularly

List your targets using Appendix I on page 303. Assign priorities to your targets, with the most important ones coming first

Select specific financial products, either yourself or with the aid of financial advice

Work out what resources you have using Appendix I\ on page 308: income less expenses, capital less debts

Identify the financial tools you can use to achieve your targets (see Chapters 4–17)

What resources can you commit to your financial targets? Take into account any foreseeable changes in your resources: e.g. a likely inheritance, a high risk of redundancy etc. Do you need to revise your targets in the light of the resources available?

Consider how your personal circumstances – e.g. tax position, attitude towards risk – should influence your choice of financial tools

Typical phases of life

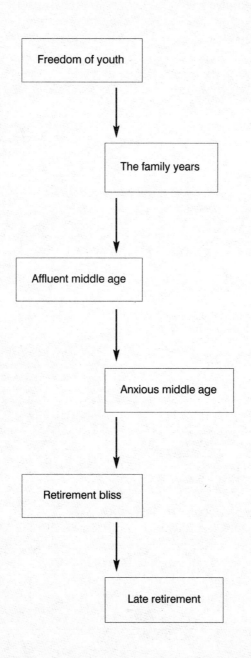

Your objectives and the way you prioritise them should reflect not just what you would *like* to achieve financially, but also what you *need* to do given your family commitments, what the state provides, and so on. For example, though you might prefer not to dwell on the risks of life, if you have dependants you should consider how they would cope if you were no longer there. Similarly, it is very easy to ignore pension planning until it is too late to build up the level of income you would ideally like to enjoy when you retire.

You might be surprised to see that throughout many of the life phases described below, protecting your income should you fall ill is given higher priority than life insurance. Yet this is perfectly logical, given that you are roughly 15 times more likely to be off work sick for a prolonged period than you are to die during your working years.

Typical phases of life

Freedom of youth

This is the early phase of life, when you cease to rely on your parents and, all being well, start to earn your own living. Typically, no one is dependent on you, and your main priority is having a roof over your head. Quite possibly, rented accommodation fits in with your desire for mobility. Other commitments are likely to be few, but might include, say, paying off loans taken out during student days. The net result is likely to be a surplus of income over necessary expenditure. The temptation of youth is probably to spend the excess, but there are some bones you can build into your skeleton even now. In a realistic order of priority, these are:

- emergency fund to draw on if you face unexpected expenses
- protecting your income in the event of your falling ill
- pension planning: it takes a lot of investment to build up an adequate pension, so the earlier you start the better
- short-term saving, for example for a car, holidays, and so on
- medium- to long-term non-pension saving for eventual house purchase plus other, non-specific reasons.

The family years

At some stage, most people find a partner whom they either live with or marry. This immediately creates a changed situation. Even if your partner is financially independent, you are likely to develop some joint commitments. These may be major items, such as sharing the costs of buying and running a home. In this case, you have to consider what would be the financial impact on your partner if, say, you fell ill or died, and similarly what the impact on you would be if your partner were affected by such events. For those with children, the shared commitments are even more demanding and complex, requiring financial forethought and planning. Children are likely to exert greater pressures on your resources than will occur at any other stage of your life. If you or your partner stop or cut back your work in order to care for the children, these resources will be further depleted.

In this situation, it is essential to decide what your financial priorities are. They are likely to take on this sort of shape:

- emergency fund
- protecting your own and your partner's income in the event of illness, at least to the extent that joint expenses would be covered
- life insurance on your own and your partner's life
- borrowing to buy a home
- planning for education, for example school fees if you opt for private-sector schooling, or the cost of maintaining your child(ren) at university
- pension planning: ideally, this should have higher priority but this might not be possible if funds are tight
- short-term saving for family events, for example presents, holidays, and so on
- medium- to long-term saving, if you have surplus funds.

Many couples separate or divorce, and, if children are involved, the financial pressures can become particularly severe. Often the same overall resources must be stretched to finance two households, extra childcare costs, solicitors' bills, and so on. Although money may be tighter, the overall needs and priorities associated with the family years are likely to be much the same as shown above. In particular, bear in mind that if you are relying on maintenance from a former husband or wife for part of your income, you probably still have a need for life insurance which would pay out if he or she were to die.

Affluent middle age

When eventually the financial demands of a family subside, you may enter a phase of relative wealth. This would be a good time to anticipate future events. But if you choose simply to concentrate on the present, increased spending and personal ambitions are likely to dominate your priorities after basic needs have been met. Typically, your priorities might look like this:

- emergency fund
- protecting income against illness
- life insurance if you have a partner or other dependants
- fun targets – more holidays, hobbies, a second home, and so on
- pension planning
- other saving.

Anxious middle age

Unfortunately, the relaxed feeling of early middle age tends to give way as you enter the late forties and fifties. Realisation grows that retirement is just around the corner, and perhaps you should be doing more to prepare for it. Pension planning should now move up your priorities and, for the first time, your thoughts might turn to the health problems of old age. At this phase of life, you might also find elderly parents becoming more dependent on you, though, equally, your resources might be boosted through inheritance.

The following profile of priorities is possible:

- emergency fund
- protecting income against illness
- life insurance if you have a partner or other dependants
- pension planning
- long-term care planning, if you are not confident of continuing state provision
- serious investment.

Retirement bliss

By the time retirement arrives, your earlier planning should be bearing fruit. With luck, this should be another relaxed phase of life. But it pays to have a weather eye on the future, making sure that your income will be sustained as retirement progresses and that you will be able to cope with increased costs due to health problems. At retirement, you are likely to receive a lump sum which you may want, at least partly, to invest rather than spend.

Priorities could be:

- emergency fund
- continuing income if you or your partner were to die
- replacing perks that went with your job, for example a car, medical insurance, and spending on capital items expected to see you through retirement
- fun targets, for example increased travel, new hobbies, indulging grandchildren
- investment for income either now or later on
- long-term care planning, if you are not confident that the state will provide
- inheritance planning – taking steps to reduce a potential inheritance tax bill at death.

Late retirement

The last phase of life. Your priorities now depend very much on how well your earlier financial planning succeeded. For some, a shortage of income might be the top concern; for others, how to pass on their assets. Very loosely, then, priorities might be:

- emergency fund
- continuing income if you or your partner were to die
- investing for income/boosting income
- inheritance planning.

The impact of other factors on your targets

As well as responding to your life phase and personal ambitions, you will also have needs that arise because of the risk of outside shocks upsetting your financial plans. These shocks range from near-certain events, such as changes in interest rates and periodic changes to the tax system, to others that might not come to pass at all, such as being made redundant. Whether or not you respond to the threat of these shocks depends on how likely you think they are to happen to you and the severity of the impact they would have. You can gather statistics about the probability of certain events happening – how likely you are to have a fatal heart attack at age 40, how likely you are to be off work sick, how likely you are to live to a hundred, and so on. These may help to frame your perception, but different people will come to a different conclusion about the risks they think they personally face, coloured by their own temperament (optimistic or not) and circumstances (for example, a family history of illness). Likewise, the impact of a shock on your finances will vary from person to person depending on the resources you have, the expenses you have, how important it is to you to protect a particular lifestyle, and so on.

Changes in government policy can have a big impact on how you perceive risks. For example, a reduction in support for mortgage payments in the event of having to claim income support has prompted more people to consider taking out insurance to cover their mortgage payments in case of unemployment. Presumably, they do not think it is more likely that they will face unemployment, but the damage unemployment could cause to their finances is now expected to be greater. Similarly, debate on whether the health service can continue to provide free (at the point of use) treatment for all indefinitely does not increase your likelihood of falling ill. However, it might encourage you to take out insurance to pay for private treatment, because you perceive a potentially worse impact on your finances if you were to need treatment.

Your perception of the risks posed by outside shocks will tend to vary according to the general economic climate. For example, in a recession people tend to save more because they perceive a higher risk of becoming unemployed and want the means to keep going financially if their main income is lost. Inflation can have a complex influence on financial planning – in the early stages, people often save more to cope with rising prices but, if inflation persists, they may save less as they become aware that the value of their savings is being eroded.

All in all, the way you arrive at your list of financial targets and the priority you give to each one is a subtle and complex process. Although some targets should be built into everyone's financial skeleton, there can be no single rule which universally applies. In Appendix I on page 303 is a checklist prompting you to clarify your own targets and priorities – this is the essential first step in financial planning.

Assessing your resources

If you had unlimited resources, you could meet all your financial objectives without problem and would have little need for financial planning. For most of us, life is not so straightforward. Usually, it is impossible to achieve instantly all we would wish, hard choices have to be made and targets have to be approached step by step.

The second stage in your planning has to be a frank assessment of what resources you have, what claims there are on them, to what extent resources are already being used to meet your targets and what surplus (if any) is available to further your plans. Appendix II on page 308 contains Resources Calculators to guide you through this process.

It is important that you are as accurate as possible when filling in these Calculators. If you have doubts about any entries, check back to any relevant documents, such as pay slips, mortgage statements, bills and so on.

Once you have completed this stage, you should have a reasonably clear idea of what resources – both assets and money set aside out of income – are currently available for meeting your targets. You are also invited to consider how your resources might change in the foreseeable future, since this could influence your choice of financial tools, for example borrowing (that is, committing future resources to current spending), insurances with the option to increase payments later on, and so on.

Revising your targets

At this point, you might come to the conclusion that your targets are too ambitious in the light of the resources you have available. Something will have to give. You have several choices:

- boost your resources: for example by taking on extra work to increase your income
- alter one or more targets: for example if you had pencilled in a tour of India for next year, defer the trip for a year or two; if you had planned to retire at 55, consider retiring at 60 instead
- abandon one or more targets at least temporarily. If you have prioritised the targets realistically, the ones you abandon should be those to which you have given the lowest priority.

Alternatively, you might find that you have more resources than you had anticipated. This opens the way to increasing the scale of one or more targets, accelerating the time-scale over which you plan to meet the targets or adding further targets to your plan. Once again, if you have allocated your priorities correctly, any new targets should be added after existing targets and would be the first to go if resources became tighter.

As you can see from the chart on page 32, your financial targets are like a ladder, with your most fundamental priorities at the base and less important objectives on the higher rungs. The more resources you have, the higher up the ladder you can climb. A temporary fall in resources would mean retreating down the ladder a little; a windfall inheritance or unexpected pay rise would let you climb a bit higher.

Personal factors

In practice, measuring up your targets against available resources can be done only in a broad-brush fashion, if you have not thought about what financial tools could be used. After all, you need to know how quickly an investment might grow, or how much it might cost to buy a particular type of insurance. But there is another important stage to go through before you can pick the tools: you need to consider the personal factors that will tend to make some financial tools more appropriate than others for you. There are four key factors: tax, your attitude towards risk, your time-scale for investment and your state of health.

A ladder of targets

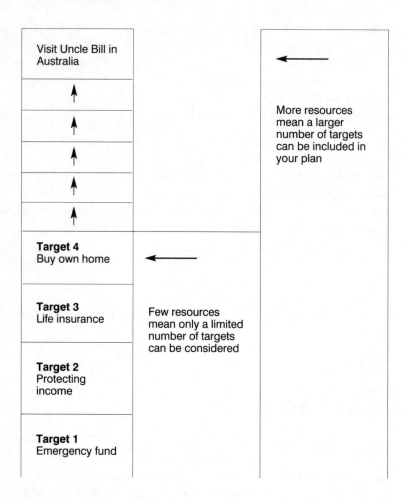

Your tax position

Three main taxes will influence your financial planning: income tax, capital gains tax and inheritance tax.

Income tax is charged on most types of income, including earnings, profits, interest and dividends from most investments, pensions, and so on. It is charged at one of three rates – the lower, basic and higher rates. In the 1997–8 tax year, these are 20 per cent on the first £4,100 of income, 23 per cent on the next £22,000 and 40 per cent on anything over £26,100. However, you do not pay tax on all your income because:

- some types of income are specifically tax-free, for example the return from National Savings certificates and, until 1999, dividends on shares held in a personal equity plan
- you are allowed to deduct certain expenses from your income before tax is worked out, for example donations to charity under a Give-As-You-Earn scheme, amounts you pay into a pension scheme or plan
- you get allowances which let you have your first slice of income either tax-free or only partially taxed.

The main tax allowances for 1997–8 are shown in the table on page 35. The personal allowance is deducted from your income before tax is worked out and so gives you tax relief up to your top rate of tax. The married person's allowance (and other allowances related to it) gives you tax relief at just 15 per cent and is given as a deduction in the tax you would otherwise pay.

You get higher personal and married allowances from the start of the tax year in which you reach age 65, but the extra amount is progressively lost if your income is more than a given amount (£15,600 in 1997–8). You lose £1 of allowance for each £2 by which your income exceeds the threshold, making an effective tax rate of 34.5 per cent. You carry on losing the extra allowance until your allowances have been reduced to the standard levels which apply to people under 65.

Tip

If your income is in the region where you risk losing the extra age allowance (see the table on page 35), be very wary of increasing the taxable income you get: for example, by cashing in a single-premium life insurance bond (see page 263). Avoid the problem by choosing investments which give a tax-free return.

Capital gains tax (CGT) is charged on profits you make from selling or disposing of assets, such as investments, second homes, antiques, and so on. At the time of writing, the government was reviewing the way this tax works, but in 1997–8 the regime is as follows. Chargeable gains are added to your taxable income for a given tax year and CGT is levied at the same rates as income tax would be, if the total were all income. Many capital gains escape tax though, because:

- gains on some assets are tax-free: for example, your main home, British Government stocks
- some transactions are tax-free: for example, gifts of assets to your husband or wife
- expenses associated with buying and selling the asset can be deducted before tax is worked out
- gains due purely to inflation are not taxed
- the first slice of otherwise taxable gains each year (£6,500 in 1997–8) is tax-free
- losses on other assets can usually be deducted.

It is essential that you consider the impact of tax on your financial planning, especially when looking at various types of investment. The way in which the proceeds are taxed will have a big impact on the return you get and will heavily influence your choice of investments. Throughout Chapters 4–17, your attention is drawn to the tax treatment of the various financial tools, and guidance is given on how this should influence your planning. For a more detailed discussion of tax, see *Which? Way to Save Tax*, published by Which? Books.★

Inheritance tax may be due on what you leave when you die and occasionally on gifts you make during your lifetime. Chapter 17 provides a brief introduction to inheritance tax planning, given the tax regime as it stands in 1997–8, but this tax is also the subject of a government review under way at the time of writing. For more information about this aspect of financial planning, see *The Which? Guide to Giving and Inheriting*, published by Which? Books.★

Income and capital gains taxes are administered by the Inland Revenue,★ which produces a wide range of explanatory pamphlets, some of which are referred to in this book. You can obtain all the pamphlets through local tax enquiry centres or your own tax office. Inheritance tax is the province of the Inland Revenue Capital Taxes Office.★ The tax system is reviewed each year by the government in the Budget. The Budget speech – which used to be made in November but has reverted to March from 1998 onwards – is broadcast on television and radio, and changes are widely reported in those media and in the press. Make sure you keep abreast of the changes and understand how they might influence your financial plans.

Your attitude towards risk

Everyone's temperament is different. Some people give high priority to security and predictability. Others are relaxed with, or even crave, a high degree of uncertainty. The degree of uncertainty – or risk – with which you are comfortable will shape your financial planning and the financial tools you select, especially in relation to saving and investing.

Main income tax allowances in 1997–8

	Allow-ance	Saves you up to this much tax if you are a:		
		lower-rate taxpayer	basic-rate taxpayer	higher-rate taxpayer
Personal allowances				
Under 65	£4,045	£809	£930.35	£1,618
Age 65–74	£5,220	£1,044	£1,200.60	£1,618*
75 and over	£5,400	£1,080	£1,242	£1,618*
Married couple's allowance				
Under 65	£1,830	£274.50	£274.50	£274.50
Age 65–74	£3,185	£477.75	£477.75	£274.50*
75 and over	£3,225	£483.75	£483.75	£274.50*

Income bands in which extra age allowances are being lost

Single: age 65–74	£15,600–£17,590
Single: age 75 and over	£15,600–£18,310
Married: age 65–74	£15,600–£20,660 (£15,600–£20,740 if your spouse is aged 75 or over)
Married: age 75 and over	£15,600–£21,100

* Income too high to qualify for the age-related addition

Your attitude towards risk is not simply a reflection of temperament. It depends also on such factors as:

- **your income**: if you have little cash to spare, you might quite rightly be reluctant to take risks with it; the more 'surplus' income you have, the more adventurous you might be financially
- **your age**: in later years, especially after retirement, it may be difficult or impossible to replace any money you lose, which will tend to make you cautious; when you are young and earning, you can usually make good your losses
- **your responsibilities**: if, for example, you have a young family dependent on you, it might be unacceptable to risk their financial security; with only yourself to consider, the consequences of a gamble going wrong may not seem as important.

Throughout this book, we highlight the areas where risk is a key element in your choice of financial tools and suggest ways in which you can attempt to match risk to your own attitude.

Your time-scale for investment

This factor is in many cases intrinsic to your financial targets. For example, if you are saving for a holiday or to pay for a wedding, you generally have a set date in mind by which you need the proceeds of your investment. Some financial tools are completely inappropriate for such financial targets, either because they tie up your money for too long a period or because their capital value fluctuates and you could not be sure of getting back the amount you need at a precise point in time. On the other hand, some financial aims are either long term or open-ended and give you scope to choose from a much wider range of investments.

Your health

Health is a factor you need to consider when you take out many types of insurance and when you buy some types of annuity (a form of investment which is basically an educated gamble on how long you will live). Poor health can push up the cost of many insurances or even bar you from having them and should make you think twice about lifetime annuities. The chapters that follow discuss the health factor wherever appropriate.

Chapter 3

You and the financial system

Advice about financial products and how they are sold are still causes for concern today, but matters were far worse before the implementation of the Financial Services Act 1986. For the first time, the Act set in place a cohesive structure for the regulation of investment businesses. However, regulation under the 1986 Act has been heavily criticised both by the industry which has to operate within its scope and by consumers who are the intended beneficiaries. Financial firms argue that regulation is costly and overly burdensome. Consumers are bewildered by the array of different regulators and the delays in sorting out financial scandals, such as the mis-selling of pensions. As a result, financial regulation in the UK is, at the time of writing, embarking on a metamorphosis from which a new 'super-regulator' is to emerge. Below, the regulatory system is set out as it was operating in 1997 and was set to continue until 1999, and an outline is given of the new approach which is then due to take over.

How investments are regulated in 1997

The scope of regulation

The scope of the Financial Services Act is currently limited to investments. This means that quite a range of financial products are not covered, including deposits, most term insurance (see Chapter 4), some types of health insurance (see Chapter 5) and mortgages (apart from any investment element linked to them; see Chapter 8), and no equivalent legislation covers these products. You should also realise that you will not enjoy the full protection of the Financial Services Act in all situations, in particular if you opt not to receive advice before entering into a transaction.

The existing regulators

The Financial Services Act 1986 put into place a system of self-regulation within a tight statutory framework. Although a government department, the Treasury, is ultimately responsible for policing the investment industry, it delegated the bulk of this task to the Securities and Investments Board (SIB), which on 28 October 1997 was renamed the Financial Services Authority (FSA)★ in preparation for the advent of the new regulatory regime.

Initially, the FSA has taken over the existing duties of SIB. It lays down the broad rules, but most of the day-to-day regulation is handled by a series of Self-Regulating Organisations (SROs)★ which specialise in particular areas of investment business. The main advantage of this type of system is supposed to be that the regulators are close to the industry, often being practitioners themselves, and so have a good understanding of the practices they are trying to control.

It is illegal for an investment business to operate unless it is authorised by either the FSA or one of the three SROs – the Personal Investment Authority (PIA),★ the Securities and Futures Authority (SFA)★ or the Investment Managers Regulatory Organisation (IMRO).★ In addition, some non-investment businesses nevertheless advise on or arrange investments as a corollary to their mainstream business: for example, solicitors and accountants. They are allowed to carry on the investment side of their business, provided that they belong to one of the Recognised Professional Bodies (RPBs)★ responsible for regulating both their mainstream and investment business. The nine RPBs are the three Institutes of Chartered Accountants★ (for England and Wales, Scotland and Northern Ireland), the three Law Societies,★ the Institute of Actuaries,★ the Insurance Brokers Registration Council★ and the Association of Chartered Certified Accountants.★

The system of investment regulation has evolved since its introduction in April 1988. The chart on page 40 shows the structure which was in place in late 1997.

What the regulators do

The regulators have three main functions:

- **acting as licensing authorities** An investment business must belong to one of the regulators – this is called being authorised. The regulators operate a system of 'positive licensing', meaning that businesses must meet certain standards before being granted authorisation
- **ensuring high standards within the investment industry** Within the framework established by the FSA, each SRO has drawn up an extensive system of rules governing the way investment businesses carry on their business. The rules cover, for example, minimum levels of training and competence, advertising, the information to be given to clients and prospective customers, safeguards for clients' money and investments, how complaints should be handled, and so on. The regulators also put in place measures to help them to keep a check on whether rules are being kept and standards maintained, for example requiring reports from member firms and carrying out both regular and spot checks on their businesses
- **dealing with problems** This involves having a complaints procedure for deciding what has happened in a dispute, a system for ensuring that investors who have been unfairly treated are compensated, and a system for taking disciplinary action against members who break the rules. Such action could range from warnings and fines right through to expulsion from the SRO or RPB, in which case the firm could no longer legally carry on with its investment business.

Protection in practice

At a practical level, the rules translate into a variety of specific ways in which you are protected when you do business with an investment firm. If you are buying stocks and shares or other investments through a stockbroker, the rules of the SFA will protect you. With most other investments you buy – life insurance, personal pension plans, unit trusts, and so on – you will usually be protected by the rules of the PIA (but occasionally those of IMRO or the FSA). In your dealings with advisers and salesmen, the rules protect you in the following ways:

Who are the regulators?

The Treasury
Government department responsible
for investment regulation

↓

The Financial Services Authority (FSA)
(formerly the Securities and Investments
Board (SIB))
The main regulator with overall responsibility
for standards

Recognised Professional Bodies (RPBs)
Bodies responsible for actuaries, lawyers,
accountants and insurance brokers

Self-Regulating Organisations (SROs)

Personal Investment Authority (PIA)	**Securities and Futures Authority (SFA)**	**Investment Managers Regulatory Organisation (IMRO)**
Covers most investments and packaged products sold to the public	Covers stock market investments, such as shares and options	Covers the management of investment funds

- people who advise on and sell investments must pass examinations ensuring that they have reached a minimum level of competence
- at the start of your dealings the adviser or salesperson must make clear to you his or her status and the nature of the business – for example, whether he (or she) is totally independent or tied to

just one company (see page 17) and what types of business he or she is authorised to carry out

- you must be given a 'terms of business' letter before any chargeable work is carried out for you. This sets out, for example, how the adviser will be paid (by commissions or fee) and whether the firm is allowed to handle your money (rather than your paying the product providers direct)
- if advisers or salespeople 'cold call' you out of the blue, they must make clear that they are hoping to sell you something (formerly, they may have pretended to be doing market research), they must check that you are happy to talk to them and they must end the interview if you request it
- in most cases, the adviser or salesperson dealing with you must comply with the 'know your customer' rule. This means finding out the details about your personal and financial circumstances, without which it would not be possible to give sound advice. Often this is done by filling in a systematic questionnaire called a 'fact-find'. The fact-find or its equivalent must provide the framework for the advice you are given. If you do not want to give all the details, the adviser or salesperson will confirm this in writing
- the adviser or salesperson must give 'best advice'. This means he or she is required to recommend only products which are suitable for you, given the details from the fact-find. An independent adviser must select the most suitable providers as well. If there are no suitable products in the range which an adviser or salesperson can sell you, he or she should say so and can, with your agreement, pass you on to another adviser or salesperson who can help. You do not have to follow the advice given, but if the adviser or salesperson thinks that the course of action you choose is not suitable, he or she must inform you in writing to this effect
- depending on the types of product you are looking at, there are detailed rules setting out the information you must be given (see page 46). Any projections of possible future returns must be based on standard assumptions about growth rates but, in the case of life insurance and pensions, taking account of the provider's own charges
- with some products, once you have agreed to buy or invest, there is usually a cancellation period during which you have the right

to change your mind. This is particularly useful if you have made a hasty decision as a result of a cold call

- after you have made your investment or bought a product, but no later than the date you are sent the cancellation notice, you must be sent a 'reason why' letter in which the adviser sets out his or her reasons for the particular advice given and recommendations made
- if you feel you have not been fairly treated, you can follow the complaints procedures (see page 50)
- if you lose financially because of the dishonesty or negligence of an investment business, you can claim redress from it. If the business has gone bust, the Investors Compensation Scheme (ICS)★ might step in and refund at least part of your loss.

When you are not protected

If you have developed a good understanding of personal finance, you might simply want to buy products either direct from the provider or through an adviser without going to the trouble of contributing to a fact-find and receiving advice. Doing so is perfectly feasible. It is called 'execution-only' business – in other words, the adviser or salesperson simply executes your orders without any comment or advice. However, you should be wary of buying in this way, because you give up some of the protection of the Financial Services Act:

- the 'know your customer' and 'best advice' rules do not apply. This makes it far less likely that you would be able to get compensation if things went wrong
- there is usually no cancellation period.

Some companies sell products only on an execution-only basis, for example Marks & Spencer and a number of discount stockbrokers. By cutting out advisers and middlemen, these businesses can often offer attractive low-cost deals. But you must be very clear that you are buying on a no-advice basis: there is no point grumbling later that you have been landed with an unsuitable investment or that the timing of your deal was wrong. By dealing on an execution-only basis, you are taking on full responsibility for your action. The provider will give you *information* about the product, but do not confuse that with advice. The regulators are currently worried that investors might misunderstand the nature of their dealings with direct companies and, in future, extra rules might possibly be introduced at least to ensure that very clear warnings are given.

By the way, don't assume that execution-only services are always telephone-based. This is not so – you can be an execution-only customer whether you are dealing with an adviser face to face or on the phone. Similarly, not all telephone-only services are execution-only; it is perfectly feasible for firms to conduct the fact-finds over the phone.

If you buy or invest in response to a mailshot, a prospectus for newly issued shares or through an application form included in a printed advertisement, the protection you get is restricted in much the same way as when dealing on an execution-only basis.

You should also be wary of being classified as an experienced investor. If you ask to be treated as experienced and the adviser has reasonable grounds for assuming that you have enough understanding and experience to make your own decisions and you have been notified in writing that you are being treated in this way, you will lose much of the protection under the Financial Services Act. However experienced you are, it may still be wiser to hear the advice and keep the protection.

How investments are to be regulated from 1999

The scope of regulation

Over the last decade, financial firms have changed. Banks no longer simply offer accounts and insurance companies don't sell just insurance. The distinction between different types of firm has blurred as they have moved into new areas, becoming conglomerates offering a one-stop shop for a wide range of financial products and services. It was becoming increasingly difficult for regulators who traditionally focused on particular business areas – for example, banking, building societies, insurance companies, investment funds, and so on – effectively to oversee the areas of activity relevant to them without some knowledge of operations in other parts of the firm. Therefore, under the new regulatory system, one regulator will be responsible for the vast majority of financial products and services (see below). However, at the time of writing it was not clear whether products such as mortgages and long-term care insurance would be brought within the scope of the new system.

The new regulator

At the time of writing, the FSA is simply the SIB renamed, but very rapidly the FSA is due to be transformed into the 'super-regulator'. It will take over the powers of nine existing regulators who will then cease to operate. These are: the Building Societies Commission,* Friendly Societies Commission,* Insurance Directorate of the Department of Trade and Industry,* SIB, the three SROs* (PIA, IMRO and SFA), Registrar of Friendly Societies* and the Supervision and Surveillance Division of the Bank of England.* The FSA will also take over the regulatory responsibilities for investment business currently delegated to the RPBs.* The handover of powers will take place in several stages:

- **October 1997** to **spring 1998** SIB replaced, appointment of FSA officials, consultation on key issues, organising staff etc.
- **'N1'** The date on which the FSA takes over from the Bank of England the regulation of banks
- **spring 1998 to autumn 1999** Co-ordinating supervision of firms across all SROs, co-ordinating systems, draft legislation for a new Financial Services Act circulated for consultation
- **'N2'** Date on which the new regime becomes fully operational. The FSA will have its full complement of powers, new complaints handling and compensation arrangements will come into force.

Although the FSA will be fully operational only from 'N2' – some time in late 1999 – the SROs will start to co-ordinate the way in which they regulate their members from spring 1998 onwards. However, until 1999 it is expected that you, the customer, will continue to deal with the individual SROs, as now.

What the regulator will do

The functions of the new single regulator will, in general terms, be the same as those of the individual regulators it replaces, though the emphasis will be on the regulatory functions rather than on different areas of investment business. For example, instead of having one regime for building societies and another for unit trusts, the FSA will try to identify the common ground in regulating all types of investment business and set up a regime which is – as far as possible – applicable across the board. Five regulatory functions have been identified:

- **policy formation and review** This will include analysis of new products and market developments and the early identification of possible hazards
- **authorisation of firms and vetting and registration of individuals** Authorisation will be centralised, so firms and individuals go through the same process whatever the area of business in which they operate. It is expected that all firms which are currently authorised will automatically count as authorised by the new regulator, but the FSA will have the power to require a firm or group of firms to reapply for authorisation
- **investigations, enforcement and discipline** A single unit will carry out the investigation, enforcement and disciplinary work across the board
- **relations with consumers and the public** This encompasses handling enquiries and complaints. A new single point of enquiry – the FSA Enquiry Unit* – has already been established. For a time it will run alongside the enquiry services of the individual SROs but eventually the FSA unit will be the single point of access – a welcome simplification for consumers. It is expected that there will be some consolidation of ombudsman schemes and other complaints mechanisms, but at the time of writing it was not known what form this would take or whether a single body would either be considered or even feasible
- **supervision, both prudential and conduct of business** Experts in different areas will monitor different types of business, but they will be co-ordinated by a 'lead supervisor' for each authorised firm. The lead supervisor will therefore be in a position to see and evaluate the pan-organisation structures of the firm: for example, its business strategy, the soundness of its management, its systems and controls, available resources, and so on. In the case of some large and complex organisations, a whole team gathering together a range of expertise might be assigned to a particular firm.

The FSA's published aims stress that a balance must be struck between the costs of regulation and the benefits it brings. They also state that the FSA will 'acknowledge consumers' responsibility for their own decisions, while aiming to ensure that they are not exposed to risks that they should not reasonably be expected to assume'. And there is emphasis elsewhere on the need to promote consumer education. Only as the new regime takes shape will the division of responsibility between consumers and advisers and how it is to be enforced become clear.

Protection in practice

At the time of writing, only the outline of the new system had been decided. Many months of consultation and drafting of rules lay ahead. Shifting to a single regulator should simplify regulation from the consumer's point of view, especially in areas such as making complaints and seeking compensation. In the latter case, the FSA has said that a single scheme will be adopted to replace the current mêlée of the Investors Compensation Scheme★ for some investments, Deposit Protection Scheme★ for deposit accounts, and so on.

It seems likely that the bulk of rules concerning information for investors, protection from bad sales practice, and so on – as set out earlier in this chapter – will continue largely unchanged. Instead, the focus seems more to be on improving the efficiency with which regulation is carried out.

Information about investments

Before you decide to buy an investment, such as a life insurance plan or pension, you must be given, in addition to the glossy brochure, certain information about the policy or plan in a particular form laid down in the PIA rules. This ensures that you have the information you need to make a sound and reasoned decision about whether or not to invest. The main documents you will get are described below.

Key features document

This document must be given to you before you decide to invest in a life insurance or pension product and must also be printed in 'off-the-page' advertisements – that is, ones that invite you to invest in response to the advertisement. The key features include:

- the nature of the policy or plan, including its aims, what commitment is required on your part (for example, regular monthly saving for a given period) and the risks inherent in the policy or plan
- an illustration of the return you could get based on growth rate(s) laid down by the PIA, the company's own charges and, in the case of life insurance and pensions, your own particular circumstances regarding age, sex, the amount of life cover you want, the premium you want to pay, and so on
- various statements, stressing that the illustration is only an example, broadly how it has been calculated and a warning that inflation will affect the values given in the illustration. (An illustration for a pension plan which replaces part of your state pension – see Chapter 10 – will give you figures in terms of today's money, in other words after adjustment for inflation, but other illustrations make no reduction for the effect of inflation and can look a lot more generous than they will in fact turn out to be)
- a description of the main terms of the policy or plan set out in a question-and-answer format
- tables showing the amount you could get back if you stopped the policy or plan within any of the first five years, each subsequent fifth or tenth year (depending on the type of contract) and the last year (or age 75 if it is a whole-of-life insurance), showing what charges would be deducted from the policy or plan and explaining why they would be made
- illustrations of what you might get back in the final five years of the policy. The idea behind this is to show the importance of the terminal bonus payable on with-profits investments (see page 242)
- a statement that over the lifetime of the policy the effect of charges is to reduce the rate of growth of your investment and the extent of this reduction: for example, charges might reduce expected growth from, say, 10 per cent a year to 8.5 per cent, meaning the first 1.5 per cent a year growth is needed simply to cover charges
- a warning if a plan or policy cannot be surrendered early; also a warning that, where you can surrender the policy early, you may get back less than you have paid into it in premiums or commission
- the amount of commission which will be paid to an adviser if you use one.

With-profits guide

If you are considering a policy or plan invested on a with-profits basis (see page 242), you can request this free guide, which tells you something about the insurer and its philosophy in setting the bonuses that make up the return on this form of investment. The information given in the guide includes:

- whether the insurer has shareholders (who will want to be paid dividends) or is a 'mutual' organisation, that is, owned by its pol-icyholders
- the main types of business which will generate the with-profits returns
- the factors which influence the level of bonuses – how the with-profits fund is invested, giving the proportion invested in gilts, property, shares, and so on over the last five years, the effect of inflation and tax, and the expenses of the fund
- the 'solvency margin' of the insurer. This is basically the degree to which the insurer has assets to meet its liabilities. This is important because it helps you to form a view about whether current bonus levels can be sustained in the future. But the basis on which this is defined can vary and it is not an easy figure for investors to get to grips with. If you do use a financial adviser, it is worth asking how he or she interprets the figures
- a description of how recent bonus levels have been set and what policy there is for ensuring that investors are treated fairly compared with one another even though they will have invested at different times, for different periods and some will surrender their policies or plans early
- brief details of the expenses which were set against the with-profits fund in the preceding year (but bear in mind that these vary from year to year)
- examples of how actual expenses reduce the investment return on various types of policy and plan
- examples of the returns you would have got from the provider's various with-profits policies if they had just come to an end.

Illustrations

The illustrations included in the key features documents and advertisements, or supplied in addition, must be based on set assumptions. The most important are:

- **charges** In the past, standardised charges were used. This was ridiculous because every insurer would produce identical illustrations for the same product even if one insurer's charges were really a lot higher than another's. Thankfully, this situation has changed and insurers must now base assumptions on their actual charging level. A company with high charges now looks less attractive than a company with low charges if you compare their projections. This does not mean that a high-charging policy is necessarily a bad investment, but you should certainly be questioning the grounds for selecting such a policy. It will have to have better-than-average performance to overcome the handicap of higher charges, so you want to know: how much better will performance have to be and what reasons are there for believing that performance really will be that good?
- **rates of return on your investment** Standardised rates must be used. They are currently 5 per cent a year and 10 per cent a year for most types of policy or plan, but 6 per cent and 12 per cent for tax-free business, such as pension plans, PEPs and friendly society 'baby bonds'.

Non-investment products

When you buy or invest in financial products which do not fall into the definition of 'investment', the protection of the Financial Services Act does not apply. This can be very confusing. For example, you might be taking out a mortgage (not covered by the Act) linked to an endowment insurance (covered by the Act). Although the firm you deal with will have to be authorised to sell you the endowment policy, the investment regulators do not control any aspect of the mortgage side of the deal.

There are no laws directly equivalent to the Financial Services Act to ensure that you are well advised when you take up non-investment products. Some protection exists, however, in the case of non-investment insurance products. The Association of British Insurers (ABI)★ has a code of selling practice which its members (insurance companies) require the advisers and salespeople they deal with to follow. But the code is voluntary and has no real teeth. If you go to an adviser who is a registered insurance broker (only insurance intermediaries who are registered can use the title 'broker'), he or she will be obliged to comply with a code of conduct laid down by the Insurance Brokers Registration Council.★ Breach of the code could result in the broker losing registration, but the code is by no means as strictly monitored as the Financial Services Act regulations.

Deposits – such as bank and building society accounts – are not classed as investments and so fall outside the scope of the Financial Services Act. The solvency of banks is regulated by the Bank of England★ and building societies by the Building Societies Commission,★ but there are no stringent controls on the way banks or societies market and sell their non-investment products and services. During 1997, the Council of Mortgage Lenders★ set up a code for its members selling mortgages, but whether this code will have any real teeth remains be to seen.

What to do if things go wrong

If you are not happy with the service from, or conduct of, a financial firm, you should first complain to the firm or the branch of it with which you were dealing. If you are not happy with the response, take your complaint higher within the firm, for example to the managing director or head office. If you still do not receive a satisfactory response, the company is obliged to tell you how to take your complaint further. The table opposite sets out the relevant complaints schemes. If you are still unsure about which complaints body to contact, the FSA Enquiries Unit★ can put you in the right direction.

If right from the start you are concerned that the firm acted dishonestly or has broken the rules in some other way, you should report the firm to the appropriate regulator – again, see the table opposite.

Where it is established that you have lost money because of the actions of the firm, the complaints scheme may be able to direct

Whom to complain to

Type of financial firm/investment involved	Complaints body once firm's internal procedure exhausted	Can you go to court if unhappy with complaints body's verdict?	Where to report rule breaches
Unauthorised firm selling investments	Not applicable: don't do business with the firm	Not applicable: don't do business with the firm	Police or Financial Services Authority (FSA)
Independent financial adviser	PIA Ombudsman	Yes	Personal Investment Authority (PIA) or FSA
Life insurance company or unit trust	PIA Ombudsman	Yes	PIA or FSA, or possibly the Investment Managers Regulatory Organisation (IMRO)
Stockbroker	SFA Complaints Bureau and Arbitration Scheme	No	Securities and Futures Authority (SFA) or FSA
Bank or building society selling investments	PIA Ombudsman	Yes	FSA or PIA, or possibly IMRO
Bank non-investment products, e.g. deposits, mortgages	Banking Ombudsman	Yes	Bank of England
Building society non-investment products, e.g. accounts, mortgages	Building Societies Ombudsman	Yes	Building Societies Commission
Insurance company non-investment-type insurance	Insurance Ombudsman, or PIA Ombudsman if company has voluntarily agreed to this	Yes	Department of Trade and Industry
Personal pensions	Usually PIA Ombudsman. Could be Occupational Pensions Advisory Service/Pensions Ombudsman	Yes	PIA, FSA or IMRO
Any investment	FSA Enquiries Unit can 'signpost' you to the correct body		

that the firm pays you compensation. Alternatively, you can usually take the firm to court and sue for damages – but this is a costly and protracted course of action. Many financial firms are required to have professional indemnity insurance, which might ultimately provide the compensation. The problem comes when the firm has gone out of business and does not have enough assets or insurance to pay compensation. With an investment business, the Investors Compensation Scheme★ will normally step in. It can compensate you fully for the first £30,000 of your loss and for 90 per cent of the next £20,000 lost, that is, total compensation of £48,000.

If the dispute involved an insurance contract or personal pension plan and the provider goes out of business, you may qualify for compensation under the Policyholders' Protection Act, which can pay out compensation for up to 90 per cent of your loss without any cash limit. Compensation is, however, restricted to *reasonable* losses, which means that any excessive bonuses or returns which failed to materialise are not normally counted as part of the loss.

In cases involving bank deposits, the Deposit Protection Scheme★ kicks in and can make awards of up to 90 per cent of the first £20,000 you have deposited (that is, £18,000 in total). Similarly, if building society deposits are involved, a building society compensation scheme provides the same level of protection. But where banks and building societies are selling you investment products which come under the Financial Services Act, the Investors Compensation Scheme★ would apply. If the products are those of a bank's or building society's life insurance subsidiary, the Policyholders' Protection Act might cover you.

Self-defence

Follow these ten steps to ensure that you get the best out of a financial adviser:

1. For investment advice, go only to authorised advisers. Check that an adviser is authorised by consulting the FSA Register.★ Make sure that the individual or subsidiary you deal with actually is part of the authorised firm and is not some other related business which is not itself authorised. Visit at least two advisers.

2. Know your adviser. Is the adviser tied or independent? If tied, are you especially interested in the products of that company, or do you particularly value the convenience, say, of using that provider? Consider getting advice from an independent adviser who can look at the full range of companies' products.

3. How can the adviser help you? Is the adviser authorised for the type of investment business you are interested in? Does the adviser have expertise in the financial areas you need help with? If independent, how does the adviser keep track of the available products? Nowadays, you should be wary of advisers who do not have access to regularly updated computerised systems (but don't assume that you will be guaranteed good advice just because an adviser has a computer).

4. Think twice before buying investments on an execution-only basis or off-the-page or being classified as an experienced investor – you lose some of the protection of the Financial Services Act.

5. Be prepared. Be clear about your financial objectives and the priority you attach to them – see Chapter 2. To comply with the 'know your customer' rule, an adviser or salesperson must find out a lot about you. Make sure you have the information to hand, for example in the form of the checklist in Appendix I (see page 303).

6. Be informed. Know what literature to expect, read it all – even the dreaded small print. Ask questions if there are gaps in your knowledge. Under the new system of regulation, it is likely that you will be expected to take greater responsibility for your investment decisions, so it will be all the more important to make sure that you understand the nature of the products you are choosing and how they can meet your financial aims.

7. Be sceptical. If a deal sounds too good to be true, then it is probably suspect. High returns always go hand in hand with high risk. Don't take terms like 'free' and 'guaranteed' at face value – check exactly what is on offer. And always remember that any guarantee is only as good as the company making it. Query the appropriateness of a deal if the adviser stands to get an unexpectedly large commission.

8. Never be pressurised into making a deal on the spot. Take your time and make sure that the product on offer fits in with your

financial plans. Discounts and special offers are poor compensation for bad, hasty decisions.

9. Most independent advisers are not authorised to handle their clients' money. If this applies in the case of your adviser, never hand money over to the adviser or middleman. Instead, make payments to the company or companies you are investing in or buying from. Even if the adviser is authorised to handle your money, there is nothing wrong in insisting that you make your payments direct to the provider. If the adviser holds investments on behalf of clients, check exactly what safeguards there are to protect the clients. If you are not happy with them, insist on holding your own investments.

10. Always get, and keep in a safe place, receipts, documents, records of interviews and telephone conversations, and so on. If anything does go wrong, it is essential that you have this information.

Chapter 4

Protecting your family

Your top priority if you have dependants is to ensure that they are protected financially if you were to die or be unable to work for a prolonged period. Chapter 5 looks at replacing income when you are ill. This chapter concentrates on the role that life insurance can play in your financial plan.

The chart on page 56 summarises who needs life cover. Bear in mind that not only the loss of a breadwinner's salary could cause financial hardship: if you are caring for children, your spouse or partner might need to pay for professional childcare and/or babysitters if you were to die. Similarly, you should take into account any extra costs of running the house, maintaining the garden, and so on. A government survey found that, nationwide, housework – which even today is still done mainly by women – takes up more hours each day than paid work. If all the cooking, cleaning, childcare, gardening, and so on had to be paid for at the market rates for each activity, they would be worth some £340 billion – about half of the whole national income.

Having identified that you need some life insurance, the next step is to work out how much. You might require a lump sum, for example to pay off the mortgage, as well as replacement income, which could be provided either by income-paying life insurance (known as family income benefit) or by insurance which pays out a lump sum which you could invest to produce the required income. This is discussed further on page 66. To find out the basic cash and income your family would need in the event of your death, work through the Calculator. If you are married or live with a partner, you should each work through the Calculator separately. The notes following the Calculator will help you to fill it in.

Who needs life insurance?

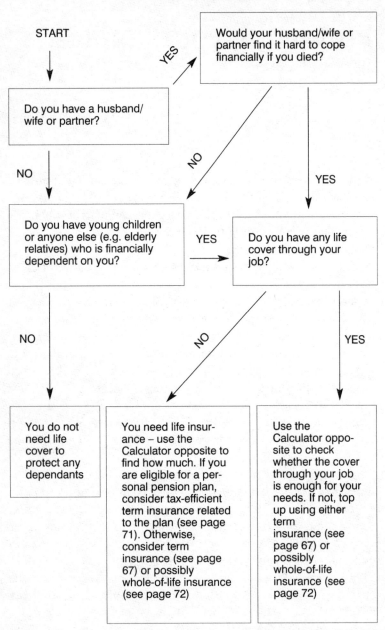

Life insurance Calculator

Part 1: Cash required and cash available		£
Funeral expenses	a	
Emergency fund to cover household expenses for, say, two months	b	
Repayment of mortgage	c	
Repayment of other loans	d	
Inheritance tax	e	
Bequests in will to people other than dependants	f	
Other lump-sum expenses	g	
TOTAL CASH NEEDED =a+b+c+d+e+f+g	A	
Payout from existing insurance to cover mortgage	h	
Lump-sum payout from any other existing insurance policies	i	
Savings and investments which would be cashed in	j	
Capital raised from sale of assets	k	
Widow's payment from state	l	
Other lump sums available	m	
TOTAL CASH AVAILABLE = h+i+j+k+l+m	B	
NET LUMP SUM NEEDED = B − A	C	

Part 2: Change in income and expenses	£/month

I: Reduction in income

Your earnings after tax and other deductions	n
Your pension	o
Your state benefits	p
Your spouse/partner's earnings if he or she had to give up work or work fewer hours	q
Income from investments which would be sold	r
Other income lost	s
TOTAL REDUCTION IN INCOME $=n+o+p+q+r+s$	D

II: Increase in income

Widow's allowance or pension from the state	t
Other state benefits	u
Other pensions	v
Income from any existing life insurance policies	w
Earnings if your spouse/partner would start work or work longer hours	x
Other	y
TOTAL INCREASE IN INCOME $= t+u+v+w+x+y$	E

III: Reduction in expenses

Mortgage and other loan repayments	z
Living expenses	aa
Life insurance premiums and pension contributions	bb
Other	cc
TOTAL REDUCTION IN EXPENSES $= z+aa+bb+cc$	F

	£/month
IV: Increase in expenses	
Cost of childcare	dd
Cost of home help/odd-job person/gardener etc.	ee
Cost of replacing fringe benefits of job, e.g. running a car, private medical insurance premiums	ff
Other	gg
TOTAL INCREASE IN EXPENSES = dd+ee+ff+gg	G

Part 3: Amount of cover required	£
Extra monthly income needed = D+G+E+F	H
Extra income needed each year = H × 12	I
Lump-sum insurance needed to produce income I (see the table on page 67)	J
TOTAL LUMP-SUM INSURANCE REQUIRED = C+J	K

Part 1: Cash required and cash available

Funeral expenses (a)

Death is a costly affair. Among other items, there could be funeral director's fees to pay, including the cost of a coffin and hearse, minister's fees, charges for crematorium and/or burial plot, gravediggers' fees, flowers, and so on. Marking a grave with a headstone is another optional but expensive item to consider. Even the smallest of funerals will swallow at least £1,000 and your survivors could easily spend a lot more. During your lifetime, you can pay either a lump sum or regular savings over, say, five years for a pre-paid funeral plan (see page 75) which guarantees to cover the cost of your chosen funeral. If you have such a plan, amount 'a' will be zero.

Emergency fund (b)

In the event of death, there is likely to be a period of confusion and coming to terms with the new situation. Your family is likely to need a financial breathing space in which to sort out long-term money affairs. There might also be delays in distributing your possessions and turning them into cash if necessary. An emergency fund will tide your dependants over during this period. It need not be provided by life insurance. It could, for example, be money which you have in a joint account with your spouse or partner. Since there could be a delay before a life insurance policy pays out, it is a good idea to have at least part of the emergency fund in an instantly available form (see Chapter 16).

Repayment of mortgage (c)

If you have a mortgage, you are likely also to have some life cover which will automatically pay off the mortgage in the event of your death (see Chapter 8). In this case, any value you put under 'c' will be balanced by the same amount under 'h' below. With a repayment mortgage (which is not necessarily sold in a package with insurance), you might not have matching life cover. At one time, some advisers suggested that you take out only enough insurance to pay off the excess of the mortgage over £30,000 (the ceiling for tax relief on mortgage interest), provided that your dependants could manage the repayments on this remaining amount of loan. This strategy ensured that you did not lose out on any tax relief. But nowadays the tax relief is so low (see page 116) that your dependants would probably prefer to do without it in exchange for the reassurance that their home is completely their own.

Repayment of other loans (d)

This covers things like the debt outstanding on your credit card(s). If you have taken out credit insurance to pay off, for example, a bank or car loan in the event of death, then the amount of loans covered by insurance will be balanced by an identical amount under 'i' below. (Note that credit insurance linked to loans does not necessarily pay the loan in the event of death; it might be limited to meeting the repayments if you are unable to work because of illness or redundancy. Check the policy to see what is covered.)

Inheritance tax (e)

Chapter 17 considers whether there is likely to be any inheritance tax to pay on your estate (your assets less your debts) when you die.

If your estate is worth less than £215,000 (in 1997–8) or you leave everything to your husband or wife, there will be no tax to pay.

Bequests to people other than dependants (f)

Your will, or the rules of intestacy if you did not make a will, may require some of your assets to be given away. See Chapter 17 for more information.

Other lump-sum expenses (g)

These might include, for example, buying a car to replace a company car which you had through your job (but not the expenses of running it – see 'ff').

Payout from existing insurance to cover mortgage (h)

This could be an endowment policy to repay an endowment mortgage or a mortgage protection policy to pay off a repayment mortgage. See Chapter 8.

Lump-sum payout from any other existing insurance policies (i)

This would include insurance taken out with a loan other than a mortgage. It would also include any other life insurance which you already have either through your work (see page 159) or policies you have taken out yourself.

Savings and investments which could be cashed in (j)

These could range from cash in a bank account to a portfolio of shares. If the investment had been producing an income, the effect of cashing it in will have to be taken into account at 'r' below.

Capital raised from the sale of other assets (k)

This could be the sale of valuable possessions, such as a car, boat, jewellery, and so on. You might consider trading down to a smaller home and so releasing some capital, but bear in mind that there could be a long delay before you manage to sell.

Widow's payment from the state (l)

This is a tax-free lump sum payment of £1,000 payable if you are under age 60 at the time you are widowed or, if older, your husband was not entitled to the basic state retirement pension. Your husband must have paid enough National Insurance contributions – otherwise you don't qualify.

Other lump sums (m)

If your income and capital are very low, you might qualify for an emergency payment from the Social Fund. Other possible sources of help are gifts or loans from relatives.

Part 2: Change in income and expenses

Your earnings after tax and other deductions (n)

This is the amount of take-home pay which your household would lose if you are employed. You should enter your monthly pay after deducting income tax, National Insurance, contributions to an employer's pension scheme and any other deductions. For a self-employed person, it is the amount of money which you draw out of your business for personal use.

Your pension (o)

Put here the amount of any pensions which would cease to be paid if you were to die. This could be state pension, pension from an employer's scheme or from a personal plan. If your spouse or other dependants would receive another pension, for example a widow's pension, enter this at 't' or 'v' below.

Your state benefits (p)

If you receive any state benefits, for example unemployment benefit/jobseeker's allowance or incapacity benefit, enter here the amount which would be lost. If your spouse or other dependants would receive other benefits instead, enter these at 'u' below.

Your spouse's/partner's earnings (q)

You are most likely to enter an amount here if you have children. Would your spouse or partner have to cut back on or stop work to look after them?

Income from investments which would be sold (r)

If you entered an amount under 'j' above, then put here any income which would be lost as a result.

Other income lost (s)

This might include, say, maintenance payments from a former spouse.

Widow's allowance or pension from the state (t)

If you have paid sufficient National Insurance contributions, your widow will qualify for widowed mother's allowance if she is caring for children (up to £62.45 a week plus extra for each child in 1997–8) or widow's pension if she is aged at least 45 at the time you die. In 1997–8 the full widow's pension ranges from £18.74 a week to £62.45 a week, depending on age. The chart on page 65 specifies those benefits for which your widow might qualify. There is no equivalent allowance or pension for a widower or unmarried partner.

Other state benefits (u)

If your spouse or partner would be left on a very low income, he or she might qualify for income support, housing benefit and various other means-tested benefits.

Single parents (including widows and widowers) used to be able to claim additional child benefit for their eldest child – formerly this addition was a separate benefit called one-parent benefit. From April 1998 the addition is no longer available to new claimants, though people already receiving the extra continue to do so.

Other pensions (v)

Enter here pensions your widow(er), partner and/or children would receive from employers' pension schemes which you belong to or personal pension plans you have. If these schemes or plans would pay out a lump sum, include it under 'i' or 'm' above.

Income from any existing life insurance policies (w)

If you already have life insurance which would pay out a regular income (that is, a family income benefit policy), record the monthly payout here.

Your spouse's/partner's earnings (x)

Would your spouse or partner take up a job, increase their hours or take up higher-paid work? Enter the likely increase.

Other (y)

Include here any other increases in income, such as rent from letting out a room in the family home. Enter the amount accordingly.

Mortgage and other loan repayments (z)

If the mortgage and/or other loans would be repaid ('c' and 'd' above), your family would no longer have to make repayments. Record the amount saved here.

Living expenses (aa)

There is likely to be some reduction in food bills, travelling expenses, entertainment, and so on. Enter the amount accordingly.

Life insurance premiums and pension contributions (bb)

If you are paying for life insurance or into a pension plan, these amounts would be saved. Don't include deductions from your pay, for example for 'superannuation', as these are already accounted for under 'n'.

Other (cc)

Any other reductions in expenses, for example maintenance payments which no longer have to be paid to a former spouse.

Help from the state for widows

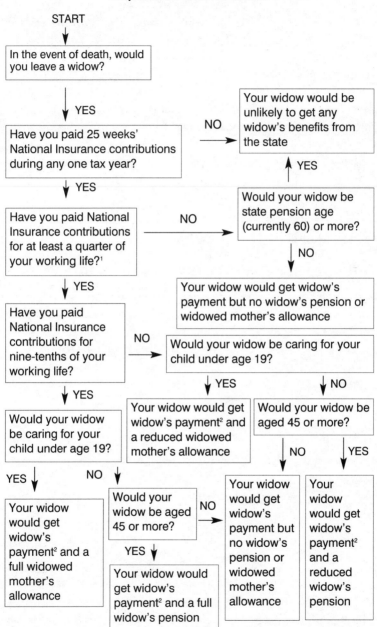

START

In the event of death, would you leave a widow?

↓ YES

Have you paid 25 weeks' National Insurance contributions during any one tax year?

→ NO → Your widow would be unlikely to get any widow's benefits from the state

↑ YES

↓ YES

Have you paid National Insurance contributions for at least a quarter of your working life?[1]

→ NO → Would your widow be state pension age (currently 60) or more?

↓ NO

↓ YES

Your widow would get widow's payment but no widow's pension or widowed mother's allowance

Have you paid National Insurance contributions for nine-tenths of your working life?

→ NO → Would your widow be caring for your child under age 19?

↓ YES   ↓ NO

↓ YES

Would your widow get widow's payment[2] and a reduced widowed mother's allowance

Would your widow be aged 45 or more?

↓ NO   ↓ YES

Would your widow be caring for your child under age 19?

YES ↓   NO ↓

Your widow would get widow's payment[2] and a full widowed mother's allowance

Would your widow be aged 45 or more? → NO →

↓ YES

Your widow would get widow's payment[2] and a full widow's pension

Your widow would get widow's payment but no widow's pension or widowed mother's allowance

Your widow would get widow's payment[2] and a reduced widow's pension

[1] Working life is officially defined to start with the tax year in which you reach age 16.
[2] Provided she is aged under state pension age (currently 60) at the time of your death.

Cost of childcare (dd)

Record here any increase in the amount the family would pay for childcare. If both you and your spouse or partner work anyway, there might not be much change from the current position. But if you stay at home to look after the children, your spouse or partner would face a hefty bill for a nanny, childminder or nursery, unless you have relatives or friends who would be willing to help. Bear in mind too that if you are the main breadwinner, your spouse or partner might have to take up work (increasing the family income under 'x') but might need to incur childcare costs in order to do so.

Cost of home help etc. (ee)

Would your dependants pay for other people to do jobs around the home which you had carried out?

Cost of replacing fringe benefits of your job (ff)

Your survivors might want to carry on enjoying some or all of the perks of your job. Replacing some fringe benefits, such as a company car, might mean paying out a lump sum and should be entered under 'g' above. But with others, regular expenditure might be required: for example, paying premiums for private medical insurance to cover hospital bills (see page 96) or petrol and insurance for your car. Bear in mind, though, that any tax on such benefits will be saved.

Other (gg)

Enter here any other extra expenses not covered elsewhere.

Part 3: Amount of cover required

Do the sums shown in the Calculator. If amount 'I' is greater than zero, you need life insurance to provide the extra income shown. Either choose a family income benefit policy (see page 71) to provide the required amount, or lump-sum insurance which could be invested to provide the income. If you opt for the latter, consider who would manage the investments. To work out what size lump sum would be necessary, you could just multiply the yearly income by the number of years for which it will be required. But this is only

Lump sum needed to provide a given amount of income each year

1: Lump sum needed to provide each £1,000 of income a year

Period for which income is to be paid	Assuming invested lump sum grows by:	
	5% a year	10% a year
5 years	£4,500	£4,200
10 years	£8,100	£6,800
15 years	£10,900	£8,400
20 years	£13,100	£9,400
25 years	£14,800	£10,000

2: Lump sum needed to provide each £1,000 in the first year increasing each year thereafter

Period for which income is to be paid	Assuming invested lump sum grows by 5% a year and income is increased by 3% each year
5 years	£4,800
10 years	£9,200
15 years	£13,200
20 years	£16,800
25 years	£20,000

a rough guide and will tend to overstate the amount of cover you need. To make a more accurate estimate, you should take into account the fact that an invested lump sum will earn some return which can also be put towards providing the income you need. To do this you'll have to take a view about future investment returns. Section 1 of the table above shows the lump sum you would need (to the nearest £100), assuming investment returns of 5 per cent and 10 per cent a year, to provide *each* £1,000 of income – so if you would need £10,000 a year to be paid out for 15 years and you think that 5 per cent a year growth is a reasonable assumption, you will need lump-sum cover of 10 × £10,900 = £109,000. Section 2 of the table shows how much you would need, assuming 5 per cent a year investment returns, if you wanted the income to grow by 3 per cent each year as some protection against rising prices.

Add the lump sum required to produce the income your dependants would need to the cash sum (if any) worked out at 'C'. This tells you the total amount of lump-sum life insurance you ideally require. The next section describes the types of policy you could choose.

Which type of insurance?

There are two broad types of life insurance: **protection-only** and **investment-type**. If your main need is for protection, there are two schools of thought:

- the first recommends that you choose protection-only insurance, which is called 'term insurance'. In its simplest form, it pays out a specified amount if you die within a selected period of years. If you survive, it pays out nothing. It is the cheapest way overall of buying the cover you need. The numerous variations on this basic theme are described below
- the second recommends that you choose a whole-of-life policy which is one form of investment-type policy. As the name suggests, this provides cover for as long as you live. Since the policy must eventually pay out, it builds up an investment value which you can cash in by surrendering the policy. But it takes many years for a surrender value to build up and, in general, whole-of-life policies are an expensive buy if your main need is protection. However, a variation called a 'maximum protection policy' lets you buy a high level of cover at a premium which is initially very low. This type of policy is discussed in more detail on page 72.

You should definitely avoid taking out an endowment policy if your primary need is protection. Endowment policies are investment-type life insurance which pay out if you die within a specified period (the endowment period) and also pay out if you survive. On the face of it this may seem appealing – something to gain whether you die or not – but such policies are an expensive way of buying life cover. Endowment policies can have a role to play in your financial planning, and this is considered in Chapters 8 and 14, but they are not a good tool for straightforward protection of your dependants.

Warning

Investment-type life insurances, such as endowment policies, are an expensive way to buy life cover.

Tip

Overall, term insurance is the cheapest way to buy large sums of life cover to protect your family. A maximum protection plan might be cheaper in the early years, but watch out for premium increases later on.

Variations on the term insurance theme

Lump-sum term insurance

You choose what level of cover you need and the period for which you require it – for example, until the children have finished their education, or beyond the time when Great Aunt Florence can reasonably be expected to rely on your support. The lump sum is paid out tax-free if you die within that term.

The premiums you pay are set at the time you take out the policy and depend largely on the level of cover, the term you choose, your age at the start and your state of health. You will normally be charged more – or even refused cover – if your work, hobbies or lifestyle are deemed to be particularly risky. Some insurance companies reserve the right to increase the premiums – often substantially – if they experience unusually high levels of claims against their term insurance policies. This is a device which was adopted in response to the problem of deaths through AIDS.

Increasing term insurance

This works much like the basic term insurance, except that the level of cover increases – and usually the premiums too – for example by five per cent a year or in line with inflation. It is worth considering this type of policy, especially if you are insuring for a long term, because increasing prices eat away at the value of a fixed level of cover as the years go by.

Increasable term insurance

This variant gives you the option to increase the level of cover either at set intervals – such as on each anniversary of taking out the policy – or when particular events occur – for example, marriage or the birth of a child. You pay extra in premiums for any increase in cover, but the premiums are worked out on the basis of your health at the time you first took out the original policy, even if your health has subsequently deteriorated.

Decreasing term insurance

With this variant, the amount of cover reduces year by year. The two main uses for this type of insurance are to repay loans, such as a mortgage (see Chapter 8), or to cover a potential inheritance tax bill on a lifetime gift (see Chapter 17).

Renewable term insurance

This version allows you to extend the insurance term when it comes to an end. The premium you then pay is based on your health at the time you took out the original policy, even if your health has subsequently deteriorated. This can be a useful variation for dealing with the unexpected, for example a child who stays in full-time education for longer than you had anticipated.

It is also a good option if you cannot, at present, afford the level of cover you need for the period you want. Instead, you could take out the cover you need but for a shorter period. At the end of the period, you could take up your option for a further period. Premiums would then be higher because you would be older, but there would be no additional charge even if you had developed health problems.

> **Tip**
>
> If you cannot afford the amount of life insurance cover you need, you do not necessarily have to insure for less. Consider taking out the full cover but for a shorter time, using renewable term insurance, which guarantees that you can take out a further policy at the end of the original term when perhaps you can afford to pay more.

Convertible term insurance

With this type of term insurance, you have the option at specified dates to convert your protection-only policy into an investment-type insurance policy based on your health at the time you took out the original term insurance. This option is of limited use. See Chapter 14 for more about investment-type policies.

Family income benefit insurance

Instead of paying out a single lump sum, this type of term insurance pays out a series of regular tax-free lump sums which you can use as income. The income starts to be paid at the time of death until the end of the policy term. Since the policy pays out less overall the longer you survive, this is generally the cheapest form of term insurance and can be a good choice for families. A useful variation allows the regular income to increase over time to counteract the effects of inflation.

Pension-linked term insurance

If you are eligible to contribute to a personal pension plan (other than one simply used for contracting out of part of the state pension scheme), you are also eligible to take out pension-linked term insurance. Chapter 9 explains who is eligible. You do not have to be actually making contributions towards a personal pension to take out pension-linked term insurance.

The big advantage of taking out this type of term insurance is that you get tax relief on your premiums at your highest rate of income tax. The drawback is that what you pay towards any term insurance reduces the amount you can put towards a pension (see page 184).

Don't assume that pension-linked term insurance will always be the cheapest cover; compare it with the premiums payable for ordinary term insurance too.

Tip

If you are eligible for a personal pension plan, you can get tax relief on what you pay for term insurance.

Maximum protection policies

Over the years, *Which?* has generally advised that you keep your protection and investment arrangements quite separate, independently choosing the best options to meet each need. However, there is one type of investment-type life insurance which does need to be considered within the context of protection: flexible whole-of-life policies which give the option of choosing maximum protection.

These are unit-linked policies (see page 262). The premiums you pay go into an investment fund which is divided up into units. The value of your policy depends on how the price of these units moves and that, in turn, depends on the value of the underlying investments in the fund. You decide how much life cover you want within limits:

- **minimum cover** Most of your premiums remain in the investment fund and hopefully build up a good cash-in value to give you a return on your investment. Alternatively, you might use the fund which has built up to pay for insurance later on: for example, to cover a potential inheritance tax bill (see Chapter 17).

- **maximum cover** Your units in the investment are cashed in each month to pay for the life cover. At this highest level of cover, and assuming a given return on the investment fund, it is expected that cover can be maintained at the same premium for, say, five or ten years. After that, it is likely that premiums would have to rise to maintain the same level of cover.

The policy is reviewed regularly, usually after the first ten years and after that every five years. At the review, the balance of premiums, investment fund and cover are checked. If your current premiums and fund are insufficient to maintain the chosen level of cover, either the premiums must increase or you must reduce your cover.

A maximum protection policy can be cheaper than term insurance in the early years and is, therefore, an option to consider if you need a lot of cover now for the lowest possible premium. But you must bear in mind that, at the policy review, your premiums are likely to rise or the cover reduce.

Other things to consider

Joint life policies

Instead of you and your spouse or partner taking out separate insurance policies, you could take out a joint life policy. A 'first death' policy covers both your lives and pays out once on the death of the first of you to die. A 'last survivor' policy pays out once on the death of the second of you to die. For protecting dependants, the 'first death' option is usually the more appropriate. A joint life policy will be suitable only if you both need to insure for the same amount. For example, a joint life policy may be ideal for paying off a mortgage in the event of one of you dying, but less suitable as a means of replacing lost income since the income needs will vary depending on which of you has died.

Writing life insurance in trust

If the proceeds of a life policy are paid to your estate on death, there can be a long delay before the money becomes available to your dependants and there could be inheritance tax to pay on the proceeds (see Chapter 17). Writing an insurance policy in trust avoids these problems by ensuring that the policy pays out direct to your dependants, bypassing your estate altogether.

Most insurance companies give you the option of writing a policy in trust at no extra charge and have standard forms for doing this. Policies on your life (but not joint life policies) which are to benefit your husband, wife or children can be very simply and easily written in trust using the Married Women's Property Act 1882.

The form of trust set up under the terms of this Act cannot be altered later, so you need to make sure that it really does suit your requirements.

Life-of-another policies

So far, this chapter has considered life insurance policies which pay out either to your estate, if you die, or indirectly to someone else via a trust. An alternative is a policy which pays out direct to someone else if you die. For example, if you want to ensure that your husband or wife or unmarried partner is financially secure if you were to die, consider one of these options:

- **own-life policy** You take out life insurance to pay out on your own death. To prevent the payout forming part of your estate and to avoid delays, you write the policy in trust for the benefit of your spouse or partner
- **life-of-another policy** Your husband, wife or partner takes out life insurance based on your life. If you die, the policy pays out direct to him or her, so there is no need to write the policy in trust.

With all types of life insurance, at the time the policy is taken out you must have an insurable interest in the life of the person covered. This means that you must stand to lose financially if he or she were to die. You are assumed automatically to have an unlimited insurable interest in your own life and in that of your husband or wife. When it comes to other people, your insurable interest is limited to the amount that you would lose if they died. Therefore, a life-of-another policy cannot be taken out on someone with whom you have no financial connection. The main disadvantage of a life-of-another policy is if your relationship breaks down: your former spouse or partner owns the policy and has the absolute right to the proceeds if you were to die, so you may need to take out your own policy to ensure that any children would be financially provided for. On the other hand, where a relationship has already broken down, a life-of-another policy taken out by a parent with care of the children on the life of the absent parent can be useful as a way of protecting the family against the loss of maintenance payments in the event of the absent parent dying.

Waiver of premium

Both term insurance and whole-of-life policies may include 'waiver of premium'. This lets you suspend your premiums for a certain period in specified circumstances: for example if you are unable to work because of illness. You need to check the policy wording carefully to see precisely what conditions apply. Not all policies offer the waiver. With those that do, the waiver is sometimes automatically included and sometimes an optional extra. Although, as an option, it could increase your premiums by around six per cent, say. Waiver of premium is a relatively cheap and straightforward way of making sure that your life cover would continue even if your finances were temporarily straitened.

Pre-paid funeral plans

Even the simplest funeral is not cheap, and the idea of paying for your own funeral *in advance* is catching on in the UK. The advantages of a pre-paid funeral are that you can choose the type of funeral you want and you don't have to feel a burden to relatives by leaving them to pick up the tab.

Typically, a plan works like this: you pay for your funeral either with a lump sum, starting at around £850, or by instalments spread over five years, say. The plan guarantees to fund your chosen funeral whenever you die, regardless of price increases. The key to these plans is that your money is invested to provide the necessary funds when they are needed. But because you are deemed to be paying for a service in advance rather than making an investment yourself, the rigorous investment laws described in Chapter 3 don't apply to funeral plans. This leaves you with little protection if things go wrong – as they have, in the case of a few plans.

There are two main concerns. The first is: how safe is the money? The second relates to the people who buy the plans, as they are often elderly and vulnerable and may be persuaded to pay for over-elaborate funerals. In the UK there was a disturbing case in Huddersfield in 1993 where £35,000 disappeared, leaving 30 elderly people's funeral arrangements in jeopardy; fortunately, another company stepped in to help.

The funeral industry has responded by setting up its own codes of practice to regulate the sale and management of pre-paid plans.

Two rival trade bodies operate these codes: the Funeral Planning Council (FPC)★ and the National Association of Pre-Paid Funeral Plans (NAPFP).★ The codes include requirements for customers' pre-payments to be held in a trust fund which is independently administered – for example, by a bank – and for a formal complaints-handling system. The FPC has set up a Funeral Ombudsman★ who can direct member firms to make awards of up to £55,000. However, codes of practice are only as good as their monitoring and enforcement. Moreover, firms that choose not to belong to the trade bodies are not covered by the codes. So be wary if you are attracted to taking out a funeral plan.

More information

To find out more about the state benefits for which your dependants might qualify, see the relevant leaflets published by the Benefits Agency,★ an agency of the Department of Social Security

---

Planning in practice

Susann and Murray have two young children. Susann thinks she might need extra life insurance but is unsure how much. They use the *Which?* calculator to work out the figures.

They both work full-time and Susann has some death-in-service benefit from her employer. Their mortgage is covered by an insurance policy so, if Susann died, the mortgage would be repaid. Susann and Murray calculate that there would be enough cash available to cover immediate expenses if Susann died (in fact, there would be £8,500 left). But, in the longer term they need life cover to replace her lost income. Murray would need to pay for a housekeeper while he was at work.

Using the Calculator, they reckon that Murray would be £9,888 worse off each year if Susann died. They need a 20-year policy to cover Susann's life until their youngest child is 21. As a rough guide, Susann and Murray multiply £9,888 by 20, making a total of £197, 760. Finally, they subtract the £8,500 cash that would be left from initial expenses (see above) making the total cover needed £189,260.

Which? August 1996

(DSS),★ which are available from your local Benefits Agency, many public libraries, some post offices and by post. See in particular NP45 *Widow's Benefits*, FB2 *Which Benefit*, FB27 *Bringing up children?*, CH1 *Child benefit*, CH8 *About child benefit* and CA09 *National Insurance contributions for widows*.

To find out which insurance companies offer the best-value protection insurance, see the regular surveys in *Which?*★ and specialist personal finance magazines. If you have a fax machine, you can get rates from the *Moneyfacts* service (see Fax services★). Having narrowed down your choice to a few companies, contact those companies direct (some may refer you to an independent adviser) and ask them to send you literature about the policies you are interested in and to give you a quotation of how much you'll have to pay for the cover you want.

Chapter 5

Protecting your income

It has been estimated that for each person of working age who dies, there are 15 people suffering from long-term illness or a disability. Few people question the need for life insurance to protect their dependants if they were to die, but only one working person in ten has any specific long-term financial protection if they are unable to work because of sickness.

According to government statistics, in 1993 182,000 people aged 20–64 had been off work sick for between six months and a year, 470,000 between one and three years and 757,000 for more than three years. As the chart on page 80 suggests, few people would find it easy to cope with the financial impact of a prolonged illness. So why is this area of financial planning so often neglected? There are three main reasons:

- a mistaken belief that the state and employers will provide. A survey by Swiss Reinsurance and The Henley Centre found that well over half of working people think that their employer would carry on paying sick pay if they were off work ill for more than six months, yet very few companies can afford to do this
- a lack of understanding about how you can arrange protection privately. This is not helped by the somewhat obscure name 'permanent health insurance' given to the main tool for protecting your income
- the relatively high cost of this form of protection.

> **Warning**
>
> Do not rely on the state to provide you with a reasonable income
> if you were unable to work for a long period due to illness or dis-
> ability. You have to pass strict medical tests to qualify for inca-
> pacity benefit. The alternative – means-tested income support –
> does not give you much to live on.

What help can you expect if you fall ill?

The table on page 81 summarises the main types of health crisis that
might damage your income. The two middle columns tell you
broadly what help you might get from the state and from your
employer. The final column suggests ways in which you can provide for yourself. The various sources of protection are described
more fully starting on page 85.

Protection from the state

Most people assume that the state provides a safety net to catch anyone who is unable to earn a living and has no other income to rely
on. After all, is that not why we pay National Insurance? But you
might be surprised at how little the state would provide if you could
not work because of a long-term illness or disability. Since April
1995, the main help you can expect if you are off work sick is incapacity benefit, paid as described below.

For the first 28 weeks

No benefits are payable for the first three days of illness. After that,
most employees qualify for Statutory Sick Pay (SSP) which is paid
by your employer – see page 85.

If you are self-employed or you are an employee who does not
get SSP, and provided you have paid enough National Insurance
contributions (see the chart on page 84), you can claim the lower
rate of short-term incapacity benefit. In 1997–8 this is a tax-free
£47.10 a week. There is no extra if you have children. You can claim
an increase for your husband, wife or partner, but only if:

79

Do you need to protect your income in case of illness?

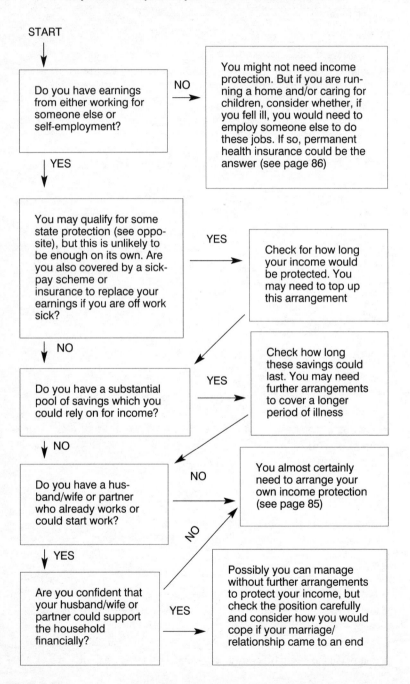

START

Do you have earnings from either working for someone else or self-employment?

NO → You might not need income protection. But if you are running a home and/or caring for children, consider whether, if you fell ill, you would need to employ someone else to do these jobs. If so, permanent health insurance could be the answer (see page 86)

YES

You may qualify for some state protection (see opposite), but this is unlikely to be enough on its own. Are you also covered by a sick-pay scheme or insurance to replace your earnings if you are off work sick?

YES → Check for how long your income would be protected. You may need to top up this arrangement

NO

Do you have a substantial pool of savings which you could rely on for income?

YES → Check how long these savings could last. You may need further arrangements to cover a longer period of illness

NO

Do you have a husband/wife or partner who already works or could start work?

NO → You almost certainly need to arrange your own income protection (see page 85)

YES

Are you confident that your husband/wife or partner could support the household financially?

NO ↗

YES → Possibly you can manage without further arrangements to protect your income, but check the position carefully and consider how you would cope if your marriage/relationship came to an end

How your income might be protected if you fall ill

What can go wrong	Help from the state	Help from your employer	Possible private health insurances
You are off work sick for between 4 days and 28 weeks	• Incapacity benefit (lower rate) if you don't qualify for Statutory Sick Pay • Income support if your income is very low	• Statutory Sick Pay (unless your earnings are very low) *or* • Employer's own sick pay, if more generous than statutory scheme	• Sickness and accident insurance • Permanent health insurance
You are off work sick for more than 28 weeks	• Incapacity benefit (higher rate/long-term rate) but you must pass a strict medical test • Income support if your income is very low • Disability benefits • Attendance allowance	• Sick pay if your employer runs a long-term scheme • Pension through early retirement on ill health grounds	• Sickness and accident insurance – unlikely to extend beyond two years • Permanent health insurance • Personal pension plan – benefits can be paid from any age if you retire because ill, but the pension could be very low, especially if you are young
You have an accident which seriously maims you	• Benefits as above if you cannot work • Industrial injuries benefit if accident is work-related and you are an employee	• Protection as above if you cannot work • Lump sum if your employer has taken out accident insurance for employees	• Accident insurance • Critical illness insurance – some policies • Insurances as above if you are unable to work
You are diagnosed with a life-threatening illness	• Benefits as above if you cannot work	• Protection as above if you cannot work • Retirement pension might be replaced by a lump sum if you are not expected to live long	• Critical illness insurance

- you have dependent children in the family (an increase of £29.15 a week in 1997–8), or
- your spouse or partner is aged 60 or more (an increase of £35.90 a week in 1997–8), and
- if working, your spouse or partner earns no more than the amount of the increase.

During this first stage, you can qualify for incapacity benefit because you are unable to do your normal job – you will need sick notes from your doctor. But from week 29 onwards, you must pass a strict medical test, called the 'all work test'. This takes the form of a detailed questionnaire and possibly an examination by a Benefits Agency doctor. Information from your own doctor may also be taken into account. The test looks at your ability to perform certain functions, such as standing, seeing and reaching. You'll have to be found incapable of doing *any* work, not simply your normal job, in order to continue getting benefit.

From week 29 to week 52

Provided they satisfy the medical test, both employees and the self-employed switch to higher-rate short-term incapacity benefit (£55.70 a week in 1997–8). Although the amount is higher, it is now taxable. This means that, if you have income from other sources, you could actually receive less than you did during the first 28 weeks. If applicable, you still get the increase for your partner. You can now also claim extra (which is tax-free) for any children in your family:

- £9.90 a week in 1997–8 for your only or eldest child, and
- £11.20 a week for each additional child.

These additions for children are lost or reduced if your husband, wife or partner earns more than a given amount (£135 a week in 1997–8 if you have one child, increased by £17 for each additional child).

After a year

You switch to long-term incapacity benefit (£62.45 a week in 1997–8). If you are terminally ill or you are very severely disabled, you can get this rate of incapacity benefit from the twenty-ninth week onwards.

There is also an increase if you are under age 45 at the start of the illness. If you are under 35, you get an extra £13.15 a week in 1997–8. Between the ages of 35 and 44, you get less – £6.60 a week in 1997–8.

If you have children, you still get extra for your husband, wife or partner, though this is paid at a higher rate than previously (£37.35 a week in 1997–8) provided he or she earns no more than £49.15 a week. The same additions as before are payable in respect of children. Benefit (apart from increases for children) continues to be taxable.

Long-term incapacity benefit is not payable if you are over state pension age, but you will usually qualify for state retirement pension instead (see Chapter 9).

Other help from the state

If you have not paid enough contributions to qualify for incapacity benefit, you might be able to get severe disablement allowance instead. This is a non-taxable benefit available to people who have been off work sick for at least 28 weeks and count as seriously disabled.

Whatever other benefits you qualify for, if your income is deemed to be too little to live on, you might qualify for income support and other means-tested benefits instead. Income support is based on the amount that the state deems you need to live on, and the rates are not generous: for example, a single adult aged 25 or more is expected to be able to survive on £49.15 a week and a couple on £77.15 a week in 1997–8. You can qualify for extra if you count as severely disabled. There are also supplements for children and for families, disabled people, pensioners and single parents – though this last supplement is due to be abolished. To qualify for income support at all, you must have no more than £8,000 in savings (£16,000 if you live in a nursing or residential home), and the amounts you get are scaled down if your savings exceed £3,000 because your savings are assumed to produce some income (whether or not, in fact, they do).

Who can get incapacity benefit?

START

Were you under state pension age (see Chapter 9) at the time the illness started?

NO → You cannot get incapacity benefit. Check whether you qualify for state retirement pension (see Chapter 9).

YES ↓

Have you been ill for more than three days?

NO → You cannot claim incapacity benefit yet

YES ↓

Do you work for an employer?

YES → In most cases you do not get incapacity benefit for the first 28 weeks; instead claim Statutory Sick Pay from your employer (see opposite). After that, incapacity benefit continues provided you satisfy the rules – follow the arrow

NO ↓

after 28 weeks

Have you:

● paid at least 25 Class 1 or Class 2 National Insurance contributions during any one tax year, and
● paid or been credited with at least 50 Class 1 or Class 2 National Insurance contributions in each of the last two complete tax years?

YES → You qualify for incapacity benefit. But after the first 28 weeks of illness you must satisfy a strict medical test and be found incapable of doing *any* work

NO ↓

Are you a widow or widower?

YES → Even though you have not paid enough National Insurance contributions, you might still be able to get incapacity benefit. Check at your local DSS office

NO ↓

You are unlikely to qualify for incapacity benefit. You might qualify for other state benefits instead (see page 83)

Protection through your job

By law, your employer must usually pay you at least a minimum amount if you are off work sick for more than three days; this is called Statutory Sick Pay (SSP). In 1997–8 SSP is set at £55.70 a week. It is taxable just like ordinary pay, so income tax and National Insurance may be deducted from it if you also have some other income. SSP is payable for up to 28 weeks.

If you earn less than the 'lower earnings limit' – a figure set by the government each year, equal to £62 a week (or its equivalent) in 1997–8 – your employer does not have to pay you SSP. A few other groups of employees are not covered by the scheme, including workers over state pension age, anyone on a contract lasting less than three months and people working for overseas employers. If your employer does not pay you SSP, he or she must give you a claim pack SSP1. This includes a claim form for incapacity benefit, which you might be able to get instead.

Your employer may run a sick-pay scheme which is more generous than the minimum SSP: for example, maintaining your full pay for several months and then perhaps half-pay for a few more. Some employers take out insurance to provide income for sick employees over a longer period; this is called 'group permanent health insurance' ('group PHI'). The insurance works in a similar way to the private insurance you can arrange for yourself (see below), except the income it pays out is taxable. PHI through your job is a fringe benefit which is usually tax-free.

If you are unlikely to be able to return to work at all, you may qualify for early retirement on the grounds of ill health. This could trigger an immediate pension from your employer's pension scheme if it runs one – see Chapter 10.

Check your contract of employment to see what arrangements apply to you.

Arranging your own protection

The main way in which you can make sure that you would still have enough to live on if you could not work because of illness is by taking out insurance. There are three types of policy to consider, which are described below.

Permanent health insurance (PHI)

PHI replaces part of your income if you are unable to work because of illness or disability. Since 6 April 1996, income from a PHI policy has been tax-free.

Traditional schemes replace up to three-quarters of your income (adjusted for any benefits from the state, etc. – see below) either until you get better or until you reach retirement, whichever happens first. But PHI is expensive and, in an effort to reduce premiums, some policies offer a lower maximum income and a few limit the pay-out period to a maximum of, say, two or five years. Research by *Which?* has found that these options do not necessarily save you money – by shopping around you may be able to find a traditional policy for an equivalent or lower premium. In addition, there are several other steps you can take to cut the premium you'll pay.

You choose how long after the onset of an illness you want the policy to start paying out. This is called the 'waiting period' and can normally be 4, 13, 26, 52 or even 104 weeks. Choosing a longer waiting period reduces the premiums you pay. You can fit the waiting period to your other resources, for example a sick-pay scheme at work, or savings.

When choosing the amount of income you want the policy to provide, you do not have to opt for the maximum allowed under the policy rules. Typically, the limit is three-quarters of your before-tax earnings less any state incapacity benefit and income from other similar insurance, but you can choose a lower amount.

The payout can be at a flat rate. Alternatively, you can opt for an increasing income – worth considering, since otherwise inflation will erode the value of the income. There are two aspects to this: first, you want to know that the amount you would start to get if you made a claim is being increased each year; secondly, once an income is being paid, you want to be sure that it will be increased.

At one time the premium you paid at the outset of the policy was guaranteed to continue for the whole lifetime of the policy (assuming the level of cover was unchanged). This type of policy is now very rare, and nowadays premiums are usually reviewed every five years and can be increased if the insurance company finds that claims by its policyholders are higher than it had expected. But any increase in premiums as a result of a review will apply to *all* policyholders as a group, not just to selected individuals. How premiums are set at the start of the policy depends on a wide range of factors:

- **your sex** Usually, women have to pay substantially more (for example, around half as much again) as men for the same cover. This is because, as a group, they tend to make more claims and for longer periods
- **your age** at the time you first take out the policy. Permanent health insurance is more expensive the older you are, because older people tend to have more health problems
- **your job** Some jobs carry bigger risks to health than others. For example, your premiums will be lower if you have a relatively 'safe' job, such as a bank manager, civil servant, computer programmer, or secretary, than if you are a manual worker or driver, say. Some workers, for example bar staff and divers, might find it hard to get cover at all. Some plans offer cover to housewives and househusbands, deeming the value of their work to be equivalent to earnings of, say, £10,000 a year. The insurance providers set their job categories according to their own experience of claims. A job treated as high risk by one insurer might be assigned a lower risk by another, so it is definitely worth shopping around
- **your state of health** Expect to pay higher premiums or be refused cover altogether if you already have health problems. However, PHI's strange name – *permanent* health insurance – underlines the fact that, with most policies, once you have been accepted for cover you will not be turned down or have your premiums loaded because you *subsequently* claim on the policy. However, while all PHI insurers refuse claims related to AIDS or HIV, a few will not continue your cover at all if, having taken out PHI, you are subsequently diagnosed as HIV-positive – a move which is at odds with the original 'permanence' of the insurance
- **your hobbies** Expect additional premiums or restrictions on cover if you enjoy flying, rock-climbing or other sports which insurers consider dangerous
- **your lifestyle** Smokers are often charged more, you'll usually have to give details of how much alcohol you drink regularly and insurance companies want to find out whether there's a risk of your contracting AIDS

- **the chosen level of payout** The higher the income you choose, the higher the premiums
- **the waiting period** The sooner you want the payout to start, the higher the premiums
- **other policy options**: for example, you pay more for increasing policies than ones paying out a level benefit.

PHI policies can either be pure insurance, in which case your monthly premiums go directly to buy the cover you've selected, or they can be investment-linked. With the latter, your monthly payments are invested and the cost of the insurance is paid from your investment fund. Your plan is reviewed, typically, every five years. If the investments have grown by a target rate or more, cover continues at the standard price (and you might receive a cash sum when the policy comes to an end). But if the investments have not grown as well as expected, your premiums are increased or the cover might finish earlier than you had originally intended.

Sickness and accident insurance

Accident insurance pays out a tax-free lump sum if you suffer a specified injury or die: for example, you might get £5,000 for the loss of a finger or a big toe, £10,000 for the loss of hearing, £100,000 for permanent disability. Although this type of insurance is very cheap – sometimes it is even offered free as an enticement to you to take up some other financial product – the probability of your suffering the particular injuries which are covered is very low. On the whole, accident insurance on its own is not worth buying.

However, accident insurance is often included with other insurances, such as travel policies and car insurance. It is also sometimes combined with sickness insurance (the latter is not offered on its own). The sickness insurance element of the policy typically pays out a limited income, usually from the first week you are ill, for a maximum of two years, if you cannot work because of illness or an accident. As with PHI insurance, the income has been tax-free since 6 April 1996. Unlike PHI, there is no 'permanent' element to sickness insurance; you simply take out the policy for a year at a time. At renewal, the premiums can be increased or cover refused if you have built up a record of claims or suffered a deterioration in your health. For this reason and because of the limited period for which the benefits are payable, sickness insurance is a poor substitute for PHI.

Critical illness insurance

Critical illness cover (CIC) pays out a sizeable tax-free lump sum if you are diagnosed with a specified life-threatening condition or have to undergo certain types of surgery. Over the last ten years or so, CIC has become increasingly popular due to its relative cheapness and its simplicity.

CIC policies are now often sold as part of a mortgage package and are also sold as stand-alone policies. CIC is also commonly combined with life insurance, with some policies paying out either on diagnosis of a specific illness or on death and others paying out in both events. With the latter type, and with some others, there is often a waiting period between diagnosis and payout: for example, 28 days or even as long as six months or a year for certain conditions, such as total permanent disability. However, if the diagnosis is clear cut, the insurer might be prepared to waive the waiting period.

The maximum payout varies from policy to policy, with £500,000 or £1 million being common, though cover for higher amounts might be available on request. Where the policy is linked to your mortgage, the lump sum is obviously designed to pay off the mortgage but, with other policies, there are no restrictions on how you use the money. For example, you might use it in the same way as a PHI policy to cover living expenses while you are off work, but equally you could pay for private medical treatment, buy the services of a carer, adapt your home, put it towards retraining for a less stressful career, help your dependants or even take a holiday.

Nearly all policies cover six core conditions: cancer, heart attack, stroke, kidney failure, coronary artery bypass and major organ transplant. After many years of confusion, most CIC providers have agreed to use standard definitions of these conditions, giving a consistent approach to the circumstances under which a claim will be met. There is less agreement about defining the many other conditions that might also be covered: for example, multiple sclerosis, loss of hearing or sight, severe burns, Alzheimer's disease, Parkinson's disease, total permanent disability and so on. Beware of exclusions: for example, some policies do not cover Alzheimer's or Parkinson's disease if it is first diagnosed after the age of 60, which is very likely to be the case. Also, do not be overly impressed by long lists of ailments; often another policy will cover the same conditions but under one of its broader headings. For example, in recent years some insurers have added Creutzfeldt Jakob disease (CJD) as a specified condition, but this would almost certainly be covered under another section, such as coma, terminal illness or total permanent disability.

Heart attacks and cancer account for over three-quarters of all claims. Government statistics show that about one person in three develops cancer and around a fifth of the population have a cardiovascular disease, ranging from angina and high blood pressure through to heart attacks and stroke. Overall, nearly two-thirds of the population suffer a critical illness at some stage in their lives. In the past they would often have died, but survival rates are now reasonably good. For example, 40 per cent of cancer sufferers survive for five years or longer, and nearly half of the 130,000 people a year who suffer their first heart attack will survive for 13 years or more.

CIC is substantially cheaper than PHI, which makes it look a tempting substitute. However, although a large lump sum from a critical illness policy could be used to provide a replacement income for an extended period, the range of conditions it covers is by definition limited. If you are unable to work because of, say, a back injury, a critical illness policy will not be any help.

More information

To find out more about the state benefits you might qualify for if you are ill, contact your local Benefits Agency.* In particular, see the following Benefits Agency leaflets: IB202 *Incapacity benefit*, NI252 *Severe disablement allowance*, IS1 *Income support* and DS703 *Disability working allowance*.

Check your contract of employment or talk to your personnel department to find out what arrangements your employer has for paying sick employees.

Magazines such as *Money Management*★ and *Planned Savings*★ publish regular surveys of PHI policies and critical illness insurance. Having identified suitable policies, you can contact most companies direct. However, because of the complex nature of PHI and the many factors influencing premiums, this is an area where it is probably worth visiting an independent financial adviser. A good adviser will have access to a database of most or all of the policies available and can arrange quotations of those which would be most suitable for you.

Planning in practice

To illustrate the gap between state provision and PHI, take a fictitious example of catering manager Peter Smith. Peter is 45, married with two children and earns £35,000 a year. Here, we compare how much he'd be entitled to from the state if he fell ill and couldn't work with how much he could get from a PHI policy – and how much he'd pay for one.

If Peter fell ill and had no insurance, he'd be eligible for incapacity benefit after the first 28 weeks. This would amount to a basic £55.70 a week plus £29.15 for his wife (because she has no income of her own), £9.90 for their first child and £11.20 for their second. The total weekly allowance would therefore be £105.95.

This would mean that, if he were to rely on state benefits alone, Peter's income would fall by about 80 per cent. However, if Peter had PHI and his policy were index-linked, he could receive a payout of up to 75 per cent of his salary. Payouts from his policy would be tax-free.

Peter would have been best to choose a policy which would pay out only after 26 weeks (the 'deferred period') because his employer will cover him for the first six months he's off work. Had he chosen a policy which would run until he was 65, it would cost him around £40 a month (£480 per year) and give him a weekly benefit of £400.

PHI for Peter would therefore give him a benefit of about four times that which he would get from the state

Which? February 1996, updated to November 1997

Chapter 6

Insuring against illness

Around six million people in Britain are covered by insurance to pay for private hospital treatment. Two-thirds have this cover as a perk of their job or the job of the family's breadwinner. This means that only one person in nine actively takes the decision to buy private medical insurance (PMI). The low priority most of us give to private treatment is perhaps a tribute to the National Health Service. But increasing demands on the NHS may encourage more of us to consider the private alternative, and the providers of medical insurance are ever coming up with new variations to address the problems of providing the cover consumers want at a price they can afford to pay.

Who needs private treatment?

Traditionally, the NHS provides cradle-to-grave care largely free at the point of use. This means that, in one sense, nobody in this country *needs* private treatment. But the NHS is by no means perfect. The attractions of being treated privately depend on how important these imperfections are to you.

Like any service which is free to users, there is a built-in tendency for demand to mushroom. Resources are limited, so some form of rationing or queuing is inevitable. This is a situation which is tending to become worse over time, with the number of people waiting to be admitted to hospitals in England having increased by 13 per cent over the year to the end of June 1997, resulting in long queues all over the country: see the table on page 94.

The official figures for hospital waiting-lists tell only part of the story and underestimate the length of waiting for treatment. The figures measure the time from hospital treatment being prescribed to admission; you may still have a long wait from the time you first go to your GP to being seen by a specialist. The government has conceded that this time should also be taken into account, and the most recent Patient's Charter sets a target of 26 weeks for a first out-patient appointment.

Clearly, waiting months for treatment is likely to be unpleasant, especially if you are in pain. But in some cases it can be a financial disaster as well. For example, if you run your own business, you simply may not be able to afford to be off work for months pending treatment. According to a survey by the Institute for Health Policy Studies, 61 per cent of people choose private treatment in order to avoid NHS waiting-lists.

Since 1991, District Health Authorities and an increasing number of GPs have been controlling their own budgets, which they use to buy the treatments their patients need from hospitals and other units. These 'fundholders' choose where and how to spend their budgets, so they have an incentive to look for value for money and to seek ways of cutting costs. This can have good effects, encouraging better use of resources. For example, GPs might place more empha-sis on preventive medicine, which helps to reduce future spending on more costly treatment. And a survey by the National Audit Office found that most fundholding GPs achieve shorter waiting times for treatment for their patients than non-fundholders.

But fundholding may have detrimental effects too. Whether decisions are made centrally or at a local level, where resources are finite, some patients will always be denied treatment on the grounds that the likely benefits are outweighed by the costs involved. The problem with local fundholding is that such deci-sions inevitably will be influenced by local factors – the alternative uses of funds can be quite different in busy urban areas, for exam-ple, from those in quiet rural ones. In the absence of a national pol-icy to ensure that spending priorities are consistent across the NHS, patients may perceive getting treatment on the NHS as something of a lottery. By paying for private treatment, you are restored to the role of consumer and may feel more able to demand the treatment you want.

This sense of being able to exercise your consumer rights is inherent in the other advantages of going private. You can choose a time to go into hospital which is convenient for you, given your family, work and other commitments. You can expect quality treatment because you will be seen by a consultant rather than a more junior doctor, as is often the case on the NHS. Going private also lets you enjoy hotel-style facilities, such as your own room, TV and private bathroom, though many NHS hospitals compete on this score by offering pay beds with better-than-normal facilities.

On the minus side, most private hospitals do not have on-site emergency facilities, so even if you opt for the private route you will still be treated on the NHS in a crisis. This means you might have to be moved to another hospital if your condition became critical.

Waiting to be admitted to hospital

Region	Number of patients waiting more than 12 months
North Thames	10,520
South Thames	9,784
Anglia & Oxford	4,030
Northern & Yorks	2,750
Trent	7,403
West Midlands	831
South & West	4, 921
North West	6, 749

Source: Government figures, as at June 1997

Who needs medical insurance?

A major drawback of private treatment is its high cost (see the table opposite), although some private hospitals do offer fixed-price deals and special offers for some treatments.

One way to cope with the cost is to set aside some savings to draw on if you need or want private treatment. There are two draw-backs to doing this. The first is that a need for treatment might arise soon after you had started saving and before you had built up a large enough fund. The second is that, however much you saved, there would always be an outside chance that you would need very costly treatment – for example, a series of operations – that would require more than you had set aside. You could resign yourself to falling back on the NHS if your savings are not enough. Alternatively, taking out appropriate insurance can cope with both the drawbacks.

The most direct way to insure yourself against the possible costs of private treatment is to take out private medical insurance (PMI), but comprehensive policies are themselves expensive. There are various cheaper options which you can consider. In deciding whether the cost is justified, you need some feel for the likelihood that you might make a claim. The table on page 96 shows how the chances of needing hospital treatment vary with age. Overall, one woman in nine and one man in twelve was a hospital in-patient during 1992, though by no means all the conditions they were treated for would have been covered by a typical medical insurance policy.

The chart on page 97 summarises who needs medical insurance.

All-in cost of some common private treatments

Treatment	Cost
Appendectomy	£2,000–£7,200
Cataracts	£2,000–£2,800
Hernia	£1,200–£2,000
Hip replacement	£5,200–£7,200
Hysterectomy	£3,000–£4,000
Knee replacement	£5,200–£8,200

Source: PPP

Proportion of people going into hospital

Age	Percentage of people	
	Men	Women
0–4	9%	8%
5–15	5%	4%
16–44	5%	12%
45–64	9%	8%
65–74	15%	11%
75 and over	21%	20%

Source: *General Household Survey*, data for 1995-6

Private medical insurance (PMI)

What is PMI?

PMI is insurance to cover the costs of receiving private hospital treatment. It has a long history, dating from pre-NHS days, when people paid into friendly societies which then helped members financially in times of need. The largest PMI providers – BUPA and Private Patients Plan (PPP) – are still non-profit-distributing bodies. But a number of commercial insurance companies also offer PMI nowadays.

It is important to realise that no PMI policy covers every possible private treatment cost. PMI is designed to cover only 'acute illnesses', that is, conditions which can be cured or substantially alleviated by treatment. In particular, 'chronic illnesses', such as arthritis or multiple sclerosis, which would require long-term treatment, are excluded. However, treatment for an acute problem related to a long-term illness might be covered: for example, a hip replacement to ease pain and immobility caused by arthritis. Cover for mental conditions – which in one form or another affect one person in four in Britain – is generally very restricted or excluded altogether.

Other common exclusions are cosmetic surgery, treatment for alcoholism or drug abuse, treatment for infertility or normal pregnancy, and AIDS. Most standard policies also do not cover seeing a GP privately, routine check-ups and dental work (unless carried out in a hospital), although some of the more comprehensive policies do.

Who needs medical insurance?

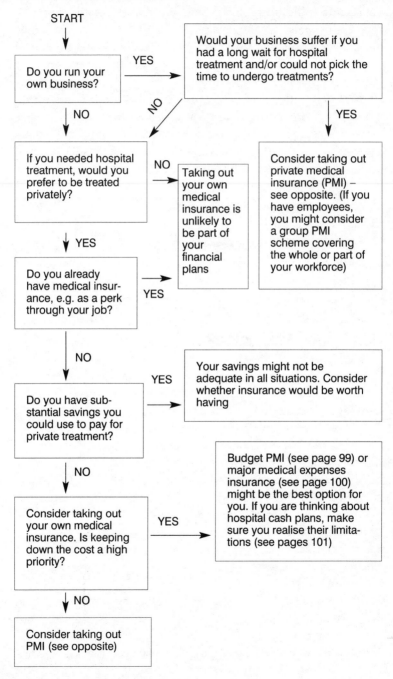

START

Do you run your own business? — **YES** → Would your business suffer if you had a long wait for hospital treatment and/or could not pick the time to undergo treatments?

NO ↓

If you needed hospital treatment, would you prefer to be treated privately? — **NO** → Taking out your own medical insurance is unlikely to be part of your financial plans

Would your business suffer... — **YES** ↓ Consider taking out private medical insurance (PMI) – see opposite. (If you have employees, you might consider a group PMI scheme covering the whole or part of your workforce)

Do you already have medical insur-ance, e.g. as a perk through your job? — **YES** →

NO ↓

Do you have sub-stantial savings you could use to pay for private treatment? — **YES** → Your savings might not be adequate in all situations. Consider whether insurance would be worth having

NO ↓

Consider taking out your own medical insurance. Is keeping down the cost a high priority? — **YES** → Budget PMI (see page 99) or major medical expenses insurance (see page 100) might be the best option for you. If you are thinking about hospital cash plans, make sure you realise their limita-tions (see pages 101)

NO ↓

Consider taking out PMI (see opposite)

97

One other important exclusion is so-called 'pre-existing conditions', that is, health problems you already have at the time you apply for insurance. A few PMI providers 'underwrite' these conditions. That means that they look at the likelihood of such conditions causing a claim and either charge you a higher premium or put special rules into your policy, such as refusing to cover any treatment related to the condition. Most providers use a 'moratorium' instead. How this typically works is that the PMI provider refuses to pay for any treatment relating to the condition until two full years have gone by without your needing treatment for it. After that, the health problem is covered just like any other.

Warning

If you have a health problem which is covered by an existing PMI policy, you should be very wary about switching to another policy because you would lose cover for that health problem.

What does PMI cover?

PMI covers the cost of treatment as an in-patient or day-patient in a private hospital or a private ward or pay bed in an NHS hospital. Out-patient treatment might also be included.

Top-of-the-range plans cover treatment, whether as an in-patient or an out-patient, in most or all private hospitals and wards, and the full cost of treatment is paid by the insurance. These plans usually include extras such as complementary medicine (for example, osteopathy and chiropractic) and home nursing. Some add in the cost of seeing GPs privately and dentists' and opticians' charges. Cover may extend abroad. A top-of-the-range plan can easily cost you hundreds of pounds a month. Not surprisingly, then, there is a whole spectrum of policies offering less cover in exchange for lower premiums.

What might be dubbed 'standard plans' cover fewer extras than the top-notch plans, and out-patient treatment is often covered only if related to a spell as an in-patient. But a major way of keeping down cost is to restrict the range of hospitals you can use. A common way of doing this is to offer you a choice between three lists (or more) of hospitals. One list covers most or all private hospitals and wards, the next excludes the most costly of these (generally the more expensive London hospitals) and the third is limited to the hospitals and wards which are least expensive. If you use a hospital which is not on the selected list, there is no guarantee that the full cost will be met; instead, you get an 'out-of-band' benefit of a specified cash sum for each night in hospital. The more restricted the hospital list you choose, the lower your premiums. If you live outside London, you are unlikely to need the most comprehensive list. The important point to check is that the list you choose includes the private facilities that you would want to use – because they are convenient to your home, for example.

'Budget plans' keep down costs by limiting cover further still. This can be done in one or a combination of the following ways:

- capping the amount which the policy will pay out overall each year
- capping the amount which the policy will pay out for certain areas of cover: for example, surgeons' fees, out-patient costs
- excluding cover altogether for some treatments: for example, physiotherapy, out-patient care
- restricting you to a single and fairly limited list of private hospitals and wards
- 'six-week waiting plans'. These cover private treatment only if the waiting-list for NHS treatment is longer than six weeks. But as NHS waiting-lists for many conditions have become longer than six weeks, this type of plan is becoming rare.

There are many variations on the theme, so you need to check carefully what's on offer. Magazines such as *Which?*★ publish regular comparisons of the policies available.

What does PMI cost?

With PMI, you get very much what you pay for. If you want a comprehensive plan, you pay a high price. If you want to pay less, you must accept restrictions.

Apart from the type of cover you choose, age is the other major influence on price. This reflects the fact that the older you are the more likely you will need hospital treatment. The government used to give an incentive to people aged 60 or more to have PMI by allowing tax relief on the premiums provided the policy met certain rules. However, the tax relief has been abolished for plans taken out or renewed on or after 2 July 1997. In response, some plan providers have further limited the cover under these plans as as alternative to policyholders having to pay extra.

Some companies offer numerous discounts on premiums under certain circumstances: for example, if you belong to a particular profession, have a certain credit card, belong to a particular motor-ing organisation, and so on. An increasing number of policies have 'voluntary excesses'; this means that you get a discount on the pre-miums if you agree to pay the first part of any claim.

The cost of medical insurance can rise rapidly from one year to the next, reflecting overall claims experience and increases in the cost of private treatment.

Major medical expenses insurance (MME)

What is MME?

MME is a type of insurance which pays out a tax-free cash sum if you undergo surgery. It costs significantly less than PMI and can be treated as an alternative if you are happy for cover to be limited sim-ply to surgical treatment and nothing else, and you realise that there is no *guarantee* that the payout will be enough to cover the cost of private treatment. MME is more flexible than PMI, because although you could use the cash sum to pay for private treatment, you do not have to. What you spend the money on is entirely up to you: for example, childcare while you are in hospital, home nurs-ing, a recuperative holiday, or something entirely unrelated to your health problem. At present, only a couple of companies offer stand-alone policies, though MME is available as an option with some other types of health insurance.

What does MME cover?

Some versions pay out whenever you undergo surgery; others restrict cover to a list of treatments for specified conditions. The cash sum is broadly enough to cover the cost of private treatment; one policy, for example, has payouts ranging from £1,400 for a minor operation, such as a hernia repair, to £14,000 for complex surgery, such as a coronary artery bypass. Some MME policies halve the payout if you are treated on the NHS rather than privately.

What does MME cost?

Premiums generally vary with your age, sex and the term of the plan. Some plans are investment-linked; this means that what you pay each month goes into an investment fund from which the cost of the insurance is paid. The plan is reviewed regularly and, provided the fund grows by a given amount, your premiums and the duration of the plan can continue unchanged. If the fund has grown by less, the premiums must increase or the plan will last for fewer years than originally intended.

> **Tip**
>
> If private medical insurance looks a bit expensive, major medical expenses insurance could be worth considering instead.

Hospital cash plan

What is a hospital cash plan and what does it cover?

This pays out a tax-free cash sum for each day you are treated as an in-patient or day-patient in either an NHS or a private hospital. This type of insurance may be combined with a range of other cash benefits: cash payments if you need dental treatment or chiropody, for example, or become pregnant.

Hospital cash plans are not a substitute for PMI or MME: the cash payments are typically small – for example, one leading plan pays from £10 up to £60 a night, depending on the premium level you choose – and they are not enough to cover the cost of private treatment. Usually, they are marketed as useful for covering the incidental costs of being in hospital: childcare or relatives travelling to visit you, for example. It is sometimes suggested that they are also useful as a way of replacing earnings lost because of being off work, but once again the low payments and the fact that the size of the sum paid out is totally unrelated to the income you personally may need to replace mean that such plans are a poor substitute for proper permanent health insurance (see Chapter 5).

How worthwhile a hospital cash plan will be depends crucially on the amounts it pays out and the probability that the events which trigger the payments will occur. Particular points to note are:

- it is crucial to read the small print: for example, it is common for there to be 'waiting periods' of, say, six months or a year before any benefits will be paid. And one plan which boasts that a family of four could receive nearly £650 a year towards dental treatment actually contracts to pay half the dental bill up to the maximum, so each family member would have to incur a bill of £324 for the full cash benefit to be paid
- of people who were treated as in-patients in British hospitals in 1992, the average stay was eight nights
- with more people being treated quickly as day-patients rather than having to stay in hospital overnight (see the table opposite), these cash plans look less attractive than they might have done in the past.

What a hospital cash plan costs

This largely depends on the level of benefit you choose. One advantage is that a single premium may cover a whole family.

Warning

Hospital cash plans appear to be fairly cheap but can be poor value for money when you look at the restrictions and the low probability of claiming some of the benefits.

Critical illness insurance

Critical illness cover (CIC) is described in Chapter 5. It pays out a tax-free lump sum if you are diagnosed with a life-threatening condition or you have to undergo certain specified types of surgery. Since there is no restriction on how you use the money, it could fund private treatment. However, you should not view CIC as an alternative to PMI. The latter pays out when you suffer an acute illness which can be cured or relieved by hospital treatment. CIC pays

The increasing number of 'acute' day-patients

Year	Number of day-case attendances '000s
1981	817
1986	1,207
1991–2	1,894
1994–5	3,049

Source: *Social Trends* 1997

Planning in practice

A PMI policy from a leading health insurer offers older customers additional benefits over its standard policy at no extra cost and looks like a good idea. People who are 60 or over can receive up to £1,000 for home nursing care, up to £1,000 for nursing home treatment and £50 towards chiropody treatment. But the small print reveals a downside too.

With the standard policy, you have a choice of 800 hospitals in which to be treated. With the policy for older customers, your choice is limited to just 148 hospitals. If the hospital you want isn't on the list, you'll need the insurer's prior agreement to attend. Without this agreement, you will lose the added benefits for two years and risk being responsible for treatment you receive, according to the brochure.

Depending on where you live, the difference in the number of hospitals could be huge. *Which?* reader Lester Marks considered switching to the policy – until he discovered that doing so would reduce the number of hospitals available in his area from thirty to two.

Which? August 1996

out mainly in the case of chronic or terminal illness. There is some potential overlap – for example, both policies might be triggered if you had a heart attack – but, on the whole, PMI and CIC are best viewed as complements, rather than substitutes, for each other.

More information

Read the regular surveys of private medical insurance in magazines such as *Which?*,* *Money Management** and *Planned Savings*.* The Association of British Insurers* can provide details of companies offering particular types of insurance. You can also gather this information from business directories kept in the reference sections of most public libraries.

Chapter 7

Care in your old age

This century has seen great improvements in life expectancy. A woman of 60 can expect on average to live another 22 years, and a man of 65 another 14 years. However, 'healthy life expectancy' – the number of years we can expect to enjoy without serious long-term illness or disability – has remained remarkably stable at around 59 years for the average man and 62 years for the average woman. So, as we live longer, we can expect more health problems and, as you might expect, the older we get, the greater the likelihood of failing health – see the table on page 106. Many of us will eventually become unable to cope on our own with normal daily activities and will require help and support from others.

This support might come from members of the family, though some experts predict that, as more women are now working, they will abandon their traditional role as carers of elderly parents and other relatives. And families are often geographically fragmented, making it harder for relatives to provide the regular support that might help an elderly person to stay in his or her own home. Some people need to move into an institutional home, particularly in later life. According to healthcare experts Laing & Buisson, just over a quarter of people aged 85 or more live in a residential or nursing home or hospital compared with one person in a hundred in the 65–74 age-group.

Many people imagine that if they did need to move into a home, the state would look after them. In fact, this is not so unless your income and savings are very low. In the main, you would have to foot the bill yourself – and the bill is high, as shown in the table on page 110.

On average, a person moving into a home spends about three years in it, though of course this length of time varies considerably from person to person. This means that, *on average*, you could get through nearly £52,000 in nursing home fees (even ignoring any fee increases). In your own particular case, the figure could range from nothing (if you did not need to move to a home at all) to a sum far in excess of the average £52,000. So how can you plan sensibly for this phase of later life?

Proportion of people whose activities are limited by long-term illness

Age	Percentage
0–4	4%
5–15	8%
16–44	12%
45–64	27%
65–74	37%
75 and over	48%

Source: *General Household Survey*, data for 1995–6

One tool available is long-term care insurance, which is relatively new in the UK. In return for a series of regular premiums or a lump sum, the insurance company pays out if you become too disabled to cope alone. The snag with this type of insurance is its high cost. Given this fact and the present rules about state provision of long-term care (see opposite), it is highly debatable whether long-term care insurance currently has a part to play in the majority of people's financial plans. However, the position is likely to change at some stage in the future. Successive governments have been concerned at the high cost to the state of caring for elderly people – a cost that is projected to increase as the population over retirement age climbs from the present level of around 10½ million to a projected 16½ million by 2040. The previous Conservative government put forward some ideas for encouraging people to plan ahead to pay for their own care later in life, which set the debate going. The Labour government has taken matters a stage further by setting up a Royal Commission to examine this whole area. The Commission may well take two to three years to carry out its investigation and publish its proposals. In the meantime, the Labour government has suggested that all people in work could, in future, be forced to pay into a fund to finance their own long-term care.

Help from the state

Since the NHS and Community Care Act 1990 came into effect in April 1993, local authorities have become largely responsible for providing state support for elderly people whose physical or mental health is failing. The system as it stands at present works as follows.

Types of care

If you can no longer cope alone at home or your carer needs help, you can contact the social services department of your local authority. If you need financial help from the state, social services will carry out an 'assessment of needs'; social services will also carry out an assessment of needs on request from people who do have enough money to pay for care themselves. Based on this assessment, a care plan will be drawn up. This sets out the level of care which social services reckon you need and the ways in which your needs can be met. There are three main options:

- **staying in your own home** Social services might suggest special equipment to make life easier – for example, grab rails and bathroom aids – and services such as a home help, meals-on-wheels, care assistance (such as someone calling each morning to help you get washed and dressed), home visits from the community nurse and a place at a day centre. In 1994–5 about 9 per cent of people aged 65 to 69 and 30 per cent of people aged 85 and over received help from a local authority care assistant or home help. Around 3 per cent of the 65-plus age-group receive meals-on-wheels
- **moving to a more suitable home** Social services cannot force you to move, but they might suggest it as something worth considering. For example, you could move to sheltered housing with a resident warden available to give emergency assistance, or to a bungalow, say, if you have trouble with stairs, or somewhere closer to relatives who can help

- **going into a care home** Again, you cannot be forced to go into a home, and social services will generally try to help you stay in your own home for as long as possible. If their recommendation is that you move into a residential or nursing home, you will need to be realistic about your ability to carry on if you are determined to stay in your own home. Where possible, you will be offered a choice of homes, though, if the local authority is paying in full for you, cost will be a constraint.

Who pays?

Some equipment and services provided by your local authority are free to everyone or offered at a minimal charge. But in the main you will be expected to pay for home helps, carers, care homes, and so on, unless your income and savings are relatively low. If you have been in hospital and need continuing medical care but provided instead in a nursing home, the NHS usually foots the bill regardless of your income or savings.

Social services can require your husband or wife to contribute towards the cost of your care, but no one else: for example, adult children cannot be asked to pay.

If you go into a care home temporarily – to give your carer a break, say – the normal income and savings rules don't apply but, at its discretion, your local authority can make a 'reasonable charge'. It must take into account any outgoing costs you still have to meet in running your own home – standing charges for fuel bills, council tax, and so on.

The cost of living in a care home

If your local authority is paying the full cost of your living in a residential or nursing home, it sets a limit on the fees it will normally pay. Most local authorities base their limits on a national scale used for income support purposes (see the table opposite), though they have the discretion to set different amounts. If you want to live in a home which has higher fees, you will need to top up the maximum the authority will pay: for example, through the help of relatives or a charity. The limits in the table fall short of the average fees for a residential or nursing home shown on page 110.

Maximum fees payable through income support* for accommodation and meals in a care home

	Weekly maximum	
	Greater London	Rest of country
Residential home		
If you are elderly/elderly and physically disabled	£249	£208
If you are elderly and very dependent	£281	£240
Nursing home		
If you are elderly/elderly and physically disabled/terminally ill	£357	£311
If you are mentally handicapped	£364	£318
Other		
Allowance for personal expenses	£14.10	£14.10
Meals where not included with accommodation (daily rates):		
breakfast	£1.10	£1.10
midday/evening meal	£1.55	£1.55

* Income support continues to meet the cost where claims predate the Care in the Community rules.

Assessing your income and savings

The rules for assessing your income and savings are set nationally. Local authorities have some limited discretion, but broadly speaking the same rules apply wherever you live.

In working out whether or not you have enough income to pay for long-term care yourself, all your income will be taken into account, including pensions and any state benefits, but not the actual income you get from your savings (see below). If someone else is dependent on your income, the assessment will allow enough to cover that person's reasonable living costs. There is an exception to this approach: if you get a pension from a former employer's scheme, half of it will be disregarded as belonging to your husband or wife provided you normally share your pension with them.

If your capital and savings come to no more than £10,000, they are ignored altogether. If they come to more than £16,000, you will get no financial help at all, until your savings have been run down below that limit. In between these two limits, you are assumed to receive £1 a week of income from each £250 (or part) of your capital. This is added to your other income to determine whether you can afford to contribute something towards the fees.

The value of your home is included as part of your capital unless your stay in the care home is only temorary or one of the following people will still be living in the home:

- your husband or wife or a partner who lives with you as husband or wife
- a relative who is aged 60 or more or is incapacitated
- a relative under the age of 16 for whom you are legally responsible.

The local authority has discretion to ignore the value of your home in other circumstances: for example, if your carer lives with you and has nowhere else to go. Where none of these exceptions applies, you might have to sell your home in order to pay the care home fees. If it takes a while to sell, the local authority might agree to pay the fees for you for now, but to take a 'charge' over the home so that it can recoup the money once the property is sold.

You might be tempted to give away some of your capital or make some expensive purchases before being assessed, but if the social services department thinks you've done this deliberately to manipulate the rules, it can treat you as still owning the capital.

Fees for private nursing and residential homes

Type of home/ region	Average weekly fees	Average cost per year
Nursing homes		
London	£438	£22,776
Average: UK	£333	£17,316
Residential homes		
London	£313	£16,276
Average: UK	£239	£12,428

Source: *Which?* February 1997

Who needs long-term care insurance?

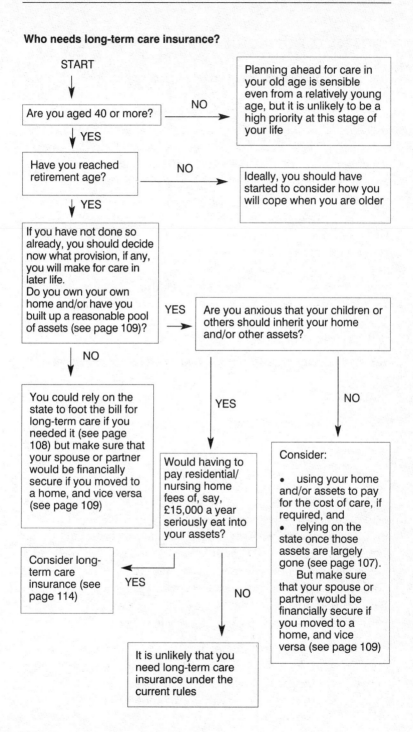

START

Are you aged 40 or more? — **NO** → Planning ahead for care in your old age is sensible even from a relatively young age, but it is unlikely to be a high priority at this stage of your life

YES

Have you reached retirement age? — **NO** → Ideally, you should have started to consider how you will cope when you are older

YES

If you have not done so already, you should decide now what provision, if any, you will make for care in later life.
Do you own your own home and/or have you built up a reasonable pool of assets (see page 109)? — **YES** → Are you anxious that your children or others should inherit your home and/or other assets?

NO

You could rely on the state to foot the bill for long-term care if you needed it (see page 108) but make sure that your spouse or partner would be financially secure if you moved to a home, and vice versa (see page 109)

YES → Would having to pay residential/ nursing home fees of, say, £15,000 a year seriously eat into your assets?

NO → Consider:

• using your home and/or assets to pay for the cost of care, if required, and
• relying on the state once those assets are largely gone (see page 107).
But make sure that your spouse or partner would be financially secure if you moved to a home, and vice versa (see page 109)

Consider long-term care insurance (see page 114) ← **YES**

NO → It is unlikely that you need long-term care insurance under the current rules

111

Concern for the future

Much concern has been expressed about our ageing population and whether the state can continue to provide the present level of support. The table below shows how the proportion of retired people to people of working age is expected to change over the next 50 years or so. Some forecasters suggest that this falling ratio means that either the workers of the future will have to bear much higher taxes than at present or that state help for the elderly will have to be reduced. This is, however, too simple an analysis. More important is the ratio of non-working elderly to active participants in the workforce: that is, after allowing for those of working age not actually in work and those of pension age who continue to work. It is also alarmist to assume that future workers would not be prepared to pay tax at higher rates, since the wealth of the nation might be considerably greater than at present and forms of distributing part of that wealth to non-workers, other than transfers through taxes, might have been devised.

Expected number of people of working age for each pensioner

Year	Number
1991	3.3
2020	3.3
2030	2.7
2050	2.5

Source: DSS

However, the signs are that all political parties will support some form of compulsory system, requiring people of working age to take out insurance or make savings to pay for their own care in old age should they need it. The Labour government has yet to spell out a policy on this and will first await the report of the Royal Commission set up to investigate the whole subject and advise on the options. Before losing office, the previous Conservative government had suggested two possible approaches:

- introducing partnership schemes for long-term care. These would work by letting people who take out insurance up to a given amount keep more of their wealth – on top of the normal capital limits – at the point where state funding kicks in

- giving members of employers' pension schemes (see Chapter 10) the option of taking a pension once they retire which increases in the later years of retirement, thus giving them more income at those times when they are most likely to face long-term care costs.

The wisdom of this latter option has to be questioned – in most cases, people do not invest enough in their pension schemes to provide an adequate standard of living in retirement, let alone to fund long-term care needs as well. In practice, it is likely to be some time before the government brings forward proposals that will have much impact on personal decisions about funding long-term care. The key question for the present remains: how anxious are you to pass on your wealth to your heirs? In the longer term, it seems possible either that it will become compulsory to make at least some advance provision for yourself or that a two-tier system will develop where those who are forced to rely on the state have less choice and enjoy lower standards than those who can directly buy the care they need.

Helping yourself

If your income and/or capital are above the limits for state help, you will have no choice but to rely on your own resources. Family members can be an important source of private care. Currently, one in five men and one in four women aged 45–64 is caring for a relative, friend or neighbour; over a third of these are looking after a parent.

However, as already noted, the outlook for the future is uncertain. There is a strong possibility that, if you do need long-term care later in life, you will have to pay for professional care either in your own home or in an institutional setting. This could quickly run down your assets, but that should not necessarily be viewed as a problem. There are two main questions to consider:

- if you have a husband, wife or unmarried partner, would he or she be financially insecure if you had to move into a residential or nursing home? Similarly, would you have too little to live on if he or she went into a home?
- are you particularly keen to preserve your assets, for example to hand on to your children? This is an issue which perhaps you

should discuss with your family. In a poll by Mintel, eight out of ten adults said that their parents should spend their money on looking after themselves in old age rather than storing it up to be passed on in inheritance.

If your answer to either of these questions is 'yes', long-term care insurance could be worth looking at.

Long-term care insurance

What is long-term care insurance?

This type of insurance pays out an income – often after a waiting period, such as 90 days – if you become unable to cope on your own. The income can be used to pay fees to a nursing or residential care home or to provide help in your own home. Since April 1996, the income has been tax-free. Typically, you'll have a valid claim if you are unable to carry out two or three out of five 'activities of daily living' (ADLs) – such as personal hygiene, dressing, feeding yourself, mobility and continence.

Although aimed mainly at paying for care in old age, this type of plan pays out whatever your age if you meet the disability test. But bear in mind that you might need care even though you are not so disabled as to qualify under the long-term care insurance tests, in which case the policy would not pay out.

What long-term care insurance costs

Premiums vary with your age, sex and health, and the payout you choose. Rather than paying the full cost of care, the payout is used typically to top up your other resources to the required level. For example, in 1997 a woman aged 60 might pay around £70 a month for a plan paying out £1,000 a month if she could not manage three ADLs. This would not be enough on its own to cover nursing home fees, but would when combined with her pension income, say.

Alternative strategies

Some long-term care plans are not insurance-based but are 'equity release schemes'. You hand over a lump sum from the sale of your home and in return receive a regular income which you can use to pay for long-term care. You can achieve the same result by using a lump sum from whatever source to buy an annuity. In a sense, this is a straight consumer decision: should you purchase immediate long-term care using whatever resources are available to you? The answer will depend largely on perceived value for money at that time.

More information

You can find out what help is available from your local authority by contacting its social services department (look in the local telephone directory under the entry for your local authority). For details of the income and capital assessment rules, see *Charging for residential accommodation*, a manual which you can inspect at any social services department and many local advice centres (such as a Citizens Advice Bureau). Long-term care insurance is developing only slowly in the UK and there are as yet relatively few plans on offer. *Which?*★ and various money magazines, such as *Money Management*★ and *Planned Savings*,★ publish regular surveys of the long-term care plans available.

Planning in practice

Mr X is 74 years old and recently widowed. He owns his own house and has no children. Taking out a long-term care insurance policy is not likely to be the best bet for Mr X – he has no dependants so is probably less worried than he might otherwise be about protecting his assets. Also, if he takes out a policy at his age, the premiums will be extremely high. If he does want to take precautions, Mr X would be better off with an equity release scheme. Otherwise, he may as well just pay for any care he ends up needing from his assets.

Mr and Mrs Y are retired, in their 60s, in good health and own their own house. They have three children and are keen to be able to leave them their house and savings. The best bet for the Ys would be to apply together for long-term care insurance policies. They could end up paying over £100 a month to be guaranteed of covering average care costs outside London. But at least they'll know that the policy will pay out for as long as required, and that their remaining assets will be protected.

Which? February 1997

115

Chapter 8

Mortgages

In one form or another, borrowing plays some part in most people's lives, whether it be a mortgage to buy a home or credit cards as a convenient way to shop. Borrowing enables you to bring forward the time at which a financial target can be met and is worth considering if there is not enough time available to use the savings route or if the cost of borrowing is lower than the return you would get on saving.

Few people can afford to buy a home outright, and it would be totally impractical to save up the full cost of your home before you bought it; after all, you need somewhere to live in the meantime. Therefore, the usual practice is to take out a mortgage – a loan secured against the property you are buying. This practice has been encouraged by past governments through the giving of tax relief on the interest paid on a mortgage to buy your only or main home. However, this tax incentive has been progressively cut back over the years and, although still useful, is now far less important than it was in the past. For the 1997–8 tax year, mortgage interest relief is given at a rate of 15 per cent in respect of the first £30,000 that you borrow. This means that, if you are paying around 8.7 per cent a year interest on a mortgage of at least £30,000, you will get tax relief of less than £33 a month. From 6 April 1998, the relief is due to be cut to just 10 per cent, reducing its value to less than £22 a month in this example.

There is a wide range of mortgages to choose from, though they fall into two main groups:

- **repayment mortgages,** where you gradually pay off the amount you have borrowed over the term of the loan, together with interest

- **interest-only mortgages,** where you pay only the interest on the loan during its term. Usually, you simultaneously make other arrangements for paying back the capital at the end of the term. The most common loan of this type is the 'endowment mortgage' (see page 119). Other less well-known variations are personal equity plan (PEP) mortgages and pension mortgages.

If you were moving home today, which type of mortgage would you end up choosing? A couple of years ago, the answer for more than half the people taking out a mortgage would have been an endowment type. But it looks as if the bad press this sort of mortgage has received has begun to take effect. In 1997 only a third of mortgages taken out were endowments. That's still fairly high, and there remains some concern that endowment mortgages are being mis-sold by advisers and salespeople who are keen to pick up the commission that goes with the endowment policy. The most popular type of mortgage overall – accounting for four mortgages out of every ten – is the repayment mortgage. This is a generally flexible, low-risk type of mortgage suitable for a wide range of borrowers. But there are other options, and which type of mortgage is right for you depends on a variety of factors such as tax treatment and your attitude towards risk.

Most popular types of mortgage

Type of mortgage	Percentage of first mortgages on a home	
	All buyers	First-time buyers
Repayment	41%	42%
Endowment	34%	33%
Interest-only	19%	18%
Pension	1%	1%
PEP	5%	6%
Other	1%	0%

Source: Council of Mortgage Lenders, data for first quarter of 1997

Repayment mortgage

This is the most straightforward type of mortgage. Your monthly payments pay off both interest and capital, which, provided you keep up the payments, ensures that the whole loan is paid off by the end of the term – see the table on page 124.

A further advantage of repayment mortgages is that they are very flexible and can easily be adapted if you run into temporary difficulties in making the repayments. For example, the most common mortgage term is 25 years at the outset, but, if you ran into problems, your lender might agree to extend the term. This would have the effect of reducing the monthly payments, making them more manageable. Another option might be to add arrears to the amount of the loan outstanding and then adjust the monthly payments, so that the arrears as well as the original loan are repaid by the end of the term.

The way these repayment mortgages are structured means that your payments in the early years are almost completely devoted to paying interest, and very little goes towards reducing the outstanding loan. Critics point out that a move in the early years of the mortgage leaves you back at square one with no reduction in the amount you need to borrow.

A point also to bear in mind is that, unlike some other types of mortgage, there is no built-in life cover to pay off the mortgage in the event of your death. If you have dependants, you will need to arrange separate life insurance, though this is easily done through a relatively cheap mortgage protection policy (a type of decreasing term insurance; see page 70).

In general, a repayment mortgage is most suitable for people who do not like to take risks and who, on a one (lowest risk) to ten (highest risk) scale, would place themselves around one to three.

Interest-only mortgage

With most other types of mortgage, you pay off only the interest on the loan and, in most cases, simultaneously pay into an investment which is intended to pay off the mortgage at the end of the term, but usually there's no guarantee that it will be sufficient to do so. The risk attached to these types of mortgage depends heavily on the type of investment to which they are linked. But you don't need to have an investment-link at all. Some lenders are prepared to make interest-only loans and leave entirely up to you how you will repay the capital at the end of the term. This might be suitable if, say, you expect to be able to sell the property at that time and repay the loan out of the proceeds, or you already have substantial investments which can be used eventually to repay the loan, or you run a business and anticipate using the proceeds of selling your interest in it. However, in 1997 it came to light that some people had been sold interest-only mortgages with no corresponding investment, thinking that they had taken out endowment mortgages (see below). Make sure that you understand what type of mortgage you have and that, if there is no investment linked to it, you are comfortable with the situation.

Interest-only mortgages linked to an investment tend to be less flexible than repayment mortgages if you run into repayment difficulties. Although it is possible to adjust the mortgage element to alter the term and repayments, the investment might not be so flexible and would no longer be properly matched to the loan. You might be allowed to switch to a repayment mortgage, but you would have to decide separately what to do with the investment; stopping payments to it early would not necessarily be the best action.

On the other hand, interest-only mortgages linked to a suitable investment are useful if you move a lot. If you take out a new mortgage, you continue with the same investment, topping it up if you take out a larger loan and simply switching it to the new mortgage – most lenders allow this. Your investment grows steadily, however many times you move, so you make continuous progress towards eventually paying off the mortgage.

The most common types of interest-only mortgages are discussed in the next few sections. The table on page 124 summarises their key characteristics.

Low-cost endowment mortgage

This comprises an interest-only mortgage linked to an endowment policy, which can work either on a with-profits or a unit-linked basis (see below for more about this). If the investment in the endowment policy grows at a reasonable rate, it is anticipated that the policy will produce enough to pay off the loan at the end of the mortgage term and even leave you a bit of extra cash as well. But there is no guarantee that this will happen: if investment returns are lower than expected, either the policy proceeds might fall short of the amount needed or you might have to increase the amount you pay into the policy.

A useful aspect of linking your mortgage to an insurance policy, if you have dependants, is that the policy automatically gives you life cover, which would pay off the loan if you were to die during the term. In practice, the amount of life cover under a low-cost endowment policy starts at less than the amount of the loan and grows gradually during the term. To ensure that the whole mortgage would be repaid in the event of death, an endowment mortgage always includes an element of decreasing term insurance (see page 70). The term insurance and endowment insurance combine to give enough cover for the whole mortgage loan.

The major drawback with an endowment mortgage is the very low cash-in value of the endowment policy if you stop paying the premiums in the early years. The costs associated with selling the policy (which include any commission paid to an adviser or salesperson) are intended to be spread over the full term of the policy. But if the policy stops early, these charges are set against the policy in full, even though the policy has had little time in which to build up much investment value. The result is that stopping the policy early can mean that you get back far less than you have paid in premiums, or even nothing at all. This makes endowment mortgages particularly inflexible if you run into problems keeping up the mortgage repayments. You may be able to alter the interest payments on the mortgage loan itself, but reducing or missing payments into the endowment policy might bring the policy to an end. A waiver of premium option (see page 75) might be at least a partial solution to this problem.

With-profits version of low-cost endowment mortgage

This is the traditional form of low-cost endowment mortgage. At the start of the mortgage, the endowment policy has a guaranteed value (payable at the end of the term or on earlier death), which is far smaller than the amount of your mortgage loan. But bonuses are added to this guaranteed sum. There are regular bonuses, usually credited each year, called 'reversionary bonuses', and normally a 'terminal bonus' added when the policy reaches the end of its term. Once added, the bonuses cannot be taken away and so the value of the policy grows steadily and is intended by the end of the term to be worth at least as much as the amount of the mortgage loan. A low-cost with-profits endowment mortgage could be suitable if you assess your risk profile at around four to five on a ten-point scale. For more information about with-profits insurance, see Chapter 14.

Unit-linked version of low-cost endowment mortgage

With a unit-linked endowment mortgage, instead of the value of the policy depending on bonuses, it is linked directly to one or more funds of investments managed by the insurance company. The fund typically will be invested in shares, and you can often switch between the funds (see Chapter 15). The value of your policy will go up – and down – with the value of the underlying investments. Although share prices tend to grow over the long term, at any point in time stock markets can be riding high or in the doldrums. If share prices happen to be low at the time your mortgage comes to an end, the value of your policy will reflect this and might not be enough to pay off the loan. This makes the unit-linked version of endowment mortgages more risky than its with-profits cousin, and on a ten-point risk scale it scores around six upwards.

Even if you are happy with this level of risk, a unit-linked endowment mortgage is still unlikely to be the best choice, because a PEP mortgage will give you a very similar level of risk but has three important advantages:

- PEP mortgages benefit from favourable tax treatment; endowment mortgages do not
- the charges (even allowing for the cost of buying life insurance if you need it) for a PEP mortgage are usually much lower than the charges for an endowment mortgage
- there are no surrender penalties if you cash in a PEP before the end of the mortgage term.

Given these differences, it is very difficult to justify choosing a unit-linked endowment mortgage nowadays. If you want a share-linked investment to pay off your interest-only mortgage, choose a broadly invested PEP.

Personal equity plan (PEP) mortgage

With this type of interest-only mortgage, you pay into a personal equity plan (PEP) to build up enough to pay off the mortgage at the end of its term. PEPs – which are described in detail in Chapters 14 and 15 – are a tax-efficient way in which to invest in shares, unit trusts and certain other investments: tax-efficient, because all the income and growth from the underlying investments is completely tax-free.

However, the days of PEPs are numbered. In December 1997, the government published its proposals for replacing PEPs with a new form of investment, the Individual Savings Account (ISA). ISAs will be tax-favoured arrangements letting you invest in a range of investments, including shares, unit trusts and National Savings. Assuming the proposals go ahead unchanged, from April 1999, no new PEPs can be started and existing PEPs will lose their tax privileges. There will be a six-month period of grace during which existing PEPs can be transferred to an ISA. But there will be an overall maximum on the amount you can hold in an ISA of £50,000. If your PEP investment is over that limit, the excess cannot be transferred. In addition, there will be a limit of £5,000 on the amount you can add to your ISA each year.

Even before the recent uncertainties, PEP mortgages have been slow to find favour. Cynics suggest that this is because the commission paid to mortgage advisers is lower on a PEP mortgage than on a traditional low-cost endowment mortgage, but there is more to it than that. People are cautious by nature about new ideas and, until the introduction of bond-based PEPs, a PEP mortgage was always a higher-risk option than a with-profits endowment mortgage. Unlike the with-profits endowment, where the addition of bonuses gives you steady growth over the years, the investments in a share-linked PEP can fall in value as well as rise. Over the long term, shares, unit trusts and investment trusts are likely to show good returns and might be expected to beat the more broadly based investment funds underlying with-profits endowment policies. But, at any point in time, stock markets may fall, and the value of your PEP along with them. So although your payments into a PEP will be pitched at the level expected to produce a fund large enough to pay off the mortgage at the end of the term, there is a significant element of uncertainty about the future. However, since there are no restrictions on withdrawing money from your PEP, as the end of the mortgage term approaches you could make a practice of cashing in part or all of your investment when share prices are high and reinvesting in a lower-risk alternative. Share-linked PEP mortgages are suitable only for people who would place themselves around six or more on a ten-point risk scale.

The picture changed in 1995 with the extension of the PEP rules to allow investment in bonds (see page 239) and preference shares (see page 241) issued by companies quoted on the Stock Exchange. In this country, the average investor is perhaps not very familiar with these, though they are more widely used in some other European countries. Although the value of bonds can rise and fall, they tend to be less volatile than the ordinary shares which form the basis of most share-linked PEPs. A bond-based PEP mortgage, therefore, gives a lower-risk way of making use of the tax advantages and is worth considering as an alternative to a with-profits endowment mortgage. On a ten-point risk scale, a bond-based mortgage scores around five, say, depending on the range of bonds held in the PEP. In other words, a bit more risky than a with-profits endowment mortgage, but against that you must balance the favourable tax treatment.

There is no built-in life cover with a PEP mortgage. If you have dependants, consider taking out term insurance – see Chapter 4.

Payments into a PEP are generally very flexible. This has the advantage that, if you run into temporary difficulties, it is easy to cut down or suspend payments into the PEP for a while. But the flip-side of this is that you need the self-discipline to ensure that you pay steadily into the PEP enough to build up the sum needed to repay the mortgage at the end of the day.

Tip

PEP mortgages are tax-efficient, but, as proposed, the new ISAs will be able to pay off only up to £50,000 of mortgage – you will need to top up with other investments if your mortgage is larger.

How different mortgages compare

	Repay- ment	Low-cost with-profit endowment	Unit-linked endowment	Pension	PEP
Guarantees to pay off loan	YES	NO	NO	NO	NO
May give you extra lump sum at maturity	NO	YES	YES	YES	YES
Tax advantages	NO	NO [1]	NO [1]	YES	YES
Life insurance built in	NO	YES	YES	NO [2]	NO
Monthly payments can be reduced easily	NO	NO	NO	MAYBE	YES
Monthly payments can be increased easily	YES	NOT USUALLY	NOT USUALLY	YES	YES
Mortgage can be completely paid off whenever you choose without penalty[3]	YES	LOAN: YES POLICY:NO	LOAN: YES POLICY:NO	LOAN: YES PLAN: NO	YES

[1] Unless you are a higher-rate taxpayer.
[2] But can be added tax-efficiently.
[3] With some loans, there is an early redemption charge if you pay off in the early years.

Pension mortgage

A pension mortgage is the most tax-efficient mortgage of all, but it does not suit everyone. You take out an interest-only loan and simultaneously pay into a personal pension plan. (In theory, an employer's pension scheme works just as well, but is rarely used in this way.) The idea is that the tax-free lump sum payable at retirement – see page 176 – will be used to pay off the mortgage. This gives you a number of tax advantages:

- your payments into the pension plan qualify for tax relief at your top rate; no other type of mortgage has this advantage
- if you need life cover, you can use a term insurance policy linked to the pension plan, which means you get tax relief at the top rate on your premiums
- your investment in the pension plan builds up tax-free
- the lump sum used to pay off the mortgage is tax-free.

Against this, you must set the following disadvantages. First, if you become no longer eligible for the pension plan – because you decide to join a pension scheme at work, for example, or because you become unemployed – you will have to find some other method of building up the sum needed to pay off your mortgage. Secondly, using a pension plan in this way reduces your scope for building up retirement income. Trying to use one financial tool to meet two targets inevitably causes a conflict.

What sort of interest rate to choose

As well as choosing between the basic types of mortgage, there is a wealth of interest rate options too:

- **variable rate** The 'standard' option in the UK. The interest you pay rises and falls with interest rates generally in the economy, making it hard to know from one year to another what your payments will be. Interestingly, this is not the norm in some other countries, where the uncertainty of variable rates is considered too risky
- **fixed rate** You lock into a set interest rate for a fixed period of time, which could be just a year or two or as long as ten years. At the end of the term, you usually revert to the normal variable rate. Usually an arrangement fee has to be paid when you take out this type of mortgage, and there will be hefty penalties if you want to pay off the mortgage: for example, to switch to a cheaper lender. The penalty period often extends beyond the fixed-rate term: for example, you might fix the rate for three years but face early redemption penalties for five years in all. This means that you are not only locked into the fixed rate but also into whatever variable rate that lender subsequently charges. In the UK, opting for a fixed-rate mortgage has become more popular due to the rise in interest rates throughout 1997. Choosing a fixed rate can be a speculative move – you choose a fixed rate if you expect interest rates generally to rise. If you are right, you will be quids in; if you are wrong and variable rates fall, you will have lost the gamble and be stuck with the higher fixed rate. But fixed rates also have the advantage that you know what your payments will be, which helps you to plan your budgeting

- **discounted rates** Some mortgages, particularly those aimed at first-time buyers, have a lower rate of interest in the early years. This is useful if money is tight at present but you expect the situation to improve, for example as you work your way up the promotions ladder at work. But make sure that what is on offer is a genuine discount. Beware of deals where the interest saved in the early years is simply deferred and added to the outstanding loan – this is an expensive way to cut costs in the early years and can cause problems when you come to move house if the outstanding loan has become larger than the value of your home. As with fixed-rate deals, there are early redemption penalties if you pay off a discounted-rate mortgage in the early years, and usually the penalty period extends beyond the discount period. For example, even a discount for just one year may go hand in hand with redemption penalties in the first five years. This means that you may be locked into the lender's standard variable rate for some time
- **capped rates** A capped rate varies in line with general interest rates but is subject to a limit: the rate is guaranteed not to rise above the interest rate cap. There might also be a floor below which the interest rate will not fall, even if general rates go lower; this is called an interest rate 'collar'. The deal runs for a fixed period of time, after which you revert to the normal variable rate. Capped rates give you some of the certainty of fixed rates, helping you to plan your budgets, without so much risk of being locked into a punishingly high rate. As with fixed-rate mortgages, expect to pay an arrangement fee for a capped mortgage and to face hefty early redemption penalties if you try to get out of a collared deal in the first few years
- **cashback deals** with some standard variable-rate mortgages, you get a cash sum when you take out the mortgage. This can be a sizeable sum: for example, 5 or 6 per cent of the amount you are borrowing. You can use the cash however you like, so it can be handy to put towards the costs of moving, decorating your new home, and so on. Although a cashback is not strictly speaking an interest rate option, it is useful to look at it here because one use for the cashback would be to invest it to give you a sum to call on if your mortgage rate rises. For example, if you borrowed £50,000 and the mortgage rate rose by 2 per cent over the first year of your mortgage, you could pay up to an extra £910

interest that year. This would be well covered by a 5 per cent cashback deal, giving you a £2,500 lump sum. After paying the extra interest you would still be in profit to the tune of £1,590. This looks a better option than, say, a one-year fixed-rate mortgage taken out at the same initial interest rate with an arrangement fee of £250 which would have saved you £910 – £250 = £660. This is a very simplified example; real life is more complex and your sums will need to take into account the difference in interest rates between deals and longer time periods than one year. With cashback deals, there is usually an early redemption penalty period of five years or so. If you pay part or all of the mortgage during that time, you generally have to pay back the cashback you received.

Flexible mortgages

Most mortgages, whether variable rate or fixed rate, tie you into making contractual payments each month. You can pay more than your contractual amount, though often any excess you pay will be set against your mortgage loan on only one date a year, so there may be a long delay before your contractual payments adjust. And, generally, there is no scope for paying lower amounts or skipping payments, unless you are in default and have agreed some temporary emergency measures with your lender to stave off losing your home.

However, a few lenders have for some time now offered flexible mortgages which give you the scope to vary your monthly payments and to skip a limited number of payments altogether. Recently, the idea has been taken even further, and, in 1997, two or three lenders operated financial packages which combined a mortgage, a current account and credit facilities – the ultimate flexible mortgage.

Warning

Be very wary of taking out a mortgage which keeps interest payments low in the early years by deferring the interest and adding it to the outstanding loan. The amount you owe can grow alarmingly, increasing future costs and causing particular problems if the value of your property is falling.

The new breed of flexible mortgage works like this: you pay your salary or other income direct into your mortgage account, where it pays the interest and reduces the outstanding mortgage balance. You then borrow from the account the money you need to cover your spending (and investment in, say, unit trusts). A result of this arrangement is that any excess of your salary over your spending – that is your short-term savings – in effect earns the current mortgage rate because it is reducing the mortgage balance. There is no tax to pay on this return (because it is in reality interest saved on the mortgage rather than interest income as such), and the mortgage rate you are 'earning' will usually be higher than the rate you can get on straightforward savings with a bank or building society.

Flexible mortgage arrangements have been welcomed by the government as more suitable to modern lifestyles where people less often stay with a job for life and may take career breaks – perhaps to spend time with their families or to retrain.

Mortgage packages

As if deciding the type of mortgage and the nature of the interest rate were not enough, mortgages often come packaged with other products, some of which may be worth having, others not.

Mortgage protection insurance

This is term insurance to pay off your mortgage if you die during the term. (It is not required with endowment mortgages, which have built-in life cover.) If anyone is financially dependent on you – your wife, husband, partner, children, elderly relative – this type of insurance is usually well worth having. However, if you have no dependants, there is no need for this cover and you might prefer to do without it (in which case your home would be sold on your death and the mortgage paid off out of the proceeds).

Mortgage payment protection insurance

One of the biggest problems, if you lose your job or fall ill for a prolonged period, is how to pay the mortgage, because failing to keep up the payments could end in your losing your home. Until

October 1995, if you became unemployed and your income and savings were low enough, you could qualify for income support to cover half your mortgage interest payments during the first 16 weeks and the full amount thereafter on up to £100,000 of loan. Since then, anyone taking out a mortgage on or after 1 October 1995 is excluded from this safety net for the first nine months of claiming benefit. For existing borrowers, there is no cover at all for the first two months, and thereafter only half of the interest payments is covered for the next four months. To plug this hole in the state safety net, the government expects people taking out new mortgages simultaneously to take out mortgage payment protection insurance, which pays out if you are unable to work because of sickness, disability or unemployment.

This insurance has been around for some time, though in the past it had limited appeal because of the many restrictions, often including a waiting period of, say, three months after taking out the policy before claims could be met, no cover for claims related to medical problems you had at the time you took out the policy, pregnancy, drugs or alcohol, HIV, and so on. Even more of a problem has been the list of people who are not normally welcomed by insurers for this type of policy, for example:

- part-time workers, meaning those who work fewer than 16 hours a week
- fixed contract workers
- people with no fixed income
- newly self-employed who haven't yet built up a track record
- people with risky jobs, for example divers
- people who already know that they are likely to lose their job.

Since the restriction on state support, insurers have been experimenting with less restrictive policies. However, you should take special care to read the terms of this type of policy to ensure that it provides cover which is suitable for you.

Whether or not you need mortgage payment protection insurance depends on what arrangements are already in place to protect your income in case of illness (see Chapter 5) or unemployment. In general, it is probably a wise precaution to take out this cover. A few lenders offer it free as part of the mortgage package.

House insurance

Insurance companies pay commission to agencies which arrange the sale of their policies. Banks and building societies have found this to be a useful source of extra income, so you may well find that you are expected to take out house buildings and even house contents insurance through the society or bank as part of the mortgage package. But check both the cost and cover carefully: you may be able to get better value insurance elsewhere, especially if you qualify for discounts with some companies because of your job. The house insurance may be a compulsory part of the particular mortgage package, in which case you will have little choice but to take it up if you are keen on the rest of the mortgage deal. Another ruse is where the bank or building society makes an administration charge if you choose to buy your house insurance elsewhere – you will have to weigh up the impact of the charge against the amount you stand to save by insuring elsewhere. Check whether the new insurer will pay the administration charge for you – at least one company does this.

Switching your mortgage

Having taken out a mortgage, you are not locked into that particular loan for the full mortgage term. Lenders compete fiercely for your custom and you may be able to reduce the cost of your mortgage by switching to a new lender. Against this you must set the costs of making the switch. These might include: valuation, legal and land registry fees; arrangement fee and mortgage indemnity insurance premium charged by the new lender; discharge fee, deeds fee and any early redemption charge levied by the old lender. The costs can easily come to £1,000 or more, but the savings can be substantial too. For example, each 1 per cent cut in the mortgage rate on a £50,000 loan would save you around £450 in interest each year. Although not widely advertised, rather than losing you to another lender, your existing mortgage lender might be willing to give you a better deal: for example, by extending to you discounted rates normally available only to first-time buyers. It is certainly worth talking to your existing lender before going ahead with any switch, since it will cost you less to stay put.

If you are interested in switching mortgage, check what deals are currently on offer (see 'more information' on page 133). Get quotes for the loans you are interested in, including the associated charges. Check what fees your existing lender might charge and check out whether your existing lender might be prepared to offer you a better deal than your current loan in order to keep your custom.

Bear in mind that switching mortgage counts as taking out a new loan, so you would be entitled to less help from the state if you ran into problems keeping up the payments – see page 129.

Mortgage problems

Payment difficulties

According to government figures, as a nation we owe more than £400 billion in mortgages. For a minority of people this debt becomes a problem. Usually this happens because of some unforeseen crisis, such as redundancy or divorce. It can be very tempting to close your eyes to mounting bills and simply hope the problem will go away. But debt problems nearly always get worse the longer you leave them. It's essential that you take action as soon as you can.

Your mortgage is a priority debt, because failing to tackle the problem could mean losing your home. Contact your lender immediately and let them know that you're having problems. They are as anxious to find a solution as you, and in most cases will take drastic action only as the very last resort. Some building societies and banks run in-house debt counselling services which will help you to prioritise your debts, advise on any state benefits for which you might qualify and will try to set a realistic target for clearing your mortgage arrears, taking into account your whole financial position. Most mortgage lenders stress that repossessing your home is the last thing they want to do. Extending the term of the loan and thus reducing the monthly payments is a possible solution. Where repossession is unavoidable, a few societies have successfully used mortgage-to-rent schemes to allow people to stay in their old home but as tenants of a housing association.

You can get independent help with your debt problems from your local Citizens Advice Bureau★ and from National Debtline,★ and your local authority might run a money advice centre.

Negative equity – where the mortgage on your home is greater than the value of your home – can be a problem, because even if your home is repossessed, there may still be a big mortgage debt outstanding. Your lender may insist on your paying for 'mortgage indemnity insurance' when you first take out your mortgage; this ensures that your lender can recover its money if you default on the mortgage, but it does not protect you. The insurance company which reimburses the lender can still chase you for the outstanding mortgage debt.

Mortgage complaints

If you are unhappy about the actions of your mortgage lender, you should complain initially to the branch where you took out the loan. If you are not satisfied with the response, take your complaint to the lender's head office. If this still fails to produce a satisfactory resolution to the problem, you can go to the Building Societies Ombudsman★ or Banking Ombudsman★ or Mortgage Code Arbitration Scheme,★ who can examine the evidence, make a judgement and, if appropriate, recommend that the lender pay you compensation up to £100,000.

If you are unhappy about any dealings with an independent mortgage adviser, complain to the firm. Unfortunately, if that does not work, there are currently no formal complaints channels. Try complaining to the lender involved, if the mortgage deal got that far. You could resort to court action, but it can be very hard to prove that poor advice was given and resulted in loss to you, and court cases are notoriously expensive and slow. From 1 July 1997, mortgage lenders have introduced a 'Mortgage Code' which sets out good practice in mortgage lending. Lenders themselves must comply with the code and, from April 1998, some 50,000 brokers, financial advisers, estate agents and other mortgage intermediaries are to be covered by it too. The code sets out the information to be given to prospective borrowers (including disclosure of commission to be received by the adviser from the lender if it comes to more than £250), requires advice to be confirmed in writing and requires membership of the Mortgage Code Arbitration Scheme (see above). It is expected that most major lenders will deal only with intermediaries who have agreed to abide by the code. However, the code is voluntary, so many advisers might choose not to join and, as intermediaries' compliance with the code is not expected to be monitored until 1999, we have yet to see how effective the code will be. Nevertheless, from April 1998 onwards, it would be wise to deal only through lenders and intermediaries who are covered by the code – their stationery should make this clear.

If you were advised by an estate agent, you might be able to complain to the Ombudsman for Corporate Estate Agents,★ but only if the agent you used is a member. You could also try complaining to any professional body to which the estate agent belongs: the National Association of Estate Agents,★ the Royal Institute of Chartered Surveyors★ or the Incorporated Society of Valuers and Auctioneers.★

Warning

If you run into difficulties in paying your mortgage, contact the lender immediately. Debt problems have a nasty habit of getting worse if you ignore them.

More information

Get details of particular mortgages direct from lenders. See the regular surveys of mortgages in *Which?*★ *an*d specialist personal finance magazines. *What mortgage*★ gives listings of mortgages on offer, as does *Moneyfacts*★ magazine. Moneyfacts also operates a fax information service. For information about tax relief on mortgages, see Inland Revenue leaflet IR123 *Mortgage interest relief – buying your home.*

Mortgages in practice

Roger Reade went to X Direct because its rate was competitive. But his mortgage offer took almost six weeks, partly due to problems with the valuation. When it arrived, it contained errors that took several letters and phone calls to resolve. Roger was unimpressed with X Direct's efficiency. He found that it asked him for information it already held and he felt that the staff lacked experience.

Alex van Tricht needed a new mortgage before he redeemed his existing one. He used a broker which suggested Y building society. He received a verbal agreement within a day, but the written offer took nearly six weeks because Y had so many applications to process. The broker helped Alex to find a lender who could meet all his special needs. But he feels that his mortgage offer took too long and that he was let down by Y's service.

Eleanor Stokoe went to Z building society for her mortgage. She was pleased with its service, but encountered delays with her application. The mortgage valuer asked her to get a report from an arboriculturist because of two trees close to the property. This delayed her mortgage offer by a month. This shows how important it is to chase all the people involved, not just the lender. When she finally received the offer, the buyer for her home pulled out at the last minute.

Which? April 1997

Chapter 9

Pensions

One of your highest financial priorities should be ensuring that you will have an adequate income in retirement. In many areas of personal finance, the aim is to protect yourself against the *possibility* that certain events will happen. But with pension planning you are dealing with the very near *certainty* that you will retire and you will need an income.

Virtually everyone will need a pension. A few people are rich enough not to worry too much about where their retirement income will come from, but even they should take advantage of the tax incentives available for pension planning. If you run your own business, you might think that you do not need to make special plans for retirement. After all, you'll sell the business and live off the proceeds, won't you? But this is a very risky strategy: your business might fail before you reach retirement, or you might be unable to sell it at the time you want to retire or for enough to provide a comfortable income.

Do not underestimate the financial resources you will need for retirement. This is a phase of your life which can span two or three decades: see the table on page 136. To build up the resources you need, you should start your retirement saving as soon as possible.

This chapter looks at the basic strategy of planning how much retirement income you will need, what part of it might come from the state and how this might change in future. Chapters 10 and 11 look at the role of employers' pension schemes and personal pension plans.

How much retirement income will you need?

One of the difficulties in looking ahead to what income you might need in retirement is that price levels are likely to be very different. But as a first step you should consider what income you might need in terms of today's prices. Your income needs are likely to be substantially different from your current needs. For example, in retirement you might no longer be paying out on a mortgage, and you will not have work-related expenses (although you might need to replace, say, running costs of a car previously met by your employer, out of your own pocket); on the other hand, you might spend more on travelling and holidays (being able to go away at off-peak times could reduce the outlay). Health problems tend to be more prevalent the older you are, so you might spend more in that area too, and so on. You should also consider how you will meet capital outlays once you are retired – for example, the cost of replacing a company car, the washing machine or the fridge. You may need to set aside a little of your income each month to meet such capital needs. Try to envisage what your expenditure patterns might be in retirement and fill in the Calculator starting opposite, estimating how much you might spend each month, assuming *today*'s prices, on each type of expenditure.

Average length of retirement

If you retire at this age:	On average, you can expect this many years of retirement:	
	women	men
50	30	26
55	26	21
60	22	17
65	18	14
70	14	11
75	11	8
80	8	6
85	6	5

Source: Government Actuary's Department

The impact of tax

The Calculator makes no allowance for income tax. Both state pensions and pensions you build up for yourself are taxable, though you may enjoy higher age-related allowances once you reach 65 (see page 35). It is fairly pointless going into detailed calculations at this stage to estimate how much extra income you might need to foot the tax bills. After all, the tax system could be wildly different by the time you retire. As a very rough rule of thumb, you might adjust the value at F in the Calculator as follows to make some allowance for tax on your pensions:

- if the value at B is £5,500 or less if you are single, or £14,000 or less if you are a married couple, make no adjustment to F
- if the value at B is in the region of £5,500 to £10,000 if you are single, or £14,000 to £22,000 if you are a couple, increase F by 10 per cent
- if the value at B is more than £10,000 if you are single, or more than £22,000 if you are a couple, increase F by 15 per cent.

Retirement income Calculator

How much you might spend on:	£/month
Household expenses	
Food shopping and household basics	a
Buying and repairing household equipment	b
Newspapers/magazines/books	c
TV licence/videos/music	d
Dog/cat/other pets	e
Clothes/shoes/cosmetics/hairdressing	f
Other home-related expenses	
Mortgage/rent	g
Repairs/service charge/decoration/furnishing	h
Building and contents insurance	i
Council Tax/water charges	j

	£/month
Gas/electricity/heating oil/solid fuel	k
Home help/window cleaner/other paid help	l
Gardening	m
Telephone	n
Leisure and treats	
Sports and hobbies: materials/lessons/other	o
Dining out/theatre/cinema/concerts/exhibitions	p
Holidays/holiday home/second home	q
Other (e.g. smoking, drinking)	r
Transport	
Owning a car: tax/insurance/servicing/repairs/ breakdown insurance	s
Renting a car: rental charges/insurance	t
Running a car: petrol/oil/diesel	u
Train fares/bus fares/coach fares	v
Other	w
Health-related	
Dentist	x
Optician	y
Private medical insurance/hospital cash plan	z
Long-term care insurance	aa
Other health-related expenses	bb
Caring for others	
Spending on children and grandchildren	cc
Financial help for elderly relatives	dd
Christmas/birthday/other presents	ee
Gifts to charity/church collections	ff

	£/month
Protection-type life insurance	gg
Other	hh
Saving and borrowing	
Saving to replace car/major household equipment	ii
Saving to finance home improvements	jj
Saving to cover higher health spending later on	kk
Other regular saving	ll
Loan repayments (other than mortgage)	mm
Other spending	
Postage/stationery etc.	nn
Other	oo
TOTAL (Add items a to oo)	A
Multiply A by 12 to give yearly amount. This is the yearly income you need to cover your retirement spending at today's prices	B
Yearly pension you expect from the state – see page 140 onwards	C
Subtract C from B. This is the yearly retirement income, at today's prices and before tax, that you need to provide for yourself – e.g. through employers' pension schemes and/or personal pension plans and/or other savings	D
Choose an inflation factor (see page 142)	E
Multiply D by E. This is the yearly retirement income, at before-tax prices at the time of retirement, which you need to provide for yourself	F

The impact of inflation

Even relatively low rates of inflation can eat heavily into the spending power of your income. For example, if prices were to rise by just

3 per cent a year over the next 20 years, a loaf of bread costing 60 pence would then cost £1.08 and you would need an income of over £18,000 to be able to buy the same things that you can today with just £10,000.

The effect of inflation is important in pension planning for two reasons:

- the amount of income you receive at the start of your retirement could be totally insufficient in your later retirement years, unless the income is guaranteed to increase regularly to either wholly or partly protect you against inflation. This point is considered in more detail within the context of the different types of pension savings available
- the starting amount of retirement income you expect to need in terms of today's prices must be converted to an amount in terms of tomorrow's prices if it is to have the same buying power at the time you retire. Many methods of building up retirement income offer no guarantee that they will compensate you for the effects of inflation between now and when the pension starts to be paid; the exceptions are the state pension (see below) and salary-related pension schemes run by employers (see page 150).

To convert your required retirement income to future prices, you need to decide when you want your pension to start and what rate of inflation you expect between then and now. The table on page 142 gives the factors you should enter at E in the Retirement Income Calculator. For example, suppose value D in the Calculator is £12,500. If you are planning to retire in 25 years' time and you expect inflation to average 4 per cent a year, multiply D by an inflation factor of 2.666 to tell you what yearly income you will need, that is, £12,500 × 2.666 = £33,325.

A pension from the state

You would be very unwise to rely on the state pension alone for your retirement income; on its own it is too low to support a comfortable standard of living. However, it does provide a useful core to your retirement planning, and it is worth making sure that you maintain your entitlement to it.

How much pension?

State retirement pensions become payable when you reach state pension age (see page 142), regardless of whether you have stopped work. You can, however, choose to delay the start of your pension for a time, in which case the amount payable is increased.

State pensions have three components:

- **basic pension** This is payable to everyone who has paid enough National Insurance contributions throughout their working life – see page 142. In 1997–8 the full basic pension for a single person is £62.45 a week (£3,247.40 a year). A couple who both qualify for their own basic pension could get double this. Alternatively, a wife over state pension age can have a basic pension of up to £37.35 a week (£1,942.20 a year) based on her husband's contribution record, provided he is receiving his state pension. If the wife is under pension age, the husband gets the extra sum, but only if his wife earns no more than a given limit (£49.15 a week in 1997–8)

- **State Earnings-Related Pension Scheme (SERPS)** This is payable to employees who pay National Insurance contributions on earnings above the lower earnings limit (which is £62 a week in 1997–8) and who are not 'contracted out' of this part of the state scheme (see opposite). If you are self-employed or not working, you cannot build up SERPS entitlement. As its name suggests, how much pension you get depends on your earnings averaged over your working life, so everyone's entitlement is different. In terms of today's money and assuming you had never contracted out of SERPS and that your earnings were equal to, or more than, the upper earnings limit (£465 a week in 1997–8) throughout your working life, this would provide, at most, some £70 to £100 a week depending on when you retire. In practice, most people will get far less than this

- **graduated pension** This is an older, simpler but much less generous earnings-related scheme for employees which ran from 1961 to 1975. If you belonged to the scheme, the National Insurance contributions you paid were related to your earnings. The contributions you paid are divided into 'units'. You now get so much pension for each unit (8.11 pence per unit in 1997–8).

In 1997–8 the most graduated pension you can get is £5.84 a week (£304 a year) if you are a woman and £6.98 a week (£363 a year) if you are a man. You could have been contracted out of the graduated scheme, in which case your employer's scheme took over responsibility for paying you a pension instead and you gave up your rights under the state graduated scheme.

All the state pensions are increased each year in line with inflation, and they are taxable. If you qualify for state retirement pension, you also get a small tax-free bonus (£10 in 1997–8) just before Christmas. The amount of this bonus has been unchanged for many years.

Taking account of inflation
Multiply by the appropriate factor below to turn a sum in terms of today's money into an equivalent sum in terms of future prices

Number of years until retirement	Rate of inflation you expect between now and the start of retirement				
	2%	4%	6%	8%	10%
5	1.104	1.217	1.338	1.469	1.611
10	1.219	1.480	1.791	2.159	2.594
15	1.346	1.801	2.397	3.172	4.177
20	1.486	2.191	3.207	4.661	6.728
25	1.641	2.666	4.292	6.848	10.835
30	1.811	3.243	5.743	10.063	17.449
35	2.000	3.946	7.686	14.785	28.102
40	2.208	4.081	10.286	21.725	45.259
45	2.438	5.841	13.765	31.920	72.890

Working life and state pension age

Your entitlement to the main state pensions depends on the National Insurance contributions paid during your working life. 'Working life' is an official definition which, for most people, means the tax years from the start of the one in which you reach age 16 to the last complete tax year before you reach state pension age.

At present, state pension age is 65 for men and 60 for women. But for women born after 5 March 1955, their pension age will also be 65. There is a transitional period during which women's pension age gradually rises from the old level of 60 to the new level of 65. Women who were born between 6 April 1950 and 5 March 1955 are affected by the transitional rules. If they apply to you, your state pension age is calculated according to the following rule: pension age is 60 plus one month for each month (or part-month) that your birth date falls after 5 April 1950. For this purpose, a month runs from the sixth day of one month to the fifth day of the next.

If your state pension age is 65, you normally have a working life of 49 years. If your state pension age is 60, your working life is normally 44 years.

National Insurance contributions

Not all National Insurance contributions count for the purpose of building up state pensions: the table on page 145 specifies those that do and don't.

To qualify for the full basic state pension, you must have paid the right type of National Insurance contributions for at least nine-tenths of your working life. If you have paid these contributions for less than a quarter of your working life, you will get no basic pension at all. Contributions paid between a quarter and nine-tenths of working life qualifies you for a reduced-rate basic pension.

If you do not pay contributions for a time because you are at home caring for children or a dependent relative, you can claim Home Responsibilities Protection (HRP). This, in effect, reduces the length of your working life, so that you need fewer years in order to qualify for a given rate of basic pension.

Warning

Home Responsibilities Protection is given only for full tax years (running from 6 April to the following 5 April). You cannot claim it for part of a year during which you stopped work to care for children or an elderly relative.

Tip

If you have gaps in your National Insurance record during the last six years (whether for full tax years or just part of any tax year), check whether filling the gaps would increase your entitlement to the state basic pension. If it would, consider paying voluntary Class 3 contributions. Contact your local DSS office* for details.

Contracting out

If you belong to an employer's pension scheme (see Chapter 10), it may be one which is 'contracted out' of SERPS. If so, two things happen:

- both you and your employer pay National Insurance contributions on earnings above the lower earnings limit at a lower-than-normal rate, and
- your employer's scheme contracts to pay you a pension at retirement instead of the SERPS pension you would otherwise have built up during the period for which you are contracted out.

The rules concerning contracting out have become very complex, and whether or not the pension from your employer's scheme will turn out to be more or less than the SERPS given up depends, among other things, on the type of scheme and precisely when you are contracted out.

If you cannot contract out through an employer's pension scheme, you can choose to contract out through a special type of personal pension plan (see page 186). While you are contracted out in this way, you do not build up SERPS entitlement, but you and your employer carry on paying National Insurance contributions at the normal rate. However, part of the contributions is rebated into your personal plan, where they are left to build up and must be used to provide a specified range of benefits, including a retirement pension from state pension age. There is no guarantee that the pension you get will match the SERPS given up; it could be more or less, depending on:

- the size of the rebate paid into the plan. Since April 1997, the rebates have been set to vary with age. Up to then, men and

Which National Insurance contributions count?

Type of contribution	Description	What do you pay in 1997–8?	Do they count?
Class 1: full rate on earnings up to the lower earnings limit (LEL – £62 a week in 1997–8)	Paid by employees (and their employers), including company directors, but not by people earning less than the lower earnings limit	2% on earnings up to the LEL. (If you earn less than the LEL, you pay nothing)	YES, towards state basic pension. (If you earn less than the LEL, you do not build up any pension entitlement)
Class 1: full rate on earnings above the lower earnings limit	Paid by employees (and their employers), including company directors	10% on earnings above the LEL up to an upper earnings limit (£465 a week in 1997–8). You pay less if you are contracted out	YES, towards SERPS pension, but NO, if you are contracted out
Class 1: reduced rate	Paid by some married women and widows, both of whom can choose to switch to the full rate	3.85% on all earnings. (If you earn less than the LEL, you pay nothing)	NO
Class 2	Paid by the self-employed. Optional for people with profits below a given limit and for some married women and widows	Flat rate: £6.15 a week in 1997–8	YES, towards state basic pension but NO, if you opt not to pay them
Class 3	Voluntary contributions	Flat rate: £6.05 a week in 1997–8	YES, towards state basic pension
Class 4	Paid by the self-employed with profits above a given level	6.0% of earnings between certain limits in 1997–8	NO
National Insurance credits	You get these, without paying, if, for example, you are claiming unemployment benefit, maternity benefit or are off work sick. If your state pension age is 65, you automatically get credits from age 60 if you are not working	n/a	YES, towards state basic pension

women over the ages of, say, 40 and 35 respectively were generally better off staying in SERPS. Because the age-related rebates do still become flat-rate for people in their late 40s, there is still a 'pivotal' age at which you should normally remain in SERPS rather than newly contracting out, though it might not be worth contracting back in at these ages because of the continuing impact of charges on your contracted-out plan

- how the invested rebates grow. The more optimistic you are about investment returns, the more attractive contracting out will seem
- the charges which the plan provider deducts. These can have a large impact on small investments and, although there is no hard-and-fast rule, you should perhaps avoid contracting out through a personal plan if you earn less than about £160 a week or if you are not certain of keeping the plan going for several years
- at what rate your investment can be converted to pension at retirement.

What state pension(s) will you get?

You do not need to work out what your state pension entitlement will be; instead, you can ask the Benefits Agency★ to provide you with a retirement forecast. This states what rights to pension you have built up so far and projects what your state pensions might be by state pension age if your circumstances continue unchanged. Note that the projection is in terms of today's money. The Benefits Agency also gives advice on steps you might take to boost your entitlement: for example, by paying voluntary National Insurance contributions to fill any gaps in your record.

To obtain a retirement forecast, get form BR19 from any Benefits Agency. Complete it and send it to the address given on the form. You should receive your forecast within a few weeks.

Changes on the way

Governments worldwide are concerned about the high cost of providing pensions for future generations. In Britain, state pensions have been eroded substantially over the last 20 years through deliberate cuts, such as breaking the link between pension increases and earnings growth, alterations to SERPS and raising women's state pension age. As a result, the government does not face such a pressing crisis as do other countries when it comes to funding future state pensions.

However, the British regime leaves people heavily dependent on non-state pensions if they are to enjoy an adequate income in retirement. Those who work for a large employer consistently for many years may achieve this goal. But many others are self-employed or have low earnings, broken working patterns (especially women who are more likely to have family responsibilities) and/or prolonged periods of unemployment. These people often find it difficult or impossible to set aside enough savings for retirement. Even when they do make retirement savings, personal pension plans have proved to be inadequate vehicles for small sums, with charges eating too heavily into the investment.

The current government is committed to encouraging people to make their own provision for retirement and is likely to make saving for some form of 'second tier' pension (that is, topping up the state basic pension) compulsory. But the government recognises that people have a right to value for money in their pension savings and, at the time of writing, is consulting widely about how to establish 'stakeholder pensions'. No details have been decided on, but according to the Social Security Secretary, Harriet Harman, stakeholder pensions:

- 'would offer economies of scale through pooling savings in multi-member schemes perhaps based on an industry, an occupation, a trade group or a locality'
- 'would have a low charging regime – significantly lower than many current personal pensions'
- 'should not penalise those on modest incomes or who break their career'
- 'will need to be available to the self-employed'.

It is envisaged that stakeholder pensions would be approved or 'kitemarked' in some way to instil trust in them and that members would be involved in the management of the schemes.

Action list for state pensions

- Check what your state pension entitlement will be by getting a retirement forecast from the Benefits Agency.★
- If you have any gaps in your National Insurance record during the last six years, consider filling them by paying voluntary Class 3 National Insurance.
- If you are paying Class 1 National Insurance at the married women's reduced rate, you are not building up your own pension entitlement, though you will be able to claim a pension based on your husband's record. Check whether you would get a higher pension by switching to full-rate Class 1 contributions.
- If you are paying Class 1 National Insurance at the married women's reduced rate and your earnings are up to £20 or so more than the lower earnings limit (£62 a week in 1997–8), you may actually be paying *more* than you would if you switched to full-rate Class 1 contributions. Check whether this applies to you.
- If you have chosen not to pay National Insurance – for example, you are self-employed and your profits are low – you are not building up a state pension entitlement. Consider paying the contributions for the sake of your future pension.
- If you are out of work, check whether you are getting National Insurance credits. If not, can you do so? For example, is it worth signing on for unemployment benefit in order to get credits? If you are caring for someone at home, are you getting Home Responsibilities Protection? (It is given automatically if you are getting child benefit.) If not, make sure you claim it.
- If you have the choice, consider whether you would be better off contracted out of SERPS or staying in this state scheme (see page 144). Review this decision every year, but if you are contracted out through a personal plan be wary of stopping the plan after only a few years – by retirement, the value of the plan could have been completely absorbed by charges.

More information

Your main source of information about state pensions – both in general terms and concerning your own entitlement – is the Benefits Agency,★ which is part of the Department of Social

Security.* The agency publishes a number of useful leaflets, including: NP46 *A guide to state retirement pensions*, NI1 *National Insurance for married women*, CF411 *Home Responsibilities Protection* and NI196 *Social security benefit rates and NI contribution rates*. Your local Benefits Agency is also the organisation to contact if you want a forecast of your state pension (see above). If you want to read more about state pensions and would like to make your own check on your entitlement to them, see *The Which? Guide to Pensions*, published by Which? Books.* See also Inland Revenue leaflet IR121 *Income tax and pensioners*.

Planning in practice

Lynne Ridge's right to a full state pension has been endangered by a little-known DSS rule: she stopped work to look after her young children. Prolonged breaks from work can reduce your state pension; to qualify for the full amount, you usually need to work (and pay National Insurance) for most of your adult life.

However, Home Responsibilities Protection (HRP) means that time spent bringing up children is deducted from the number of years which you have to work to qualify. This is good news – but there is a catch. HRP applies to 'the main payee' for child benefit. Lynne's partner registered as the main payee, although the child benefit was paid into Lynne's bank account. The DSS did not point out that she would lose HRP as a result. Lynne has now registered and will get HRP in future.

Which? June 1993

Chapter 10

Employers' pension schemes

If you completed the Retirement Income Calculator in Chapter 9, it is virtually certain that any state pension you expect to get falls far short of the income you ideally want in your retirement years. A key part of your financial planning is ensuring that the shortfall is made good. In theory, there are numerous ways in which you might save for retirement. In practice, though, there is a distinct tax advantage to using either an employer's pension scheme or a personal pension plan, because with both:

- you get tax relief at your highest rate(s) on contributions paid into the scheme or plan
- capital gains made on the invested contributions are tax-free
- up to 1 July 1997, income earned by your invested contributions was also tax-free. From 2 July 1997 onwards, income from investing in shares and unit trusts is taxed at a rate of 20 per cent (reducing to 10 per cent fom 6 April 1999). Income from other sources will continue to be tax-free
- part of the proceeds from the scheme or plan can be taken at retirement in the form of a tax-free lump sum. The rest must be taken as taxable pension.

If you are eligible to join an employer's pension scheme, this will usually be the best way of building up the additional retirement income you need because it has further advantages, which do not generally apply to personal plans:

- your employer contributes to the plan. With a contributory scheme, you pay into it as well. With a non-contributory plan, your employer foots the whole bill

- you generally enjoy a package of benefits, including life insurance, pensions for widow(er)s and dependants, and regular increases to pensions once they are being paid
- the costs of running the scheme are often met directly by the employer rather than reducing the amount which is invested for your pension. Even where costs are met by the pension scheme, they will usually be a lot lower than the costs associated with a personal pension plan.

Your main pension options are summarised in the chart on page 153. The rest of this chapter considers how much pension you can expect to build up through an employer's pension scheme and what action you can take to boost the amount you will get. It also looks briefly at how variations of employers' schemes can be used if you run your own company. These options are not open to you if you are self-employed or in partnership; see instead Chapter 11, which describes the use of personal pension plans in your financial arrangements.

How much pension?

To answer this question, you need to be clear about what type of employers' pension scheme you belong to. There are two main sorts: **money purchase scheme** and **final pay scheme**. Another option for the employer, which is becoming more widespread, is to set up a **group personal pension plan (GPP)**.

Money purchase scheme

This is the most common type of scheme but, as such schemes often cover only a small number of members, they in fact cover a minority of the workforce. They operate in a very straightforward fashion. The contributions your employer makes on your behalf, and yours if it is a contributory scheme, are invested and allowed to grow. The resulting fund is specifically earmarked for you and, when you reach retirement, it is used to buy a pension (subject, though, to limits set out by the Inland Revenue: see the table on page 157).

The appeal of money purchase schemes is a very strong sense of owning a particular 'pension pot' and the simplicity with which the pot can be used for your benefit. In particular, if you leave the scheme before retirement, your pension pot is simply left to carry on growing or can be transferred easily to some other pension arrangement (see page 164).

The drawback of money purchase schemes is that you have no clear idea, in advance, of how much pension you will end up with and whether it will be adequate for your needs, because the pension depends on:

- the amount paid into the scheme
- the return that the invested contributions can earn
- the range of benefits to be provided – in particular widow(er)'s pension – out of your pension pot
- the annuity rate at which the fund can be converted to pension at retirement.

Typically, the contributions are invested in the stock market and, although share-based investments tend to produce positive returns over the long term, prices can – and do – go down as well as up. If the stock market has slumped near the time you are considering retirement, the value of your pension pot may be a lot less than it had been perhaps just months before and will inevitably buy a lot less pension than you had hoped for. To some extent, you can be guarded against this: for example, by switching to less volatile investments, such as British Government stocks, as retirement approaches.

Annuity rates are closely linked to the returns on British Government stocks, which in turn vary with the general level of interest rates in the economy and expectations about how interest rates will move in future given economic growth, inflation, the exchange rate, and so on. Trying to guess what annuity rates might be ten, twenty, thirty or even more years ahead is an impossible task. If annuity rates are high at the time you retire, luck is with you because you will get a relatively high pension. But if annuity rates are low at the time you retire, you will get a low pension, and you will be locked into that low pension for your whole retirement. The same problem besets personal pension plans (see Chapter 11), although a partial solution has been introduced in their case by allowing you to draw an income direct from your pension fund while putting off buying an annuity. Draft rules have been drawn up

Your pension choices

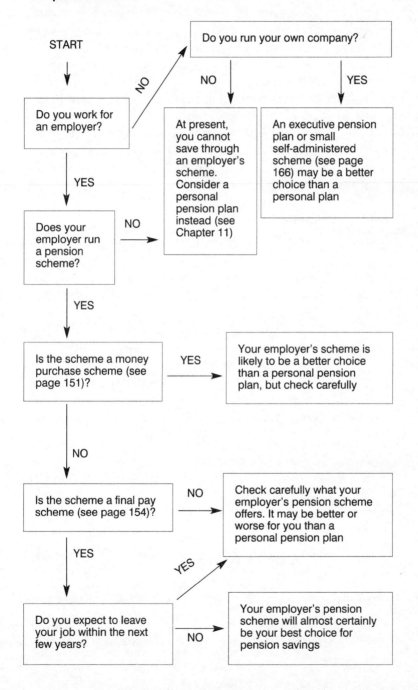

START

Do you work for an employer?

NO → Do you run your own company?

NO → At present, you cannot save through an employer's scheme. Consider a personal pension plan instead (see Chapter 11)

YES → An executive pension plan or small self-administered scheme (see page 166) may be a better choice than a personal plan

YES ↓

Does your employer run a pension scheme?

NO → At present, you cannot save through an employer's scheme. Consider a personal pension plan instead (see Chapter 11)

YES ↓

Is the scheme a money purchase scheme (see page 151)?

YES → Your employer's scheme is likely to be a better choice than a personal pension plan, but check carefully

NO ↓

Is the scheme a final pay scheme (see page 154)?

NO → Check carefully what your employer's pension scheme offers. It may be better or worse for you than a personal pension plan

YES ↓

Do you expect to leave your job within the next few years?

YES → Check carefully what your employer's pension scheme offers. It may be better or worse for you than a personal pension plan

NO → Your employer's pension scheme will almost certainly be your best choice for pension savings to allow members to draw an income direct from a money purchase employer's scheme too, but they have been put on hold while the whole issue of pension provision (see page 146) and long-term care (see page 112) is being examined. In the meantime, the Inland Revenue has issued temporary guidelines for schemes wanting to give members this option.

As far as financial planning goes, then, there is a need to make some assumptions about how your contributions will grow and what annuity rates will be at the time you retire, if you are to get a feel for whether your retirement savings are adequate or not. Your scheme will make certain assumptions when it tells you what pension you can expect (see page 162).

Final pay scheme

This is the type of scheme to which you are most likely to belong if you work for a large employer. A final pay scheme is more complex than a money purchase scheme. You do not have an individual pension pot (see above); instead, you have a 'pension promise'. The pension scheme promises to pay you a pension at retirement which is worked out according to a formula. An actuary periodically works out what contributions must be paid in to the scheme in order for the promise to be kept. You pay part of the contributions, if it is a contributory scheme, and your employer pays the balance, which the actuary says is required. In a non-contributory scheme, the employer pays the whole lot. The advantages of this type of scheme are that:

- your pension increases in line with your pay and so is protected against inflation up to the time you retire
- you get a package of benefits which usually covers widow(er)s and other dependants
- you can have a very good idea, in advance, of the amount of pension you will get relative to your earnings at the time you retire.

This last point becomes clear if you look at the typical pension formula:

pension = number of years in scheme × your final pay × accrual rate.

'Number of years in scheme' is reasonably straightforward, generally meaning the number of years for which you have been a member of the pension scheme (which might be different from the number of years for which you have been in that particular job). You can buy 'extra' years in some public-sector schemes – see Boosting Your Pension on page 161.

'Your final pay' is your pay at or near the time you retire (or your membership ends, if you leave the scheme before retirement). Definitions vary, but might, for example, be average pay over the preceding three years, the average of the best three years' pay in the preceding ten, pay on a specific date, and so on. 'Pay' can be widely defined and may include not only basic pay but overtime, commission, and even the value of any fringe benefits such as a company car. Often, a scheme aims to pay a pension to supplement what you will get from the state (see Chapter 9). In that case, 'final pay' might exclude a slice of pay broadly equal to the state basic pension or some multiple of it.

The 'accrual rate' is the proportion of your final pay which will be paid as pension for each year in the scheme. Typically, the rate is one-sixtieth, one-eightieth or one-hundredth, depending on the rules of the particular scheme. For example, if the scheme is an eightieths one, and you have been a member for twenty years, your pension would equal twenty-eightieths, that is, a quarter, of your final pay. If the scheme is a sixtieths one, you would get twenty-sixtieths, that is, a third, of final pay.

The Inland Revenue sets limits on the pension and other benefits which can be paid: see the table on page 157. Within these limits, the precise formula and definitions used by your scheme depend on the scheme's rules.

The drawback of final pay schemes is that you get far less than you might have anticipated if you change jobs frequently. This is because, instead of your pension being based on pay at the time you retire, it is based on pay at the time you left the scheme, which will generally be a lot lower. However, the lot of the early leaver is much better than it used to be: since 1 January 1991, if you leave a scheme, the pension you leave behind must be increased each year up to retirement in line with inflation up to five per cent. If the scheme is contracted out of the State Earnings-Related Pension Scheme (SERPS – see page 144), your early-leaver pension is even better protected against inflation. These increases must be reflected in the value put on your pension rights if you transfer them to another scheme or pension plan. However, the transfer value does not have to take account of 'discretionary benefits' – things that the scheme tends to provide (such as generous increases to pensions once they have started to be paid) but does not actually promise to provide. This means that you can still lose out badly if you frequently switch from one pension arrangement to another.

Tip

An employer's pension scheme is usually hard to beat as a way of saving for retirement. Not only does it benefit from favourable tax treatment, but your employer puts in money on your behalf and will often pay separately the major costs of administering the scheme instead of the costs being charged to the pension fund.

Group personal pension plan

Frequent changes in pensions legislation have made the cost of running final pay schemes ever higher and the complexity of all types of employers' schemes ever greater. This has persuaded some employers – particularly those running relatively small businesses – to organise instead a group personal pension plan (GPP).

This is an arrangement with a single plan provider (usually an insurance company) to offer personal pension plans to all, or a group of, employees. The plans might be tailored to suit those particular employees – for example, contribution payments might be flexible if there is a lot of seasonal variation in pay – but a GPP is none the less a personal pension arrangement not an employer's pension scheme. This has a number of drawbacks from your point of view:

- employers do not have to contribute anything to the GPP (whereas the law requires them to contribute to employers' schemes)
- the running costs of a GPP are likely to be much higher than those of an employer's scheme and the costs will be met out of your contributions
- the range of benefits under the GPP is likely to be more restricted than you would normally get from an employer's scheme

Main Inland Revenue limits on pensions and tax-free cash [1]

Description of scheme	Limit on pension payable at retirement [2]	Limit on lump sum at retirement
Post-1989 regime a) Scheme set up on or after 14 March 1989, or b) Scheme set up before 14 March 1989 but you joined it on or after 1 June 1989, or c) Scheme set up before 14 March 1989 which you joined before 1 June 1989, if you elect to be treated under post-1989 regime rules	Two-thirds of final pay up to a maximum cash limit (£56,000 in 1997–8) [3]	One and a half times final pay up to a maximum cash limit (£126,000 in 1997–8) [3]
1987–9 regime Scheme set up before 14 March 1989 which you joined on or after 17 March 1987 and before 1 June 1989 (unless you have opted to be covered by the post-1989 regime)	Two-thirds of final pay (without cash limit)	One and a half times final pay up to a maximum of £150,000
Pre-1987 regime Scheme you joined before 17 March 1987 (unless you have opted to be covered by the post-1989 regime)	Two-thirds of final pay (without cash limit)	One and a half times final pay (without cash limit)

[1] These limits apply to nearly all employers' schemes, regardless of whether they work on a final pay basis, money purchase basis, or some other basis. Under the 1987–9 regime and pre-1987 regime, the limits apply at the normal retirement age for the scheme. Under the post-1989 regime, limits apply at any age within the range 60–75.

[2] This is the maximum pension you can have if you do not take any of the proceeds as a tax-free lump sum. If you take tax-free cash, the maximum pension is reduced to less than the amounts shown in this column.

[3] The limit is based on an 'earnings cap' which puts a ceiling on the amount of final pay which can be used in the formula. The earnings cap is usually increased each year in line with the Retail Prices Index and is set at £84,000 for 1997–8.

- like all personal pension plans, GPPs work on a money purchase basis. This makes them more risky for you than an employer's final pay scheme (but no more or less risky than an employer's money purchase scheme).

On the plus side, under the GPP arrangement you end up with your own personal pension plan, so your pension is completely portable, being unaffected by job changes. And, although your employer does not have to make contributions on your behalf, if he does, you are not liable for any income tax or National Insurance on the amount paid in.

GPPs are governed by the rules for personal pension plans: for example, regarding the amount you can contribute and the benefits you can have (see Chapter 11). The rules outlined in this chapter do not apply to GPPs. However, if benefits are transferred from an employer's scheme to a GPP (or other personal pension plan), in some cases there will be some restriction on the benefits which can be provided by the amount transferred into the GPP. The restriction applies in order to prevent you boosting the tax-free lump sum at retirement by switching from the more rigid employers' scheme regime to the less restrictive personal pension plan regime. The employer's scheme you are leaving should tell you if such a restriction applies.

Other types of employers' pension schemes

As has been shown, both money purchase schemes and final pay schemes have advantages but drawbacks too. **Hybrid schemes** provide a mix of benefits and some attempt to have the best of both worlds by working out your pension on both a money purchase basis *and* a final pay basis and paying you whichever is the greater. This ensures a link to your earnings at or near retirement, and it also means you are less likely to lose out if you leave the scheme early.

Employers' schemes can work in other, less common ways too: for example, an **average pay scheme**, where your pension is calculated according to a formula but based on your pay throughout the whole period you belonged to the scheme. This would not be a particularly good type of scheme to belong to, because pay from the early years would seem low after a few years' inflation and would tend to pull down the average. However, an average *revalued* pay scheme (where pay from the early years is adjusted to take account of inflation before being slotted into the formula) could be even more attractive than a final pay scheme if your earnings tend to peak in mid-career rather than later on – especially if the revaluation is based on earnings inflation, rather than price inflation.

Schemes offering some link to final pay (or revalued average pay) are generally considered to be the best types of pension arrangement, offering protection against inflation up to the time you retire and some certainty in your planning, but they are expensive to provide.

Other benefits from employers' schemes

As stated on page 150, you can take part of the proceeds of a pension scheme as a tax-free lump sum. Some schemes let you swap part of your pension for this lump sum; others are structured to give you automatically a lump sum together with a pension. There is a point to note in relation to this latter approach. On the face of it, you might think that a scheme with an eightieths accrual rate would always give you less pension than a sixtieths scheme, but this is not necessarily the case. A scheme which pays you an eightieths pension but also automatically gives you a lump sum may, in fact, be offering much the same level of benefits as a scheme which invites you to give up part of your sixtieths pension in return for a lump sum. This emphasises the importance of looking at the *whole package* of benefits which the scheme is offering and not simply focusing on the pension alone.

In nearly all cases, it is worth taking the lump sum because, unlike the pension, it is tax-free. If you cannot manage on a lower amount of pension, you can use the lump sum to buy a purchased annuity (see page 236), the proceeds of which are only partly taxed.

Typically, an employer's scheme will also give you life cover. Under the Inland Revenue rules, this can be up to a maximum of four times your final pay (at or near the time of death), with an overall cash limit of £336,000 in 1997–8 regime schemes.

Schemes also usually offer pensions for your widow, widower and/or other dependants. The Inland Revenue rules limit a widow(er)'s pension to a maximum of two-thirds of the largest retirement pension to which you would have been entitled, given your membership to date and the Inland Revenue limits. No one pension for another dependant must exceed two-thirds of the maximum retirement pension to which you would have been entitled, and *all* the widow(er)'s and dependants' pension together must not amount to more than the maximum pension you could have got.

Protection against inflation

In the period up to retirement, the pension you are building up is automatically protected against inflation if you belong to a final pay scheme. A money purchase scheme has no such built-in protection. Although share-based investment returns tend to outpace inflation over the long term, there is no guarantee that share values will not have slumped at the time you need to take up your pension.

When it comes to increasing pensions once they have started to be paid, a variety of factors comes into play. A contracted-out pension built up before April 1997 will be completely protected by the state against price inflation if you are contracted out on a final pay basis, or will be largely inflation-proofed if you are contracted out on a money purchase basis. There is no legal requirement for the remainder of pre-April 1997 pensions to be inflation-proofed or increased at all. However, most final pay schemes do increase pensions, though this may be on a discretionary, *ad hoc* basis rather than built in to the rules of the scheme – you should check what the policy is in your scheme. Inland Revenue rules put a ceiling on pension increases: the starting-point is the maximum pension you would be allowed under the tax rules; this can be increased in line with the Retail Prices Index or three per cent a year if this comes to more. Members of many public-sector schemes, for example those covering NHS employees and teachers, are particularly lucky in that their pensions are fully inflation-proofed once they are being paid.

For employers' scheme pensions built up from April 1997, both contracted-out and non-contracted-out pensions must, as a legal minimum, be increased by inflation up to five per cent a year. So, for example, if inflation were three per cent, your pension would increase by three per cent; but if inflation were seven per cent, your pension would go up by only five per cent. These increases do not apply to AVC schemes (see opposite).

Checking how much pension you'll get

While it is essential that you know what type of employers' scheme you belong to and the nature of the pension you are being offered, you do not have to wade through a mass of complicated sums to find out how much pension you should expect. Your scheme must provide you with a 'benefit statement' if you ask for one (and many schemes provide these statements automatically each year). By law, you automatically get a benefit statement each year if you belong to a money purchase scheme. Your benefit statement might look like the one on the following page.

In all probability, you will belong to more than one pension scheme during your working years. You might transfer your pension rights from a former employer's scheme to another pension arrangement (see page 164). But if you leave pension rights in an old scheme, you can request a benefit statement to keep you up to date on the amount of pension you can expect at retirement.

Boosting your pension

Taking account of the state pension and your pension(s) from private arrangements, such as employers' schemes, you may still find your expected retirement income wanting. What can you do?

If, as is usually the case, your employer's pension scheme will pay you benefits which are lower than the maxima allowed under the Inland Revenue rules, you can pay extra pension contributions in order to increase your pension or most other benefits, provided you are not already up to the limit for contributions.

The Inland Revenue rules put no limit on the amount which your employer pays towards your pension. However, your own contributions must not exceed a maximum of 15 per cent of your pay. If you are covered by the post-1989 regime only pay up to the earnings cap (£84,000 in 1997–8) counts. For example, if you earn £20,000 one year, you can pay up to 15 per cent × £20,000 = £3,000 in contributions. If you earn £84,000 or more in 1997–8, the most you can contribute is 15 per cent × £84,000 = £12,600. In practice, what you pay into a contributory scheme is usually in the region of five per cent of pay. This leaves plenty of scope for paying in extra in the form of 'additional voluntary contributions' (AVCs). You get tax

Example of a benefit statement from an employer's hybrid pension scheme

Information as at 31 March 1998

Name	Jo Bloggs
National Insurance number	XY123456Z
Date of birth	7 May 1968
Date joined scheme	1 December 1993
Normal retirement date (NRD)	7 May 2023
Pensionable service to NRD	39 years 5 months
Salary	£18,500.00
Final pensionable salary	£13,659.96

Retirement benefits

State benefits – if you have a full contribution record, you can expect a pension from the state of:

Basic (single person's rate)	£3,247.40 p.a.

Scheme benefits

Final salary pension

(i) If you continue in service to retirement (65)	£5,441.22 p.a.
(ii) For service to date	£591.93 p.a.
Money purchase fund	£4,729.18
Corresponding to an approximate pension for service to date of using current annuity rates	£407.66 p.a.

Benefits on death service

Cash sum of	£74,000
Spouse's pension of 50% of your pension (with allowance for potential service) and	£2,720.61 p.a.
Dependent child pension of 25% of your pension (maximum 50% for all children)	£1,360.30 p.a.

relief on AVCs at your top rate(s) of income tax in the same way as you do with ordinary contributions.

Your employer must also offer an AVC scheme. Often this will be a straightforward savings scheme, normally investing fairly conservatively with a building society or an insurance company. The AVCs grow tax-free, and the resulting fund can be used to 'buy' extra benefits in the main pension scheme. These do not have to be a retirement pension: for example, you could use AVCs to buy increases to the pension once it is being paid, extra life insurance or a higher widow(er)'s pension in the event of death. But AVCs you started after 7 April 1987 cannot be used to provide or increase a tax-free lump sum. (However, you could take the maximum lump sum possible from the main scheme and then use AVCs to top up the pension given up.)

Some public-sector schemes have a different form of AVC scheme: your extra contributions buy 'added years', so that you are credited with more years of membership in the scheme than you really have. This works through the final pay formula to boost your retirement pension, widow(er)'s and dependants' pensions and life cover.

A scheme's own AVC scheme can be used only to boost benefits in that particular employer's pension scheme. Alternatively, you can make extra contributions to your own 'free-standing AVC scheme' (FSAVC). Although charges for an FSAVC plan may be higher than for a scheme's own AVC arrangement, there are two possible advantages with FSAVC – but you should compare your options carefully:

- the free-standing scheme travels with you so that, if you leave one pension scheme, you use it to buy benefits in a subsequent scheme to which you belong
- you choose how to invest your free-standing AVCs. This means that you do not have to be locked into a possibly over-cautious investment approach adopted by a scheme's own AVC scheme. You can choose the type of investment, for example deposit, with-profits, unit-linked, which suits you (see Chapters 13–15).

Use the Calculator on page 164 to find out how much you can pay in AVCs or free-standing AVCs in order to boost the pension you will get from an employer's scheme.

Tip

Very few people can expect a pension which is as good as the maximum allowed under Inland Revenue limits, so there is plenty of scope for making additional voluntary contributions as a tax-efficient way of boosting your retirement savings.

How much can you pay in AVCs?

	£ a year
Your earnings Include salary, commission, bonuses, overtime payments, the taxable value of fringe benefits etc.	A
Earnings cap If the 'post-1989' rules apply (see the table on page 157), enter the *lower* of your earnings or £84,000	B
The most you can contribute Multiply B by 15 and divide by 100	C
Your current contributions How much are you paying each year in regular contributions and AVCs? Your pay slips will tell you this. Also deduct any free-standing AVCs which you are already paying	D
How much you can pay in AVCs Subtract D from C. What is left is the amount you can pay to top up benefits from your pension scheme (assuming your benefits do not directly exceed the Inland Revenue limits – see page 157)	E

Leaving a scheme before retirement

If you leave a pension scheme after being a member for less than two years, the scheme does not have to give you any pension rights. Instead, it can refund your contributions (but not any paid by your employer) less income tax at a special 20 per cent rate. Up to 6 April 1997, if the scheme is contracted out (see page 144), there could also have been a deduction to buy you back into SERPS. After that date, you can no longer be bought back into SERPS.

If you leave a pension scheme after two years' membership but before you have reached retirement, you must by law be given rights to a pension. You have a variety of choices about what to do with these rights. No general rule states which choice is best. Each situation has to be looked at on its own merits. To make a rational choice, you may need the help of an expert to evaluate the relative benefits of each choice. If a large sum is involved, it would be worth seeking help from an actuary (see 'more information', below). If the cost of consulting an actuary cannot be justified, you could get advice from a couple of independent financial advisers (IFAs)★ who specialise in pensions.

Although the decisions facing early leavers cannot be generalised, there are some points worth considering:

- if you belong to a public-sector scheme, there may be a 'transfer club' which lets you transfer your pension, without loss, to another scheme within the public sector
- many public-sector schemes offer exceptional benefits, even to early leavers. Be wary of transferring your pension rights to a private-sector scheme; it is very unlikely that the new scheme could match the benefits you would give up
- it may make sense to transfer your pension rights from one private-sector scheme to another as you switch jobs. It can be easier to keep track of your pension entitlements if they are not spread too widely across many schemes. But you might lose out each time you transfer – see page 155
- be wary of transferring pension rights from an employer's scheme to a personal pension plan. The charges for a personal plan are generally a lot higher than for an employer's scheme (where the employer, rather than the pension fund, might be meeting the costs separately)
- when considering the relative merits of a possible transfer, make sure you look at the whole package of benefits under each option.

Pension choices if you run your own company

If you run your own business, you could use personal pension plans (see Chapter 11) to build up your retirement income. But if your

---

Warning

If you work or have worked in the public sector, for example for local government, as a teacher or in the NHS, you are (or were) most likely covered by an excellent pension scheme. Be very wary of giving up those benefits, even if you now work for someone else.

---

business is set up as a company, you could instead set up your own employer's pension scheme. There are two broad types of employer's scheme which are particularly suited to your situation: executive pension plans and small self-administered schemes. The tax rules and advantages are complex, and there are variants available which exploit the rules of both types of scheme, so before deciding on a course of action you would be wise to get advice from a pensions consultant, your accountant or an IFA experienced in this area. Be warned that the Inland Revenue takes a close interest in how these schemes are used and has severe penalties if the rules are breached, even accidentally.

Executive pension plans

These are offered by insurance companies and are aimed at directors of companies, both small and large. Although each plan is tailored to a particular individual, these are employers' pension schemes rather than personal plans. As such, the rules outlined in this chapter apply to executive plans. This means that there is no limit on the amount your company can contribute to the plan on your behalf, subject to the pension and other benefits not breaching the Inland Revenue limits (see page 157) and provided certain rules about funding are complied with. This gives you the scope to build up a much larger pension than you could via a personal pension plan, where the level of contributions is strictly limited.

Small self-administered schemes

Rather than being run by an insurance company, a small self-administered scheme is in the hands of trustees appointed by your company. 'Small' means covering fewer than 12 members. The trustees control how the pension fund is invested and, subject to certain restrictions, part of the fund can be invested in your company's shares and/or property. This means that the pension fund can provide a source of finance for your business; however, any loans from the fund to the business must be at a commercial rate of interest.

More information

The operation of your particular employer's pension scheme is summarised in a scheme booklet which you should have been given before or shortly after you joined the scheme. Read the booklet: your pension is a major asset which will come into its own in the years ahead, so it makes sense to understand how it is being built up. If you do not have a booklet or you have queries which the booklet cannot answer, contact your pensions administrator and/or personnel department at work. Private-sector pension schemes are set up as special legal arrangements called 'trusts'. Trustees are appointed to ensure that the pension fund is used properly according to the rules of the scheme. The trustees are also a good source of information and advice about the scheme. The scheme booklet will detail who you can contact for help. If you have no booklet, check your notice-boards at work or contact the personnel department.

The pensions administrator or personnel department is also the place to address requests for a benefit statement, whether from your current pension scheme or one in which you have left benefits built up during an earlier job. The same source can tell you what arrangement the scheme has for making AVCs and how the scheme treats transfers from a previous employer's scheme. To find out about free-standing AVCs, either contact the companies which offer them direct – see regular surveys in magazines such as *Money Management*,★ *Pensions Management*★ and *Planned Savings*★ – or consult an independent financial adviser (IFA).★

If you have lost track of a scheme in which you had benefits – for example because you have lost the address or the company has merged with another – ask for help from the Pensions Schemes Registry.★

If you change jobs and are wondering whether or not to transfer your pension rights, consider getting the advice of a pensions expert. The Association of Consulting Actuaries★ can put you in touch with an actuary. The Society of Pension Consultants★ can refer you to members who are either actuaries or specialist IFAs. Actuaries charge fairly high fees. A cheaper option is to consult an IFA. Under rules newly put in place since the scandal over the mis-selling of personal pension plans to people transferring their pensions, only IFAs who are specially authorised to deal with pension transfer business can give advice in that area, and they must now use proper transfer analysis systems before giving you advice about your options.

If you have a problem with your scheme – for example, long delays in sorting out a transfer payment – and the scheme does not respond satisfactorily to your queries or complaints, you can ask the Occupational Pensions Advisory Service (OPAS)★ for help. OPAS is an independent body which will try to clarify and conciliate. If this is not enough to resolve the problem, you can take your case to the Pensions Ombudsman,★ who can make what is known as a determination and an award, if necessary.

If you suspect there is something badly wrong with your scheme – dishonesty or maladministration, say – you might take your doubts to the trustees or your trade union if you have one. You can also take your suspicions to the Occupational Pensions Regulatory Authority (OPRA),★ which was set up under the Pensions Act 1995 to police employers' pensions.

Planning in practice

Lindley Nevers works for the National Health Service and is a member of its pension scheme. He wanted advice on AVCs, so he saw two advisers, one from X and one from Y.

The X adviser told Lindley he should invest in the NHS in-house AVC – this was good advice.

By contrast, the Y adviser gave appalling advice. He failed even to mention the NHS in-house scheme (or the option of buying added years) until Lindley raised the subject towards the end of the second meeting. Even when the adviser did compare the two schemes, he made statements that were untrue and misleading. He also failed to say that the in-house scheme's charges are considerably lower.

The adviser told Lindley there is no choice where your money is invested with the NHS scheme. In fact, the NHS scheme offers a choice of 19 funds. He also gave Lindley misleading information about when he could take the benefits from an FSAVC, saying this could be any time after 50 and up to age 75. If Lindley remains with the NHS scheme, he must take his FSAVC benefits at the same time as the main scheme benefits.

We compared the illustration the adviser gave Lindley with an illustration for the NHS in-house scheme and found that the in-house AVC scheme looks a much better deal.

Which? August 1997

Chapter 11

Personal pension plans

Like the employers' pension schemes described in Chapter 10, personal pension plans (and group personal pension plans – GPPs) provide a relatively tax-efficient way of saving for retirement. You get income tax relief at your top rate(s) on the amount you contribute and part of the proceeds can be taken at retirement in the form of a tax-free lump sum. In addition, up to 1 July 1997, income earned by your invested contributions was also tax-free. However, from 2 July 1997 onwards, that has changed. Now, income from shares and unit trusts is taxed – at 20 per cent in 1997–8, falling to 10 per cent from 6 April 1999. Income from investing your contributions in other ways – for example, in British Government stocks or corporate bonds – remains tax-free, but that is small consolation since the bulk of most personal pension plans is invested in shares and share-based investments such as unit trusts.

If you have a personal pension plan, it has been estimated that you need to increase your contributions by about a tenth to offset the introduction of this tax and so leave the eventual benefits at the same level as they would have been in its absence. Employers' schemes are affected in the same way, but in that case you have some hope that your employer might foot at least part of the tax bill. With a personal pension plan, there is usually no one else involved; you'll have to find the extra contributions yourself or accept that your eventual pension and/or other benefits will be lower than planned.

Prior to 1988, personal pensions had a low profile and were largely the concern of the self-employed. This changed dramatically when the government promoted the idea of personal portable pensions and determined to cut dependence on state pensions by encouraging many more people to opt out of the State Earnings-Related Pension Scheme (SERPS). This had several effects:

- you, the individual, were suddenly being encouraged to make complex decisions about your pension arrangements
- what can only be described as hefty 'bribes' (in the form of bonuses paid by the state into your plan) were introduced to help you choose personal pensions rather than state provision
- the insurance companies and other personal plan providers could not believe their luck as the government in effect marketed their products for them.

The outcome, as is now becoming clear, has not been a happy one. Many people mistakenly thought personal pensions were a better option than an employer's pension scheme. Many have opted out of SERPS only to find that they have little or no hope of building up an equivalent pension because of high charges for their personal plan. The pensions industry has dragged its heels over identifying the victims of pensions mis-selling and arranging compensation. Clearly, this is an area in which it is essential that you build up some knowledge and take the lead in your financial planning.

Personal pension plans might enter your financial planning in three ways. The first, as already mentioned, is as an alternative to part of the state pension; this is discussed in more detail on page 186 and summarised in the chart on page 172. The second is as your main method of saving for retirement. With a few exceptions, you cannot simultaneously belong to an employer's pension scheme and contribute to a personal pension plan. (The exceptions are a personal plan used solely to contract out of SERPS where your employer's scheme does not allow you to contract out that way, and where you have some other earnings apart from those from the employer whose scheme you belong to – in that case, you can take out a personal plan related to the other earnings source.) The chart on page 173 looks at the choices you face. Finally, if you have pensions left behind in a previous employer's scheme, the chart on page 174 considers whether you should switch them to a personal plan.

Looking ahead to the future, the government has announced its intention to introduce 'stakeholder pensions' (see page 146).

Although at the time of writing their precise form had yet to be decided, it seems that stakeholder pensions would compete with personal pension plans to offer a lower-cost, 'quality-assured' means of saving for retirement.

How personal pension plans work

There are two broad types of personal pension:

- **retirement annuity contracts** These were the form personal pensions took before 1 July 1988. Although new retirement annuity contracts have not been issued since, you might still be contributing to one (or more) which you started before 1 July 1988
- **personal pension plans** This type of plan has been available from 1 July 1988. A special type, the **appropriate personal pension plan**, is used for contracting out of SERPS; this is looked at on page 186.

All personal pension plans work on a 'money purchase' basis (see page 151), which means that the amount of pension you get at retirement depends on how much is paid into the plan, how the invested contributions grow, and at what rate (called the 'annuity rate') the pension fund you build up can be converted into a pension at the time you retire. The last two factors are to some extent in the lap of the gods, so you cannot be certain, in advance, how much pension you are going to get or whether it will be enough to fund your chosen style of retirement (see page 136). However, you can get an idea by making some assumptions.

With personal pension plans issued on or after 1 July 1988, you must be given an 'open-market option'. This lets you take your pension fund at retirement and use it to buy a pension (called a 'compulsory purchase annuity') from any provider of your choice – in other words, you are not committed to the same provider you have been saving with. Many retirement annuity contracts also give you this option (although they are not required by law to do so). You should be prepared to use this option, because some companies specialise in annuities and are likely to offer better rates than others. You can check the annuities on offer by using one of the specialist annuity advisers (see page 237), a specialist fax service,★ or checking

Do you need a personal pension plan instead of SERPS?

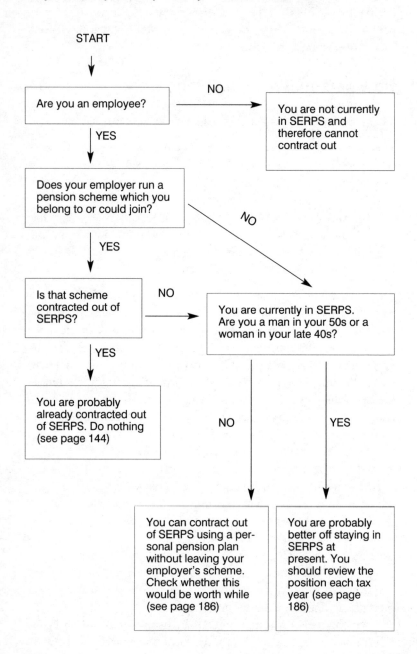

START

Are you an employee?

NO → You are not currently in SERPS and therefore cannot contract out

YES

Does your employer run a pension scheme which you belong to or could join?

NO

YES

Is that scheme contracted out of SERPS?

NO → You are currently in SERPS. Are you a man in your 50s or a woman in your late 40s?

YES

You are probably already contracted out of SERPS. Do nothing (see page 144)

NO

YES

You can contract out of SERPS using a personal pension plan without leaving your employer's scheme. Check whether this would be worth while (see page 186)

You are probably better off staying in SERPS at present. You should review the position each tax year (see page 186)

Is a personal pension plan the best way for you to save for retirement?

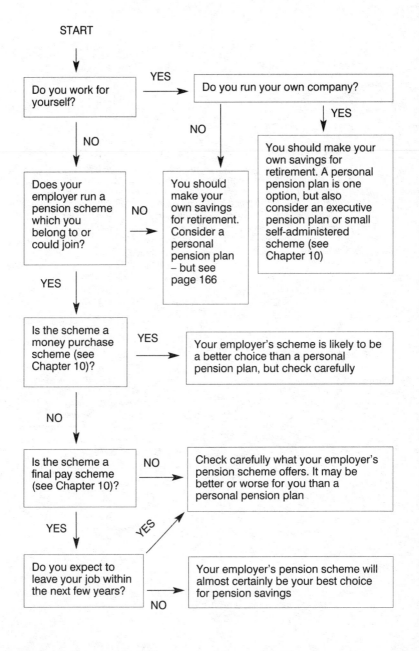

START

Do you work for yourself?

— YES → Do you run your own company?

NO ↓

YES ↓

You should make your own savings for retirement. A personal pension plan is one option, but also consider an executive pension plan or small self-administered scheme (see Chapter 10)

Does your employer run a pension scheme which you belong to or could join?

— NO → You should make your own savings for retirement. Consider a personal pension plan – but see page 166

YES ↓

Is the scheme a money purchase scheme (see Chapter 10)?

— YES → Your employer's scheme is likely to be a better choice than a personal pension plan, but check carefully

NO ↓

Is the scheme a final pay scheme (see Chapter 10)?

— NO → Check carefully what your employer's pension scheme offers. It may be better or worse for you than a personal pension plan

YES ↓

Do you expect to leave your job within the next few years?

YES ↗

— NO → Your employer's pension scheme will almost certainly be your best choice for pension savings

What should you do with pensions from a previous pension scheme or plan?

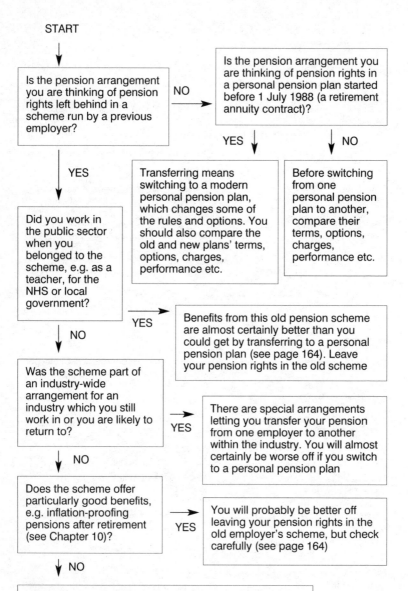

START

Is the pension arrangement you are thinking of pension rights left behind in a scheme run by a previous employer?

NO →

Is the pension arrangement you are thinking of pension rights in a personal pension plan started before 1 July 1988 (a retirement annuity contract)?

YES ↓   ↓ NO

Transferring means switching to a modern personal pension plan, which changes some of the rules and options. You should also compare the old and new plans' terms, options, charges, performance etc.

Before switching from one personal pension plan to another, compare their terms, options, charges, performance etc.

YES ↓

Did you work in the public sector when you belonged to the scheme, e.g. as a teacher, for the NHS or local government?

YES →

Benefits from this old pension scheme are almost certainly better than you could get by transferring to a personal pension plan (see page 164). Leave your pension rights in the old scheme

NO ↓

Was the scheme part of an industry-wide arrangement for an industry which you still work in or you are likely to return to?

YES →

There are special arrangements letting you transfer your pension from one employer to another within the industry. You will almost certainly be worse off if you switch to a personal pension plan

NO ↓

Does the scheme offer particularly good benefits, e.g. inflation-proofing pensions after retirement (see Chapter 10)?

YES →

You will probably be better off leaving your pension rights in the old employer's scheme, but check carefully (see page 164)

NO ↓

You might well be better off transferring your pension rights, but a personal pension plan is just one of the options open to you and might not be the best. Check the options carefully (see page 164)

the listings of annuities in publications such as *Money Management*★ and *Planned Savings*.★

If annuity rates are low at the time you retire, you are locked into a low income for your whole retirement. But you can get round this if your plan offers an 'annuity deferral' option. This lets you leave your pension fund invested – either with the original pension plan provider or with a new one – but withdraw an income direct from your fund. The plan provider organises payment of the income to you, and rules laid down by the Inland Revenue limit the amount you can withdraw so that your fund cannot be run down too fast. However, you still have a wide choice about how much income to take, and you would be wise to take advice before deciding on a particular level. At any stage, you can decide to stop taking the income withdrawals and buy an annuity instead; this could be worth doing if annuity rates rose significantly. At age 75, income withdrawal must cease and you must buy an annuity. It is crucial that your fund is soundly invested during the income withdrawal phase. If it loses value, not only will you be able to draw less from the fund, but you will have less with which to buy an annuity later on. On the other hand, if you invest in deposits, where the cash value of your fund cannot fall, the fund might grow too slowly to protect you against inflation. Unless annuity rates are historically very low at the time you retire, you should be wary of taking this 'annuity deferral' route unless you have a reasonable amount – at least £100,000 – in your pension fund. The imposition of tax on the income your pension fund earns from shares and similar investments (see page 169) means that, from 2 July 1997 onwards, your pension fund will have to work even harder to provide an income during the 'income withdrawal' phase and still protect your ability to buy a reasonable annuity later on.

When is the pension payable?

If you have a personal pension plan, you can start to take a pension from it at any age from 50 to 75. You do not have to stop work to be eligible for the pension. Bear in mind that the more you pay into your plan and the longer your contributions are left invested, the greater the fund you will build up. This means that, while retiring at 50 might seem very appealing, it could be hard to save enough by that age to retire on a reasonable income. One way to cope with this problem could be to take out a 'cluster' of plans which can be converted to pension one by one at a range of different ages. This would give you the flexibility of gradually easing back on work, replacing your earnings with pension income as you did so.

If you have a retirement annuity contract, once again you do not have to stop work to take the pension. And, once again, you can put off the start as late as age 75, but the earliest age – 60 – is higher than it is for personal plans. However, you can switch from a retirement annuity contract to a personal plan at any time, in which case you could have access to your fund from age 50 onwards.

The rules applying to contracted-out personal pension plans are more restrictive – you cannot start your pension before reaching state pension age.

Tax-free cash at retirement

You can swap part of your pension at retirement for a tax-free lump sum. The table on page 178 sets out the maximum amount of cash you can have. In general, it is worth making the switch, even if you need the maximum possible income. This is because the pension you give up is taxable income. The lump sum, itself tax-free, can be used to buy a 'purchased life annuity' (see page 236), the income from which is only partly taxable. In this way, if you are a taxpayer, you could end up with a higher after-tax income than if you had kept the full pension and turned down the lump sum.

If your personal pension plan includes any amounts which were transferred to it from an employer's pension scheme, there may be a restriction on your cash lump sum from the personal pension plan if any of the following applies:

- the transfer was from an AVC scheme started on or after 8 April 1987 or an FSAVC scheme – see page 161 – neither of which can be used to provide a tax-free lump sum. The amount transferred cannot itself be taken as a lump sum, although it can still be counted as part of the pension fund when you calculate the maximum cash as a proportion of the fund
- at any time in the ten years up to the date of transfer being made, you were a controlling director of the company whose employer's pension scheme you belonged to, or you counted as a high earner

(that is if your earnings exceeded the earnings cap – see page 157 – which applied in the year the transfer was made). The scheme you left must provide you with a certificate saying how much of the transfer value can be taken as a lump sum from the personal pension plan; this amount can be increased in line with price inflation up to the date on which the lump sum is paid out

- the transfer was from a scheme with a normal retirement date of 45 or less, or certain old schemes which you contributed to before April 1980, in which case none of the transfer value may be taken as a lump sum.

In the past it was fairly rare for any of these conditions to apply, but with growing interest among employers in providing GPPs as an alternative to bona fide employers' schemes, more people in future may find themselves in this situation. If your employer gives you the option to switch your accumulated pension rights from an employer's scheme to a GPP, make sure you check out the impact on your eventual tax-free lump sum along with the effect on your pension and other benefits.

Tip

At retirement, it is nearly always worth taking the maximum tax-free lump sum from your pension plan even if you then use it to buy an annuity to provide an income. Different tax rules mean you should usually get a higher after-tax income from the annuity than the pension you give up.

Other benefits from personal pension plans

If you were to die before reaching pension age, your retirement annuity contract or personal pension plan (other than a plan used for contracting out – see page 186) would normally pay out a lump sum to your survivors. Usually, you will be asked to nominate who should receive this money, and this does not have to be someone who is financially dependent on you. Although the pension provider is not obliged to follow your wishes, it would be very unusual for it not to do so. The advantage of this arrangement is that the payment is made direct to your survivors and does not pass

How much tax-free cash?

Type of plan and when you started it	Maximum amount of tax-free cash
Retirement annuity contracts	
Started before 17 March 1987	Three times the remaining pension, e.g. if, after taking the lump sum, you would have a pension of £5,000, then the maximum lump sum would be $3 \times £5,000 = £15,000$
Started on or after 17 March 1987 and before 1 July 1988	Three times the remaining pension up to an overall maximum of £150,000 per plan[1]
Personal pension plans	
Started on or after 1 July 1988 and before 27 July 1989	A quarter of the pension fund (excluding amounts to be used to provide dependants' pensions)[2]
Started on or after 27 July 1989	A quarter of the pension fund (except amounts to be used to provide contracted-out pensions) (see page 186)

[1]   In practice, the limit was often avoided by taking out a cluster of several smaller plans instead of just one.

[2]   Strictly speaking, an overall limit of £150,000 per plan applies. In practice, the limit is easily avoided by taking out a cluster of plans or switching to a later plan without the cash limit using the open-market option (see page 171).

through your estate, so there is no risk of inheritance tax being due on the sum, and there is no delay in making the payment while your estate is being sorted out.

The amount paid out will generally be the accumulated value of your pension fund, or alternatively the return of your contributions along with interest or bonuses. Instead of a lump sum, you could arrange for your contract or plan to pay out a pension for your widow(er), children or other dependants in the event of death before retirement. In this case, the fund would be converted into pension(s) at the compulsory purchase annuity rates prevailing at the time of death. But because of the tax treatment of annuities (see page 236), it is generally better to take the lump sum and buy a purchased life annuity.

A proportion of your retirement annuity contract or personal pension plan contributions can be used to buy life insurance. This must pay out a lump sum on your death before retirement; it cannot be a family income benefit policy (see page 71). Taking out this type of insurance means that you get tax relief at your top rate on the premiums. The downside is that the amount you contribute towards life insurance reduces the maximum you can contribute towards your pension – see page 182. You can use a pension plan to provide life insurance on its own even if you are not contributing towards a pension (provided you are eligible to have the plan). You can arrange for your dependants to receive something from your retirement annuity contract or personal pension plan if you were to die after retirement. There are two ways of doing this:

- **pension guarantee** You arrange for your pension to be paid for a set number of years after the start date, regardless of whether you survive for the whole period. The law allows a maximum of ten years. In practice, most guarantees are for five years. You nominate the person who will receive this pension if you were to die before the guaranteed period was up. The person you choose does not have to be financially dependent on you
- **joint annuity** You convert your pension fund into a pension which carries on being paid until both you and your husband or wife or other partner have both died. You can arrange for your widow(er) to receive either the full pension or some proportion – for example, half – of it. This is called a 'joint life, last survivor annuity'.

The price of both these options is a lower starting pension. A five-year guarantee costs relatively little, reducing a level pension (a pension which does not have any increases built in) by just a few pounds at age 60 up to about £40 to £80 a year at age 75 for each £10,000 in your fund. This option is fairly popular, as it ensures that at least some value is had from your pension even if you were to die soon after retirement, but it is a poor way of providing for your dependants.

For men, a joint annuity is the more expensive option. For example, at annuity rates in November 1997, a man aged 65 could buy a yearly pension of around £10,000 if he had £100,000 in his pension fund. If his wife were aged 60 and he chose a joint life, last survivor annuity, the pension would be reduced to about £7,500. (This assumes that you had opted for the pension to continue at the same rate after the first death.)

The extra cost of a joint annuity is nowhere near so great for women whose annuity will be lower anyway than that for a comparable man. This is because, on average, wives outlive their husbands. Where a man takes out a joint annuity covering his wife, the pension is likely to be paid until his wife dies – longer than a pension covering him alone. But where a wife takes out a joint annuity covering her husband, the pension is likely to be paid out for the same length of time as a pension just for herself would have been. In the example above, the joint annuity paid a pension of £7,500 a year. An annuity for a woman aged 60 alone would have paid around £8,000 a year.

Whether or not you choose a joint annuity depends on your particular family circumstances. You should consider this option if anyone is financially dependent on you. You might already have adequate life cover, or your husband, wife or other dependants might have other sources of income they could fall back on. The Calculator in Chapter 4 will help you to work out whether there would be any shortfall in the income or capital which your dependants would need.

Warning

When you start to take a pension from your plan, remember to consider what income would remain for your husband or wife if you were to die before him or her. Opting for a joint annuity would protect them from financial hardship. An annuity simply offering a five-year guarantee is not adequate for this purpose.

Another option with retirement annuity contracts and personal pension plans which is well worth considering is 'waiver of premium' benefit. This comes into play if you become ill or disabled and cannot keep up your contributions to the contract or plan. The contributions are treated as if they were still being paid, so your pension continues to build up. The waiver may be for a limited period, or can last up to your selected pension age if the illness or disability persists. With retirement annuity contracts, waiver of premium can apply only to your pension contributions, and not to any amount paying for life cover; with personal pension plans, the waiver can cover both elements of your plan.

Protection against inflation

Apart from personal plans used to contract out of SERPS, neither a retirement annuity contract nor a personal pension plan has built-in protection against inflation. In the period while you are building up your pension, you should take inflation into account when considering how to invest your pension fund. Briefly, if you opt for seemingly safe deposit-type investments, you run the risk of inflation eating heavily into the value of your fund. By choosing share-based investments, the long-term growth of your fund hopefully will outstrip increasing prices. For more on this, see Chapter 12.

Chapter 9 looked at the devastating impact inflation can have on pensions once they start to be paid out. The ideal is index-linked pensions which automatically maintain the buying power of your income. The snag is that indexed pensions are not cheap and, when it comes to personal plans, usually the only person to foot the bill is you.

Various types of annuities are available which you can choose at retirement. One which guarantees to increase the pension by five per cent a year would typically start at about two-thirds of the amount provided by a level annuity for a man aged 65. Is it worth accepting such a large cut in the pension? The factors you need to consider are:

- if you are single, are you likely to live long enough for the extra gained through pension increases to outweigh the initial cut in the pension? The table on page 136 shows *average* life expectancy. You may have good reason for expecting that you are not average: for example, you may be in poor health, in which case you should be wary of trading your pension now for future increases. On the other hand, you might come from a family notorious for its longevity, which suggests that taking the increasing pension might be a good deal. The table opposite shows how many years you would need to survive to be a 'winner' from an annuity increasing by five per cent each year. The table takes no account of the income you could have earned on the pension forgone in the early years. Taking such income into account weakens the case for choosing an increasing annuity

- if you have a wife, husband or partner to consider, are they likely to outlive you? If so, they will be the main person to benefit from the pension increases. If you opt for an annuity without increases, will they be able to cope financially in later retirement?
- could you take the higher-level pension but invest part of it to provide extra income later in retirement? This would require a certain amount of discipline on your part.

How much can you contribute?

A key factor determining the amount of pension your retirement annuity contract or personal pension plan will give you is the amount you pay into it. Because of the valuable tax reliefs, the Inland Revenue puts limits on the amount you can contribute. The limits are set as a proportion of your 'net relevant earnings'. For employees, this means your total before-tax pay, including the value of most taxable fringe benefits. For the self-employed, it means your profits for tax purposes after deducting capital allowances.

The table on page 184 sets out the limits, which are different for retirement annuity contracts and for personal pension plans. You can simultaneously contribute to both types of plan, in which case, as well as the individual limits applying, contributions to both must not exceed the limits for personal plans. In addition to the personal plan percentage-of-earnings limits, there is an overall cash limit on the amount of earnings which can be taken into account. For 1997–8 this limit is £84,000; usually, it is increased each year in line with price inflation.

Increasing annuities – would you win or lose?

Year	Pension from a level annuity (i.e. no increases)	Pension from an annuity increasing by 5% a year
Man aged 65: average life expectancy 14 years		
At retirement	£1,026	£691
Year 3: pensions equal	£1,026	£1,021
Year 20: gains through indexation match losses through lower starting pension	£1,026	£1,508
Man aged 70: average life expectancy 11 years		
At retirement	£1,194	£858
Year 11: pensions equal	£1,194	£1,207
Year 17: gains through indexation match losses through lower starting pension	£1,194	£1,618
Woman aged 60: average life expectancy 22 years		
At retirement	£794	£465
Year 11: pensions equal	£794	£795
Year 21: gains through indexation match losses through lower starting pension	£794	£1,295
Woman aged 65: average life expectancy 18 years		
At retirement	£883	£556
Year 9: pensions equal	£883	£862
Year 18: gains through indexation match losses through lower starting pension	£883	£1,338

Based on annuity rates in November 1997. The figures show annuity income for each £10,000 invested.

Limits on contributions to retirement annuity contracts and personal pension plans

| Your age at the start of the tax year (6 April) | Contribution limits as a percentage of your earnings or profits: | | Overall cash limit on contributions to personal pension plan in 1997–8 [1] |
	Retirement annuity contract	Personal pension plan	
Up to 35	17.5%	17.5%	£14,700
36–45	17.5%	20%	£16,800
46–50	17.5%	25%	£21,000
51–55	20%	30%	£25,200
56–60	22.5%	35%	£29,400
61–74	27.5%	40%	£33,600
75 and over	You can no longer contribute		

[1] Percentage limit multiplied by earnings limit of £84,000 for 1997–8.

Employers can contribute to an employee's personal pension plan (but not a retirement annuity contract), and those contributions use up part of the employee's contribution limit. Amounts paid by the government into an appropriate personal plan (see page 187) do not use up any of the limit.

Up to five per cent of your net relevant earnings can be paid in premiums for life insurance (see page 179), but this uses up part of your limit and leaves less available for making pension contributions.

If you work for an employer, you get tax relief at the basic rate by making contributions to a personal pension plan net of basic-rate tax. The plan provider then claims the amount deducted from the Inland Revenue and adds it to your contributions. You get relief at this rate even if your top rate of tax is only 20 per cent. If you are a higher-rate taxpayer, you can claim extra relief.

If you are self-employed, or whatever your work status if you are paying into a retirement annuity contract, you pay the contributions without deducting any tax and you have to claim the relief through your tax office.

As average life spans are increasing, retirement can now easily account for a third of your life. To finance such a long period, you need to start saving for retirement as early as you can.

Carrying back contributions

If you have not used up your contribution limit for the previous year, you can have a contribution paid in the current tax year treated as if it were paid in the preceding tax year. (If you had no relevant earnings in the preceding year, you can carry back contributions to the year before that, that is, two years in total.) Tax relief is given at the rates applying to the year to which you carry back. You must pay the contribution before the end of the tax year– that is 5 April – from which you are carrying it back, but you have until the following 31 January to notify your tax office that you wish to carry back the amount paid. For example, if you make a contribution in 1997–8, you have until 31 January 1999 to tell your tax office that you are carrying the contribution back to 1996–7.

Carrying back contributions is especially useful if you are in business for yourself because you can leave a decision about how much to contribute until you are clear about how much profit you made in the previous year and what tax is due.

On the other hand, there is a disadvantage to using the carry-back rules. Under the self-assessment tax system which now applies, if you are self-employed you pay your current year's tax in instalments during the year. These 'payments on account', as they are called, are set at half your tax bill for the previous year with a final instalment or refund in the January following the end of the tax year. However, although your tax bill for the year to which you carry back a pension contribution is reduced, there is no consequent reduction in the payments on account which you make for the following year. In the example above, the tax due or paid for 1996–7 will be reduced but the payments on account for 1997–8 are unchanged. This contrasts with the situation where you do not use the carry-back rules but instead pay your contribution in the year to which it applies. For example, if you had instead paid the contribution in 1996–7 and it was attributed to that same year, your tax bill for 1996–7 would be reduced and so too would your payments on account for 1997–8. You need to compare the cash flow positions both using and not using the carry-back rule to see how best you should time your pension contributions.

Provided you do not owe any tax and the tax relief on the premium comes to more than £50, you should receive a cheque from the Inland Revenue for the amount of relief due on the carried back contribution. If you owe tax or a payment on account is soon due, the tax relief may be set against this.

Carrying forward unused contribution limits

If you don't use up all your contribution limit for a tax year, you can carry the unused limit forward for up to six years. This lets you make good any shortfalls in your pension savings in earlier years. You must use up the limit from the earliest years first. Tax relief is given at the tax rates prevailing in the year the contribution is paid (or treated as paid if you have elected to carry it back). By combining the carry-back and carry-forward rules, you can use up unused limit from seven, rather than six, years earlier: for example, in 1997–8, you could pay a contribution and elect to carry it back to 1996–7. You can set the contribution against limits carried forward from as long ago as 1990–1 (that is, six years before 1996–7). Note, however, that the total contributions actually paid (or treated as paid) in a tax year must not come to more than your net relevant earnings for that year.

Tip

Using the carry-forward rules lets you partly make up for lost time and give a boost to your pension savings. Provided you have enough unused contributions and your earnings or profits for the year to which you carry forward are at least enough to cover the contributions you are paying, you do not actually have to pay the contributions out of earnings – you could, for example, use a lump sum you have inherited.

What a contracted-out personal pension plan provides

You can take out an appropriate personal pension plan only if you are an employee, and so eligible for the SERPS part of the state scheme, and you are not already contracted out, for example through your employer's pension scheme (see Chapter 10). The appropriate plan does not guarantee to match the benefits you would have got had you stayed in SERPS, but it provides a substitute package of benefits called 'protected rights'. These are:

- a pension for you payable from your state pension age (see page 142). How much this pension will be depends, like all money purchase plans, on the amount paid in, how well the investment grows, and the annuity rate at which the fund can be turned into pension at retirement. Men and women of the same age must be offered the same annuity rates and, once it starts to be paid, the pension must increase in line with price inflation up to three per cent a year (five per cent for pensions bought by contributions paid from April 1997)
- a pension for your widow or widower if he or she is 45 or over at the time you die, or younger if caring for a dependent child.

An appropriate pension plan cannot be used to provide a lump sum.

Payments into a contracted-out plan

You cannot make contributions to a contracted-out personal plan (though if you are eligible, you can – and should – run an ordinary personal plan alongside it to boost the pension you will get). The money that goes into a contracted-out plan comes from the government in the form of a rebate of part of the National Insurance which you and your employer have paid (see page 145). In addition, the government adds tax relief on your share of the rebate

Since 6 April 1997, the rebates have been age-related. This reflects the fact that it costs more to provide a given level of pension at retirement for an older person than a younger person. (A contribution for a younger person can be invested for a longer period and so can grow to a larger sum by retirement.) If the rebates continued to increase by the appropriate amount all the way up to retirement, there would be little to choose between staying in SERPS and contracting out. But the government deemed this approach to be too costly, so the rebates increase with age up to age 46, when they flatten out at 9 per cent of earnings above the lower earnings limit (£62 a week in 1997–8) up to the upper earnings limit (£465 a week in 1997–8). The result is that, if you are a man in your 50s or a woman in your late 40s, you will probably be better off remaining in SERPS rather than contracting out. But if you are already contracted out, contracting back in might not be worth while because of the impact of charges on your contracted-out plan – see below. For anyone below these ages, contracting out could be worth while.

Whether or not contracting out makes sense at these younger ages depends partly on how optimistic you are about investment returns. If you think the invested rebates will grow strongly, contracting out will look more attractive than if you are pessimistic about investment returns. The introduction of tax on pension fund income from shares and similar investments has reduced the expected return by about a tenth compared with the pre-July 1997 situation, when pension fund income was completely tax-free.

Another important factor in your decision is the charges made by the plan provider. The rebates going into a contracted-out personal plan are relatively small. Moreover, in the past, many people have been persuaded to contract out for only a few years, with the result that only a low amount overall has been paid into their plan. Charges levied by the insurance companies running these plans can eat heavily into small investments and, unfortunately, many people are likely to be disappointed at the small pension which their appropriate plan will pay out at retirement. In some cases, the pension will have been wiped out altogether.

A further factor to consider is the stability of SERPS. This pension system was introduced in the 1970s with all-party support. It was supposed to be outside the political arena and to provide a stable long-term second-tier pension system. In fact, SERPS has scarcely left the politicians' sight. Fears over the escalating costs of the system have triggered numerous changes in the form of cuts to its benefits and elaborate ways of privatising its payment. Now, it is stongly rumoured that SERPS will be phased out completely when 'stakeholder pensions' are introduced. Changes to pensions legislation are not generally retrospective, so pension rights already built up under SERPS would in theory probably still be honoured even if new rights could no longer be added. However, SERPS pensions are based on average earnings throughout your working life, so in practice any phasing out might well have a detrimental effect on rights already built up. Without a crystal ball, there is no way to predict what will happen to SERPS, but you should be aware that uncertainty does hang over its future.

Choosing a personal pension plan

Your first step is to be very clear about the pension options open to you; hopefully, the preceding pages will have helped. If you are certain that a personal pension plan is the best option for you (see page 173), your next step is to consider what you want from a plan:

- how much do you want/can you afford to invest?
- do you want to save regular amounts – a useful discipline – or would you prefer to invest lump sums as and when you can afford to do so – a more flexible option? A compromise might be to save a small sum regularly and to top up periodically with lump sums
- what benefits and options do you want?
- how do you want to invest your contributions? The main choice is between investing on a with-profits basis (see page 242) or a unit-linked basis (see page 262). Close to retirement, you might want to switch to a deposit basis (see page 262).

You should then get hold of some surveys of pension plans – for instance, those published by *Which?*,★ *Money Management*,★ *Pensions Management*★ or *Planned Savings*.★ Look for providers offering plans with the features you need, who *consistently* turn in good investment performance, and whose charges do not eat heavily into your investment. Pick out, perhaps, half a dozen providers which look promising. Now contact those companies direct and ask them to send you the information you need – see 'More information' on page 192.

Alternatively, having developed a clear idea of your needs, you might now approach a couple of IFAs★ (see page 17). Choose ones who specialise in pensions and have access to a computer database comparing the pension plans on offer. Ask the IFA to arrange for you to receive information about the plans which look best for you. Do not commit yourself to anything until you have been able to study and compare the information at your leisure in your own home.

If you are considering transferring a previous employer's pension to a personal plan, you are recommended to enlist the help of an IFA or specialist pensions adviser (see page 167). The IFA must now be specifically authorised for this type of business and must use a computerised transfer analysis system to compare the options open to you. Pay particular attention to the assumptions used in the comparison. Better still would be to seek the advice of a consulting actuary (see page 167). Follow similar steps if you are considering opting out of your current employer's scheme in favour of a personal plan, but be very wary of taking this course of action – an employer's scheme will nearly always be better than a personal plan.

Alternatives to a personal pension plan

In recent years, much attention has been paid to the high level of charges on many personal pension plans. Research by *Money Management*★ suggests that charges can swallow from as little as 3 per cent of your pension fund up to a massive 40 per cent, depending on the plan you choose and for how long you invest: see the table below.

How charges eat into your pension fund

| | % of pension fund taken up in charges if you invest for: | | | | |
	5 years	10 years	15 years	20 years	25 years
Monthly contributions of £200 per month					
Best plan	3.0%	5.3%	7.4%	8.9%	10.6%
Average plan	11.5%	13.4%	15.3%	17.5%	19.6%
Worst plan	19.2%	22.0%	24.6%	28.2%	27.8%
Single contribution of £10,000					
Best plan	3.9%	7.1%	9.2%	10.6%	10.4%
Average plan	10.1%	13.7%	16.7%	19.6%	22.5%
Worst plan	17.4%	20.5%	27.0%	32.9%	38.2%

Source: *Money Management* October 1997

Charges at these levels eat into – and can even negate – the tax advantages of using a pension plan. As a result, it has been suggested that personal equity plans (PEPs) would be a better vehicle for retirement savings. PEPs provide a tax-efficient way to invest in a range of investments, such as shares, unit trusts and corporate bonds. They are described in Chapter 15.

Since July 1997, the argument in favour of PEPs has been even greater on tax grounds, since PEP income is completely tax-free, unlike the position for pension funds. However, this advantage is short-lived. In its July 1997 Budget, the government announced that, from April 1999 onwards, income from shares and unit trusts held in a PEP would be taxed in the same way as pension fund income. Since then, the government has gone on to announce that from April 1999 onwards no new PEPs can be started. Instead, you will be able to invest in new Individual Savings Accounts (ISAs) – see page 122. There will be a six-month period of grace up to October 1999 during which you can transfer investments from your existing PEPs to an ISA. At the end of the six months, PEPs will cease to have any tax advantages. The snag is that the new ISAs will have an overall limit, expected to be £50,000, and an annual limit, expected to be £5,000, which are both low in terms of pension planning. However, you should consider building up your PEP investments to £50,000 with a view to switching the maximum possible into the new ISAs when they start.

Coping with uncertainty

The uncertainty surrounding pensions and PEPs makes it extremely difficult for anyone who is not eligible for an employer's pension scheme to make sensible decisions about his or her pension planning in the short term. If you are already making regular premiums to a personal pension plan, in most cases you should carry on doing so for now. If you have a large lump sum to invest, a single-premium personal plan may be best, but shop around carefully for a plan with low charges as well as with the other features you need. If you have a relatively small amount to invest, either as a lump sum or as regular premiums, it might be better to find a temporary home for your investment – for example, a PEP investing in low-cost unit trusts, or even a building society account if your savings are very small – with a view to investing in an ISA or a stakeholder pension once they are up and running.

More information

Depending on how the pension provider you approach operates, you might be referred to an IFA, or the provider's own salesperson or agent might arrange to meet you. There are just a handful of 'direct sellers' offering pension plans to the public without giving any advice whatsoever. But the other providers or IFAs will need to gather a lot of information about you (usually by carrying out a fact-find – see page 41), on the basis of which they will offer their own advice. If you have done your homework, you will be in a good position to evaluate this advice and ask for further details as necessary. Do not sign anything at this stage. Ask for an illustration of the benefits you might expect by contributing to that provider's plan and a copy of the key features document (see page 46). The chart on

---

Planning in practice

Malcolm Coles, who is 26, left university in 1993. His first job was with a small research company. It didn't operate a company-wide pension scheme for employees, so Malcolm decided to ask a financial adviser for advice on what to do about getting a pension. He knew that the sooner he started paying towards a pension, the more it would be worth in years to come. After seeing the adviser, Malcolm took out a personal pension and opted out of the State Earnings-Related Pension Scheme in October 1993. He paid £90 every month into the plan; with tax relief this worked out at £120.

Two years later he joined Consumers' Association (CA), where he had the chance to join a hybrid-type employer's pension scheme (see page 158), Malcolm decided to join CA's scheme. He stopped making contributions to his personal pension and is letting the money he paid in grow until he retires. However, he has to pay extra charges on top of the usual monthly ones because he won't be making any more contributions. He could have transferred the money from his personal pension to CA's pension scheme, but after finding out the transfer penalties that would be imposed by his personal pension provider, Malcolm decided not to do so.

Which? October 1996

page 195 shows a typical illustration; the wording and assumptions used are laid down by the relevant regulator (the Personal Investment Authority – see page 38). At one time, all providers would give you an identical illustration for a given scenario, which helped you to get a feel for how much pension you might get but was of no use in comparing one provider's plan with another's. Now, although all providers use the same assumptions about how your invested contributions might grow, the illustration reflects the impact of each provider's own charges. The projected pension from a provider making high charges will be lower than that from a low-charging provider. In general, avoid high-charging plans unless there are very good overriding reasons not to do so: for example, the plan has extra features which you are keen to have and which are not available elsewhere, or the provider has an outstanding and con-

---

Kate Sroczynski, who is 27, works as an events manger for a new Internet company. The company hasn't set up a pension scheme for its employees so far, and Kate hasn't made any private provision of her own either. If and when the company decides to set up a pension scheme for employees, this will take some time to get going. Kate's worried that she'll be missing out on valuable years when she should be providing for her retirement, so she's decided to take out a personal pension. She's looking for a pension plan that is flexible and that allows her to vary her payments when she needs to. She'll join her employer's scheme if it starts one, so she also wants a plan that doesn't charge heavily for transferring

Which? January 1997

Dinah Williams has built up an investment portfolio in a range of unit trust PEPs in UK and EU stock markets. Dinah runs her own business and she's using her PEPs to build up a lump sum for retirement. But corporate bond PEPs are much safer than stock market-linked PEPs. So in April 1996 she invested £6,000 in the X income corporate bond PEP. Dinah plans gradually to move more of her assets into lower-risk investments over the next few years as she approaches retirement

Which? March 1997

sistent record of investment performance which you are confident will be maintained.

The key features document is a summary of all the important aspects of the plan: the aim of the contract, what is required from you, any penalties – for example, for failing to keep up regular premiums – the risks involved, and so on. Chapter 3 describes this document in more detail. Needless to say, it is important that you read the document and check that the plan on offer does indeed match your needs.

Having compared the literature and illustrations from the various plan providers, you should now be in a position to make your choice.

For information about the tax position of personal pension plans and of personal equity plans, see Inland Revenue* leaflets IR78 *Personal pensions* and IR89 *Personal equity plans*.

Illustration for a personal pension plan

1 December 1997
Male aged under 40 years
Pension age for illustration 65

The contributions

Gross single contribution	£ 5000.00
Less income tax saved if at 23% of the contribution	£ 1150.00
Net initial outlay	£ 3850.00

This illustration uses the same rates of return as other insurance companies' illustrations, but uses the Society's own charges. The figures are only examples, none is guaranteed and they do not represent the minimum or maximum amounts. The eventual benefits will depend on how the investments perform and may be more or less than those shown. Do not forget that inflation would reduce what you could buy in the future with the benefits arising. All insurance companies use the same rates to illustrate how funds may be converted into pension income. Your pension income will depend on how the investments perform and on annuity rates at the time you retire.

The benefits on survival to illustrated pension age

	Projected benefits if future rate of return is:		
	6% p.a.	9% p.a.	12% p.a.
Projected fund	£ 18800	£ 38600	£ 77400
which could provide:			
(a) projected tax-free cash sum (N.B. this may be restricted)	£ 4700	£ 9650	£ 19300
plus (b) projected balance of fund	£ 14100	£ 28950	£ 58100

The balance of the fund not providing a tax-free cash sum must be used to purchase a pension. For example, it could provide a projected monthly pension payable throughout the member's lifetime of

£ 109	£ 268	£ 628

What the benefits might be

WARNING – this contract has no cash-in value at any time

The last three columns assume that the return on the investment is 9.0% p.a.

The early years

At end of year	Total paid in to date £	Total actual deductions to date £	Effect of deductions to date £	What the transfer value might be £
1	5000.00	215	215	5230
2	5000.00	241	260	5670
3	5000.00	269	312	6160
4	5000.00	300	371	6680
5	5000.00	334	438	7250

The later years

10	5000.00	549	928	10900
15	5000.00	872	1810	16400
20	5000.00	1350	3350	24600
25	5000.00	2080	6030	37000
Full term	5000.00	2170	6380	38600

What are the deductions for?

- The deductions allow for the Society's current charges, which are designed to cover the expenses incurred by the Society, including the cost of providing advice (where appropriate).
- The last line in the table shows that, over the full illustrated term of the policy, the effect of the total deductions could amount to £6380.
- Putting it another way this would have the same effect as bringing the investment return used from 9.0% a year down to 8.3% a year.

How much will the advice cost?

- The allocation of costs for the handling of new business at our branches (which includes the cost of providing advice where appropriate) depends upon the size of the contribution and where relevant the duration of the contract. For this contract, the cost is estimated to be £152.
- That estimate is based on the actual allocation of costs for similar policies effected in 1996. These costs are paid out of the deductions or charges in the contract, not by any separate payment.
- Any further contributions paid would normally attract a broadly similar proportionate cost for the advice provided.

Notes

1. Tax-free cash sum

   If a tax-free cash sum figure is shown overleaf, this represents the maximum cash sum which may be taken in respect of the projected fund accumulated by the contributions illustrated and any existing fund under the plan. Please note, however, that if an existing fund is shown and any part of that fund derives from a transfer value from an occupational pension scheme, then there may be a further restriction on the amount of cash sum.

2. Projected pension

   Where projected pensions are shown the illustrated figures have been calculated assuming rates of return of 5%, 7.5% and 10% apply at retirement for the 6%, 9% and 12% projected funds, respectively.

3. Waiver of contribution facility

   If you apply for the waiver of contribution facility the level of benefits purchased by each relevant contribution will be lower than those which would have been purchased if the facility had not been chosen. The benefits illustrated assume that the facility is not incorporated. Details of the waiver facility are to be found in our leaflet 'Waiver of Contribution Facility'.

Source: The Equitable Life Assurance Society

Chapter 12

Basic investment planning

Chapter 2 should have given you a good idea of your financial objectives and the priority you attach to each one. Some of these objectives will concern your protection needs and have been dealt with in earlier chapters. Pension objectives have also been dealt with separately. What you should be left with now are your mainstream savings and investment objectives. Clearly, these will vary from person to person, but essentially they will fall into three broad types:

- providing a lump sum some time in the future either by investing a lump sum now or by saving regularly
- providing an income now by investing a lump sum
- providing an income some time in the future either by investing a lump sum now or by saving regularly.

The charts on pages 200–3 suggest how you might narrow down your choice of investments and methods of saving to find the most appropriate ways to meet your financial targets. A wide range of factors should be taken into account; these are discussed on page 198 onwards. The charts concentrate largely on risk, because this is the factor above all others which most often seems to cause problems. Numerous financial scandals have revolved around investors being seduced into products which promised exceptional returns at seemingly little or no risk. Sometimes governments issue such investments, but in the commercial world risk and reward *always* go hand in hand. If you want the chance of high returns, you must be prepared to take on extra risk.

The charts invite you to think of risk as a continuous scale from one to ten. If you place yourself at one, you are very averse to risk and should select savings and investments which carry the minimum of risk. Moving along the scale, you become more comfortable with risk and, at ten, you positively enjoy taking a gamble. How you assess your attitude towards risk was looked at in greater detail on page 35. As mentioned there, for a particular financial decision, your attitude towards risk may be influenced by the extent to which you are already on course to meet your most important financial targets. You should work through the charts for *each* financial target you have identified, bearing in mind the priority attached to each one. For example, if you are at the start of your financial plan, needing to build up an emergency fund and with little cash to spare, you should normally be very averse to risk. But as your main financial building-blocks fall into place, you may be comfortable taking greater risks with the lower priority targets – see the chart opposite.

How to choose savings and investments

You need to consider a combination of factors when thinking about whether one type of savings or investments or another will best meet your needs. Here, the main factors are looked at in turn. They provide the framework for Chapters 13–15, which describe how the most common savings and investments work. Chapter 16 puts into practice matching specific savings and investments to your financial skeleton.

How much can you save or invest and how regularly?

With most savings and investments, there is a minimum amount you can invest. Sometimes, where there is no minimum, charges still make it uneconomic to pay in small sums. Where a type of saving or investment enjoys favourable tax treatment, there is usually a maximum you can invest. This can apply to other products too.

[*continues on page 203*]

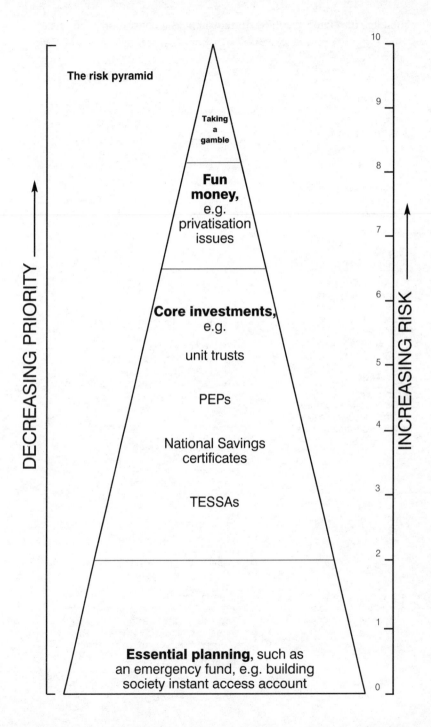

DECREASING PRIORITY →

INCREASING RISK →

The risk pyramid

Taking
a
gamble

**Fun
money,**
e.g.
privatisation
issues

Core investments,
e.g.

unit trusts

PEPs

National Savings
certificates

TESSAs

Essential planning, such as
an emergency fund, e.g. building
society instant access account

10
9
8
7
6
5
4
3
2
1
0

Building up a lump sum through regular saving

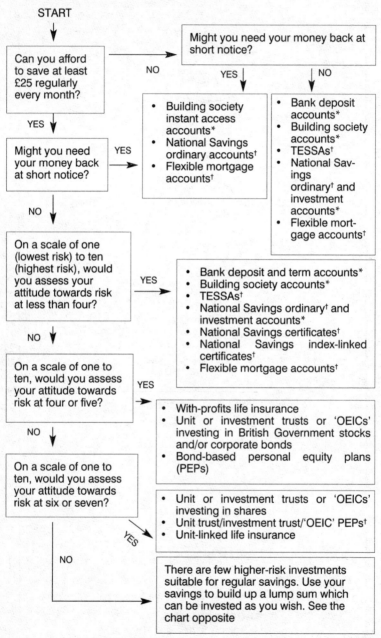

START

Can you afford to save at least £25 regularly every month?

NO → Might you need your money back at short notice?

YES ↓ — Might you need your money back at short notice?

YES ↓
- Building society instant access accounts*
- National Savings ordinary accounts†
- Flexible mortgage accounts†

NO ↓
- Bank deposit accounts*
- Building society accounts*
- TESSAs†
- National Savings ordinary† and investment accounts*
- Flexible mortgage accounts†

YES ↓

Might you need your money back at short notice?

YES →
- Building society instant access accounts*
- National Savings ordinary accounts†
- Flexible mortgage accounts†

NO ↓

On a scale of one (lowest risk) to ten (highest risk), would you assess your attitude towards risk at less than four?

YES →
- Bank deposit and term accounts*
- Building society accounts*
- TESSAs†
- National Savings ordinary† and investment accounts*
- National Savings certificates†
- National Savings index-linked certificates†
- Flexible mortgage accounts†

NO ↓

On a scale of one to ten, would you assess your attitude towards risk at four or five?

YES →
- With-profits life insurance
- Unit or investment trusts or 'OEICs' investing in British Government stocks and/or corporate bonds
- Bond-based personal equity plans (PEPs)

NO ↓

On a scale of one to ten, would you assess your attitude towards risk at six or seven?

YES →
- Unit or investment trusts or 'OEICs' investing in shares
- Unit trust/investment trust/'OEIC' PEPs†
- Unit-linked life insurance

NO →

There are few higher-risk investments suitable for regular savings. Use your savings to build up a lump sum which can be invested as you wish. See the chart opposite

* May be particularly worth considering if you are a non-taxpayer.
† May be particularly worth considering if you pay tax at the higher rate.

Investing a lump sum to make it grow

START

Might you need your money back at short notice? — YES →
- Building society instant access accounts*
- National Savings ordinary accounts†
- Flexible mortgage accounts†

↓ NO

On a scale of one (lowest risk) to ten (highest risk), would you assess your attitude towards risk at less than four? — YES →
- Bank deposit and term accounts*
- Building society accounts*
- TESSAs†
- National Savings ordinary† and investment accounts*
- Flexible mortgage accounts†
- National Savings certificates†
- National Savings index-linked certificates†
- Index-linked British Government stocks held to redemption*

↓ NO

On a scale of one to ten, would you assess your attitude towards risk at around four? — YES →
- Insurance company guaranteed growth bonds
- British Government stocks held to redemption*†
- With-profits life insurance
- With-profits friendly society plans
- Unit or investment trusts investing in British Government stocks and/or corporate bonds
- Bond-based personal equity plans (PEPs)†
- British Government stocks*†
- Index-linked British Government stocks*†

↓ NO

On a scale of one to ten, would you assess your attitude towards risk at around five? — YES →
- Personal equity plan (PEP) investing in bonds of a single high-quality company†
- Bonds of high-quality companies held to redemption

↓ NO

On a scale of one to ten, would you assess your attitude towards risk at six or seven? — YES →
- Corporate bonds
- Unit or investment trusts or 'OEICs' investing in UK shares
- Unit trust/investment trust/'OEIC' PEPs†
- Unit-linked life insurance, e.g. single-premium bonds†

— NO →
- Unit or investment trusts or 'OEICs' investing in overseas markets or specialist sectors
- Direct investment in ordinary shares†
- Higher-risk investments outside the scope of this book – e.g. traded options, enterprise investment scheme

* May be particularly worth considering if you are a non-taxpayer.
† May be particularly worth considering if you pay tax at the higher rate.

Using a lump sum to provide an income immediately

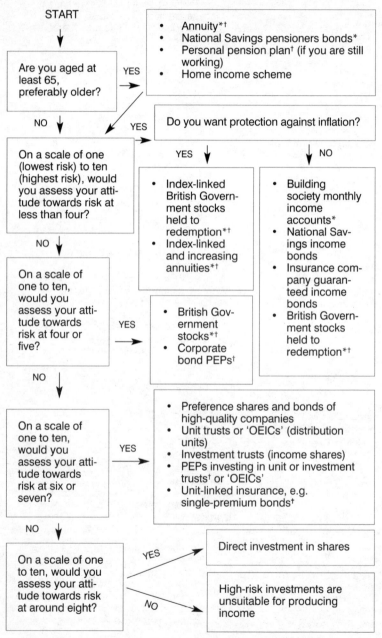

START

Are you aged at least 65, preferably older? — YES →
- Annuity*†
- National Savings pensioners bonds*
- Personal pension plan† (if you are still working)
- Home income scheme

NO ↓ / YES →

Do you want protection against inflation?

On a scale of one (lowest risk) to ten (highest risk), would you assess your attitude towards risk at less than four?

YES ↓
- Index-linked British Government stocks held to redemption*†
- Index-linked and increasing annuities*†

NO ↓

Do you want protection against inflation? NO ↓
- Building society monthly income accounts*
- National Savings income bonds
- Insurance company guaranteed income bonds
- British Government stocks held to redemption*†

On a scale of one to ten, would you assess your attitude towards risk at four or five? — YES →
- British Government stocks*†
- Corporate bond PEPs†

NO ↓

On a scale of one to ten, would you assess your attitude towards risk at six or seven? — YES →
- Preference shares and bonds of high-quality companies
- Unit trusts or 'OEICs' (distribution units)
- Investment trusts (income shares)
- PEPs investing in unit or investment trusts† or 'OEICs'
- Unit-linked insurance, e.g. single-premium bonds†

NO ↓

On a scale of one to ten would you assess your attitude towards risk at around eight? — YES → Direct investment in shares

NO → High-risk investments are unsuitable for producing income

* May be particularly worth considering if you are a non-taxpayer.
† May be particularly worth considering if you pay tax at the higher rate.

Using a lump sum or regular savings to provide an income later on

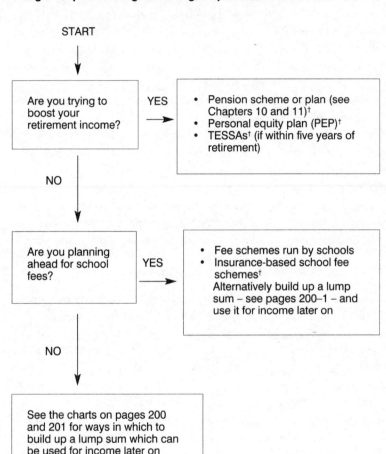

START

Are you trying to boost your retirement income? — YES →
- Pension scheme or plan (see Chapters 10 and 11)†
- Personal equity plan (PEP)†
- TESSAs† (if within five years of retirement)

NO

Are you planning ahead for school fees? — YES →
- Fee schemes run by schools
- Insurance-based school fee schemes†
  Alternatively build up a lump sum – see pages 200–1 – and use it for income later on

NO

See the charts on pages 200 and 201 for ways in which to build up a lump sum which can be used for income later on

† May be particularly worth considering if you pay tax at the higher rate

[*continued from page 198*]

Some investment products are specifically designed to accept regular savings – monthly or annual sums, for instance – and there may be penalties if you fail to keep up the payments. There is quite a debate, especially in the insurance and pensions world, over whether regular saving is a 'good thing'. Regular saving has the advantage of creating a discipline which you might find helpful. It also takes away tricky decisions about when is the right time to buy investments whose price rises and falls. On the other hand, by committing yourself to regular saving, you lose flexibility over what, when and with whom you invest, because you are locked into the savings arrangement. This can be a problem if either your circumstances change or better products come on to the market.

It is also commonly argued that charges from regular savings insurance and pensions products are higher than for equivalent single-premium products (where you pay in a single lump sum). On the face of it, this is true. However, you must consider how you would use single-premium products. If, for you, the alternative to taking out a regular-premium plan would be to take out a series of single-premium plans as and when you could afford to, you must compare charges for the *whole* series of lump-sum plans (and not just one of them) against the charges for the regular-savings plan.

For how long can you tie up your money?

Crucially important when choosing any investment is: can you get your money back, when, and are there penalties for doing so? Some products are designed to last for a specified period – five or ten years, for example. Obviously, you should not invest unless you can leave your money for the full period. Other investments do not have a specified term, but they may clearly be best suited to long-term investment, and may make an unwise choice if you know you want to save only for a year or two or might need funds in a hurry.

However sensibly you choose your investments at the outset, life can be unpredictable, so you should check what happens if you need your money back sooner: maybe you simply would not be able to have it back, perhaps you would lose interest, there might be surrender charges or, with an investment whose price rises and falls, you might run the risk of a loss.

What type of return do you need?

The need for either growth or income now or income in the future has already been considered. A further consideration is whether you want a fixed return or one which varies. Variable returns can be a problem if you are heavily reliant on them: for example as a major source of retirement income. Fixed returns, which go hand in hand with investing for a fixed period, are attractive if you expect returns on competing investments to fall. If, in fact, the competing returns rise over the period, you will lose out, so do not assume that choosing a fixed return is necessarily less risky than a return which can vary.

Even a fixed return loses value, in terms of what it can buy, if prices rise. A few products offering index-linked returns, which protect your investment against the impact of inflation, are available.

How is the return taxed?

Chapter 2 examines the tax system to help you identify your own tax position. Now, you need to marry your personal tax treatment to the tax treatment of the investments you choose. Some investments and savings have particular tax advantages for certain types of investor; these are explained more fully in the chapters that follow. Some broad points to consider are:

- look at the after-tax (net) return you will get personally, given your income tax rate and capital gains tax position, not the before-tax (gross) return
- non-taxpayers gain nothing extra from tax-free investments
- it is more convenient for non-taxpayers to receive returns from which no tax has been deducted than to have to claim back such tax
- tax-free returns are especially valuable to higher-rate taxpayers
- even if your income is taxed, you can often make capital gains without having to pay any tax on them because of the generous tax allowances
- income from most types of savings has been taxed only at the lower rate since 6 April 1996 onwards. Lower-rate and basic-rate taxpayers have no further tax to pay. Higher-rate taxpayers have extra to pay. Non-taxpayers can, in most cases, reclaim the tax already deducted. This treatment applies to interest from bank and building society accounts, income from annuities, interest from corporate bonds, and dividends and distributions from personal holdings of shares and unit trusts. From April 1999, the rate of tax on share and unit trust income will be reduced to 10 per cent, but non-taxpayers will no longer be able to reclaim the tax.

What are the costs?

Just as you need to know the after-tax return for you personally, so you need to know the after-all-charges return to build a clear idea of what you stand to gain through a particular savings or investment medium. Some products are very straightforward. For example, when you save with a building society, you are quoted a particular rate of interest. The rate has been pitched at a level which (taking other factors into account) is expected to cover the society's costs. What you are quoted is what you get net of charges. Well, almost – you do have to watch out for interest penalties if you cash in term or notice accounts.

Most packaged products (life insurance, unit trusts, pension plans) are more complex, with a variety of different charges – management fees, upfront charges, surrender penalties, switching fees, and so on. Trying to understand the impact of all these charges can be a nightmare. But since the start of 1995, life insurance and pension providers have had to provide illustrations of the possible return from their products, netting out the impact of their own charges on the return you get. That's a big improvement.

A third group of investments are those which run up dealing or transaction costs when you buy and sell them. These include most shares, British Government stocks and corporate bonds. When assessing the return you might get, you should deduct what you will pay in stockbroker's commission, stamp duty, and so on.

What are the risks?

When people talk about investment risk, they usually mean the possibility of losing some or all of their original stake. But this is only part of the picture. There are three main types of risk:

- **capital risk** If you put your money into deposit-based savings, such as building society accounts, you know that you will always get back at least the amount of your original capital – that is there is no capital risk. With investments like shares and unit trusts, which are bought and sold in a market-place, you cannot be sure of this, because their price may have fallen during the time you have owned them. Another less obvious threat to capital is where charges are deducted from that capital rather than from the return – see page 25. You also need to consider the standing of the organisation with whom you are investing. If you lend money to the British government, it is very unlikely that the government will default and be unable to pay you back as promised. But if you buy the bonds or shares of a small company struggling to break into new markets, there is a distinct possibility of your losing all your investment if the company goes out of business

- **inflation risk** The big problem with deposit-type investments is that, over the long term, their returns tend to be lower than those from investments such as shares, and can be so low that they do not even compensate you for the impact of rising prices. This means that, although you can be sure of getting back your original outlay, it may be worth a lot less in terms of what you can buy with it. A few investments are specifically designed to protect you against inflation, but are not always the most appropriate choice. In the main, if you are investing for the long term, you should consider investments either in shares or linked to shares (such as unit trusts) as a way of hedging against inflation
- **the risk of being locked in (or out)** Accepting a fixed return over a set period or agreeing to a contract with onerous early-surrender penalties can prevent you from benefiting from improved returns elsewhere. Equally, though, keeping your options open can mean that you have to accept falling returns when others have protected their position by taking on fixed-rate deals.

You can see that there is no such thing as a completely 'safe' investment. Inevitably, you have to trade risk against return, and the different risks against each other.

In the charts on pages 200–3 and Chapters 13–15 we have given each type of investment a risk rating of one (lowest risk) to ten (highest risk). These ratings attempt to take into account all the various risks and give you a rule of thumb for comparing the riskiness of one type of investment with another. However, the ratings are not based on objective measures of probabilities and volatility, and the riskiness sometimes varies depending on how you plan to use a particular type of investment: for example, holding it until repayment rather than selling in a volatile market, or combining it with other types of investment with a different degree of riskiness. Use the risk ratings as a rough guide which you can match to your assessment of the degree of risk which you are willing to take.

Building a portfolio

In general, each investment target you have will require its own strategy for achieving it. But you are not simply limited to the particular risk and return offered by each product. By combining different investments, you can build a portfolio which has its own balance of risks and rewards. This gives you the scope to tailor your savings and investments closely to your own targets, circumstances and preferences.

You can see how this works by considering the example of shares. Buying the shares in just one company would be a high-risk strategy; you would face three levels of risk:

Planning in practice

Fact-find: Robert and Mary, both aged 45, have two teenage children. Robert earns £35,000 a year; Mary has no job. Robert has been paying into his employer's pension scheme for ten years and has recently started making additional voluntary contributions. Robert has life insurance from work. They also have a joint life policy which is due to run for another ten years. They have £26,000 outstanding on their mortgage and no plans to move. They have £2,000 in an instant access savings account and a further £4,000 in a TESSA. Their immediate aim is to find the best way of investing £48,000 which they inherited from Mary's mother, who died recently.

Solution: Mary and Robert use £26,000 of the inheritance to clear their mortgage. They put £8,000 into National Savings capital bonds in Mary's name – Mary is a non-taxpayer, so there will be no tax to pay on the interest. They put £6,000 into a bond-based PEP and £6,000 into an equity income PEP unit trust – although it invests in companies which aim to provide higher-than-average dividends, they view this as a growth investment. To spread their risks, they also put £2,000 in a UK growth unit trust. In addition, they have more spending money now the mortgage has been repaid, so they decide to pay £50 a month into a high-risk unit trust investing in the growing economies of the Far East. [The subsequent economic crisis in that region in 1997/8 underlines the fact that the prospect of higher returns does indeed go hand in hand with greater risk and the importance of not investing money which you cannot afford to lose.]   *Which?* April 1995

- **market risk** The whole stock market could fall – because of economic recession, say
- **industry or sector risk** The particular industry your company is part of could suffer some blow – a sudden increase in the price of raw materials, for example
- **company risk** Your particular company could run into difficulties – for example, fierce competition from an aggressive new

Fact-find: Paul is a 40-year-old divorcee with two children. He wants some extra life cover and to save up to £50 a month on a long-term basis. He is already paying the maximum into his employer's pension scheme, has a personal equity plan (PEP) – but is paying into it less than the maximum allowed – and building society savings of £8,000.

Solution: According to a panel of *Which?* experts, best advice would be for Paul to save through a unit trust savings plan or top up the contributions to his existing PEP and to take out term insurance to provide the life cover.   *Which?* May 1995

Fact-find: In an exercise to test financial advice, a researcher posed as a 26 year-old trainee accountant earning £15,000 a year. He had no savings, life insurance or investments, but wanted to save for the next two to three years to pay for his wedding and a deposit on a home. He could set aside at most £250 a month. He had contracted out of the SERPS part of the state pension scheme but was making no pension contributions of his own. He said he could join his employer's pension scheme when he was 30.

Solution: The researcher wanted to save a fairly small amount for only a few years, so there would be little difference in the money earned from a savings account and that from a higher-return investment involving higher risk. Best advice would be to put his money in a savings account. Given his aim of saving over a short period, investments (including PEPs and investment trusts) were unsuitable. TESSAs would not generally be suitable, because there could be penalties if the savings were withdrawn within five years. However, a TESSA with a high rate of interest and low penalties could be worth considering.   *Which?* December 1995 player – and could even go bankrupt, in which case you would most likely lose all your investment.

You can reduce your exposure to company risk by investing in the shares of a number of different companies. You can reduce your exposure to sector risk by making sure those companies come from a spread of different industries. And you can lessen the market risk by investing not just in the UK stock market but in, say, Europe, Japan and the United States, and by investing in a range of other investments, such as bonds and property, which respond in a different way to economic factors. In this way you build an investment portfolio with the combination of risk and expected returns which suits you. You can buy into 'ready-made' portfolios by investing in 'pooled investments', such as unit trusts, investment trusts and investment-type life insurance.

More information

The chapters that follow outline the main investment and saving tools. For a more detailed look at them, see *Which? Way to Save and Invest*, published by Which? Books.★ Many books are devoted to developing your understanding of investment strategy and portfolio building: browse around a good bookshop or contact The Investors' Book Club.★ Regular journals to consider are *Which?*,★ *Money Management*,★ *Planned Savings*,★ *Investors Chronicle*,★ *Moneywise*★ and *Money Observer*.★

When it comes to organising your investments, you might find it helpful to use a computer. A spreadsheet programme, such as *Microsoft Excel*, is ideal if you are comfortable setting up your own system for logging your investments, calculating their values, working out any tax due, and so on. But you can also get tailor-made packages: for example, for managing a portfolio of stocks and shares, handling your tax, and so on. Have a browse around a computer warehouse or the advertisements in the various computer magazines stocked by most newsagents to see what is available. For a general outline of how computers can help, see *The Which? Guide to Computers*, published by Which? Books.★

Chapter 13

Lower-risk investments

This chapter gives you basic information about those investments that do not involve any risk of losing your original investment. However, you should bear in mind that most of them are vulnerable to the impact of inflation. This is particularly so if you are using these investments to provide an income, because the amount of your capital stays the same in money terms but gets progressively smaller in terms of what you can buy with it. If you reinvest the interest earned, not only is your capital growing by the reinvested amount, but you earn interest on the reinvested interest (a process called 'compounding'), which further boosts the value of your investment. But even if you do let the interest accumulate, the return on these investments might still fall short of inflation, and, over the long term, generally lags behind returns available elsewhere. This makes them unsuitable as the only home for long-term saving, although they might form part of a more widely invested portfolio. Balancing the risks, each product has been given a risk rating on a one (lowest risk) to ten (highest risk) scale, which should help you to match the various forms of saving and investment to your assessment of your own attitude towards risk (see also Chapters 2 and 12).

Bank and building society savings and investments

Current accounts

What they are Current accounts are the prime tool for basic money management. You deposit money – often your main source of income – and have various ways of instructing the bank or building society to make payments from the account: cheque, debit card, standing order, direct debit, for example. Access to cash is usually through visits to a branch or an automated teller machine, so convenience of these to your home/work may be a key factor in your choice of account. Most bank current accounts and a few building society accounts allow you to borrow through your current account in the form of an overdraft.

Minimum investment Often none, although the minimum investment in high-interest current accounts may be thousands of pounds.

Maximum investment None.

Type of return Many personal current accounts pay a very small rate of interest on balances which are in credit. The amount is so small that it should not be a major factor in your choice of account. High-interest accounts pay better rates but require you to keep a substantial minimum balance; you might do better to invest surplus funds in a proper savings product.

Tax treatment Interest is taxable and, since April 1996, usually paid with lower-rate tax already deducted. Non-taxpayers can reclaim tax overpaid, or, better still, arrange for interest to be paid gross by completing Form R85 from the bank, building society or your local tax office.

How long you invest for No set time. You can withdraw your money whenever you like, though there may be an upper limit on cash and/or withdrawals in any one day.

Charges With most personal current accounts, there are no charges if the account is in credit. If the account is overdrawn, there may be charges for each transaction credited to and debited from the account. Usually, there are charges for overdrafts, which are much higher if you do not arrange the overdraft in advance. A few accounts let you overdraw by a small, set limit without charge.

Risk No capital risk. Vulnerable to inflation, so do not keep surplus funds idle in a current account. Risk rating: one.

More information Regular surveys in *Which?*,★ personal finance magazines and the personal finance pages of newspapers, summaries in *Moneyfacts*,★ teletext (for high-interest accounts).

How to open an account Usually at a local branch. Some banks and building societies offer telephone or home computer banking accounts, which you can open by visiting a branch or by post.

Flexible mortgage accounts

What they are A mortgage, current account and savings facility combined. This is a new holistic approach to handling your finances. You overpay your mortgage either by paying off larger amounts than the contractual minimum or by arranging to have your whole salary or other earnings paid into your mortgage account. Using normal current account tools – cash card, debit card and chequebook, for instance – you draw against the overpayment whatever money you need to cover your normal living expenses and other spending. Any surplus remains in the mortgage account, so reducing the mortgage debt. This in effect, means that the difference between your overpayment and your spending – that is, your savings – earns whatever is the current mortgage rate (since it reduces the mortgage debt on which you pay the rate). At the time of writing, only a couple of mortgage lenders offered this type of product, but, given its flexibility and high 'return' on savings, it may become more widespread.

Minimum investment Not relevant. You must take out a mortgage and there may be a minimum for this – for example, £50,000 – and you must agree to have your earnings paid into the account. As is normal practice, the lender will usually restrict the maximum mortgage to a given multiple of your earnings.

Maximum investments In effect, the size of your mortgage.

Type of return Saving in interest on the mortgage loan if you pay off more than the minimum required. In effect, your savings are earning the mortgage rate, which is usually significantly higher than the rate on a comparable deposit account.

Tax treatment You do not receive interest as such; instead you save the interest which would otherwise be paid on the mortgage loan. Therefore, there is no tax – in effect, the return on your savings is tax-free.

How long you invest for The mortgage term, or a shorter period if you pay off your mortgage at a faster rate.

Charges Normal charges associated with taking out a mortgage (see Chapter 8).

Risk No capital risk. Inflation has both positive and negative effects, since it erodes the value of your mortgage loan as well as the value of your income/savings. If you have a variable-rate mortgage, the account is vulnerable to rising interest rates – although this in effect increases the return on your 'savings', rising rates increase the cost of the mortgage and leave a smaller surplus from your income to be 'saved'. Risk rating: one.

More information Summaries in *Moneyfacts*.★ Occasional articles in personal finance magazines and personal finance sections of newspapers.

How to open an account At the time of writing, only Mortgage Trust offered this type of account to the general public (contact the lender direct or through a broker/IFA). Virgin Direct had a similar product available to existing customers (contact the lender direct), which it planned to open up to the wider public later on.

Instant access accounts

What they are Savings accounts which let you withdraw your money at any time without notice or penalty. However, there may be limits on the amount of cash or cheque withdrawals you can make in any one day. Instant access accounts make a suitable home for an emergency fund.

Minimum investment Often none.

Maximum investment None.

Type of return Interest, which is variable. Usually tiered accounts, meaning that small balances earn little or no interest, and higher rates are paid as your balance reaches set thresholds.

Tax treatment Interest is taxable and, since April 1996, usually paid with lower-rate tax already deducted. Non-taxpayers can reclaim tax overpaid, or, better still, arrange for interest to be paid gross by completing Form R85 from the bank, building society or your local tax office. Lower-rate and basic-rate taxpayers have no further tax to pay. Higher-rate taxpayers have extra to pay.

How long you invest for No set period.

Charges No explicit charges. The bank's or building society's costs are one factor influencing the interest rates offered.

Risk No capital risk. Vulnerable to inflation. Vulnerable to falling interest rates. Risk rating: one.

More information Regular surveys in *Which?*,★ personal finance magazines and the personal finance pages of newspapers, summaries in *Moneyfacts*,★ fax services,★ teletext.

How to invest At local branch. Some building societies, particularly the smaller ones, offer postal accounts, which you can invest in and withdraw from only through the post. This means there is a short delay in making transactions, but this disadvantage may be outweighed by the higher interest rates postal accounts often pay.

Notice accounts

What they are Savings accounts which let you withdraw your money without penalty only if you give a specified period of notice, such as a month or 90 days, depending on the account. Earlier withdrawal is usually (but not always) possible on payment of an interest penalty.

Minimum investment Varies from, say, £500 to £10,000.

Maximum investment None.

Type of return Interest, which is variable. Often tiered accounts, paying higher rates if the amount you have invested exceeds specified thresholds.

Tax treatment Interest is taxable and, since April 1996, usually paid with lower-rate tax already deducted. Non-taxpayers can reclaim tax overpaid, or, better still, arrange for interest to be paid gross by completing Form R85 from the bank, building society or your local tax office. No further tax for lower-rate and basic-rate taxpayers, but higher-rate taxpayers pay extra.

How long you invest for No set term, but you should aim to give the full notice period when you want to make withdrawals.

Charges No explicit charges, apart from penalties or notice periods on withdrawal. The bank's or building society's costs are one factor influencing the interest rates offered.

Risk No capital risk. Vulnerable to inflation. Vulnerable to falling interest rates, especially since you cannot readily switch to another investment. Risk rating: two to three, depending on length of notice period.

More information Regular surveys in *Which?*,* personal finance magazines and the personal finance pages of newspapers, summaries in *Moneyfacts*,* fax services,* teletext.

How to invest At local branch. By post, if postal account.

Term accounts and bonds

What they are You invest for a set period – one or two years, say – and either cannot get your money back earlier or withdrawals are subject to strict rules: for example, you must leave a certain sum invested, or make only one withdrawal of up to ten per cent of the value of the account, and so on. There are many variations: with some, the return is paid at the end of the term when the account or bond matures; with others, you can take a monthly income.

Minimum investment Varies: £2,500, £10,000, for example.

Maximum investment None.

Type of return Interest, which may be fixed or variable, depending on the particular account or bond.

Tax treatment Interest is taxable and, since April 1996, usually paid with lower-rate tax already deducted. Non-taxpayers can reclaim tax overpaid, or, better still, arrange for interest to be paid gross by completing Form R85 from the bank, building society or your local tax office. No further tax for lower-rate and basic-rate taxpayers, but higher-rate taxpayers have extra to pay.

How long you invest for The specified term.

Charges No explicit charges. The bank's or building society's costs are one factor influencing the interest rates offered.

Risk No capital risk. Vulnerable to inflation. Variable rates are vulnerable to falling interest rates, but you would lose out if locked into fixed rates when other interest rates were rising. Risk rating: three.

More information Regular surveys in *Which?*,★ personal finance magazines and the personal finance pages of newspapers, summaries in *Moneyfacts*,★ fax services,★ teletext.

How to invest At local branch. By post, if postal account.

Monthly income accounts

What they are These can be based on several types of deposit: for example, instant access or notice account, term account or bond. Most commonly they are notice accounts. Instead of accumulating interest within the account or bond, the interest is paid out monthly as income. This form of investment is popular with pensioners seeking to boost their income.

Minimum investment Varies: can be as low as £500, but is more often £5,000 to £10,000.

Maximum investment None.

Type of return Interest, which may be fixed or variable, depending on the particular account or bond.

Tax treatment Interest is taxable and, since April 1996, usually paid with lower-rate tax already deducted. Non-taxpayers can reclaim tax overpaid, or, better still, arrange for interest to be paid gross by completing Form R85 from the bank, building society or your local tax office. No further tax for lower-rate and basic-rate taxpayers, but higher-rate taxpayers have extra to pay.

How long you invest for Depends on the type of account or bond. Most commonly, these are notice accounts where you can have your money back at any time provided you give the required notice – for example, 60 or 90 days – or alternatively pay an interest penalty.

Charges No explicit charges. The bank's or building society's costs are one factor influencing the interest rates offered.

Risk No capital risk. Vulnerable to inflation. Variable rates are vulnerable to falling interest rates, but you would lose out if locked into fixed rates when other interest rates were rising. Risk rating: one to three, depending on type of account or bond.

More information Regular surveys in *Which?*,* personal finance magazines and the personal finance pages of newspapers, summaries in Moneyfacts,* fax services,* teletext.

How to invest At local branch. By post, if postal account.

Tip

If you are a non-taxpayer, you can arrange to receive interest from your bank or building society account without any tax having been deducted by completing Form R85, which the branch or your tax office can supply. This saves you the trouble of having to reclaim tax later on. For more information, see Inland Revenue leaflet IR127 *Are you paying too much tax on your savings?*

Tax-Exempt Special Savings Accounts (TESSAs)

What they are A bank or building society account which qualifies for favourable tax treatment provided certain rules are met. To hold a TESSA, you must be at least 18. You can have only one TESSA at a time, and you cannot hold it jointly with someone else. TESSAs must be transferable from one bank or society to another, but watch out for penalties if you do switch provider. In late 1997, the government issued its proposals for Individual Savings Accounts (ISAs) – see page 122 – which will replace TESSAs from April 1999. As existing TESSAs mature, you can move the proceeds into your ISA subject to the overall limit of £50,000.

Minimum investment Varies: can be as low as £1.

Maximum investment The tax rules set the following limits: £3,000 in the first year, £1,800 in each of the following four years, up to an overall maximum of £9,000 over five years. Some providers accept a lump sum, which is put in a non-TESSA account that feeds into the TESSA year by year.

Type of return Interest, which is usually variable, occasionally fixed.

Tax treatment Interest on a TESSA is tax-free provided the tax rules are met. (Interest on an account used to feed into a TESSA is not tax-free.)

How long you invest for TESSAs are designed to run for five years. Under the tax rules, you can withdraw net interest at any time without losing the tax benefits: that is, your original capital and any tax relief must be left in the account. If you withdraw more, the account stops being a TESSA and the proceeds are then taxable.

Until 5 April 1999, at the end of five years, you can reinvest the whole of the capital (but not the interest – that is, a maximum of £9,000) from the maturing TESSA in a new TESSA running for a further five years. You must make the reinvestment within six months of the old TESSA ending. If you reinvest less than £9,000, you can add to the TESSA in subsequent years, subject to the normal £1,800 a year and overall £9,000 limits.

Charges No explicit charges. The bank or building society's costs are one factor influencing the interest rates offered. There may be penalties (lost interest, an additional fee and/or loss of bonuses) if you try to switch your TESSA from one provider to another.

Risk No capital risk. Vulnerable to inflation. Variable rates are vulnerable to falling interest rates, but you would lose out if locked into fixed rates when other interest rates were rising. Risk rating: two to three.

More information Regular surveys in *Which?*,* personal finance magazines and the personal finance pages of newspapers, summaries in *Moneyfacts*,* fax services,* teletext. See Inland Revenue leaflet IR114 *TESSAs: Tax-free interest for taxpayers*.

How to invest At local branch. By post, if postal account.

> **Tip**
>
> TESSAs can be a good investment even if you cannot tie up your money for as long as five years. This is because TESSAs often offer relatively high rates of interest. Even if you withdraw your savings before the five years are up and have to pay tax on them, the net (after-tax) return can still be higher than on accounts designed to run for shorter periods. But watch out for early-withdrawal penalties, and bear in mind that all the interest that has built up in the TESSA will be taxable in the year you make the withdrawal, which might push you into a higher tax bracket.

Children's accounts

What they are Accounts especially for children (variously defined: for example, up to age 16, 18 or 21), usually offering introductory gifts, magazines, money-boxes etc. Some accounts include cash cards for older children (aged 14 or more, say). Children's accounts are useful as a way of getting children into the savings habit.

Minimum investment Often as low as £1.

Maximum investment Usually none.

Type of return Interest, which is variable.

Tax treatment Interest is taxable and, if you do nothing, it will be paid with lower-rate tax already deducted (since April 1996). However, non-taxpayers (which includes most children) can have interest paid gross if Form R85 from the bank, building society or your local tax office is completed. Watch out for interest being treated as income of the parent (see Chapter 16).

How long you invest for Usually, these are instant access accounts, but some do not allow withdrawals before a given age.

Charges No explicit charges. The bank's or building society's costs are one factor influencing the interest rates offered.

Risk No capital risk. Vulnerable to inflation. Variable rates are vulnerable to falling interest rates. Risk rating: one.

More information Regular surveys in *Which?*,★ personal finance magazines and the personal finance pages of newspapers, summaries in *Moneyfacts*.★

How to invest At local branch.

National Savings investments

These are investments offered by the government and run by the Department for National Savings.★

National Savings ordinary account

What it is A savings account which gives you limited immediate access to your money. A small amount of interest each year is tax-free, which could be useful for higher-rate taxpayers, but overall the ordinary account is of limited use because the rate of interest paid is very low.
Minimum investment £10.
Maximum investment £10,000.
Type of return Interest, which is variable. A higher rate is paid if the balance is £500 or more and you've had the account for at least a year. Interest is credited to your account annually.
Tax treatment The first £70 (£140 from a joint account) a year of interest is tax-free. Above that limit, interest is taxable but paid out gross, that is, without the tax already deducted.
How long you invest for No time-limit. You can withdraw up to £100 instantly through post offices, or £250 if you regularly use one branch; otherwise withdrawals are made by post and take a few days.
Charges No explicit charges. National Savings' underlying costs are one factor influencing the interest rates offered.
Risk No capital risk. Vulnerable to inflation. Vulnerable to falling interest rates. Risk rating: one.
More information Post offices, the Department for National Savings,★ occasional reviews of National Savings products in *Which?*,★ personal finance magazines and the personal finance pages of newspapers, summaries in *Moneyfacts*.★
How to invest Via post offices or deal direct with the Department for National Savings.★

National Savings investment account

What it is A one-month notice account.
Minimum investment £20.
Maximum investment £100,000.

Type of return Interest, which is variable. This is a tiered account with higher rates of interest payable as your balance reaches £500, £2,500, £10,000 and £25,000. Interest is credited once a year.

Tax treatment Interest is taxable but paid out gross, that is, without the tax already deducted, making this a useful investment for non-taxpayers.

How long you invest for No time-limit, but you have to give one month's notice to withdraw any money from the account.

Charges No explicit charges. National Savings' underlying costs are one factor influencing the interest rates offered.

Risk No capital risk. Vulnerable to inflation. Vulnerable to falling interest rates. Risk rating: two.

More information Post offices, the Department for National Savings,* occasional reviews of National Savings products in *Which?*,* personal finance magazines and the personal finance pages of newspapers, summaries in *Moneyfacts*.*

How to invest Via post offices or deal direct with the Department for National Savings.*

National Savings certificates

What they are Five-year-term investment producing a guaranteed tax-free return, which makes them attractive for taxpayers, especially those paying at the higher rate.

Minimum investment £100.

Maximum investment £10,000 in the current (44th) issue, plus a further unlimited amount if you are reinvesting the maturity proceeds of an earlier issue. This is in addition to holdings of previous issues.

Type of return Interest, which is fixed and paid out at the end of the five years or on earlier encashment. The rate of interest increases each year you hold the certificates.

Tax treatment Tax-free.

How long you invest for Five years. You can get your money back earlier, but you'll get interest only at the reduced rates which apply to the earlier years. If you cash in during the first year, you get no interest at all (except on reinvested certificates). At the end of five years, make sure you cash in the certificates or reinvest in a new issue, otherwise they usually revert to a standard rate of interest called the 'General Extension Rate', which is very low.

Charges No explicit charges. National Savings' underlying costs are one factor influencing the interest rates offered.

Risk No capital risk. Vulnerable to inflation. Because you are locked in at a fixed rate, you'll lose out if other interest rates rise. Risk rating: three.

More information Post offices, the Department for National Savings,★ occasional reviews of National Savings products in *Which?*,★ personal finance magazines and the personal finance pages of newspapers, summaries in *Moneyfacts*.★

How to invest Via post offices or deal direct with the Department for National Savings.★

Index-linked National Savings certificates

What they are Five-year-term investment producing a guaranteed tax-free return which is inflation-proofed. Useful if you are concerned to protect your savings against rising prices (or if you want to take a gamble on inflation rising to high levels). The tax-free status makes them attractive for taxpayers, especially those paying at the higher rate.

Minimum investment £100.

Maximum investment £10,000 in the current (9th) issue, plus a further unlimited amount if you are reinvesting the maturity proceeds of an earlier issue. This is in addition to holdings of previous issues.

Type of return Interest made up of two elements: first, you get interest at set rates which increase for each year you hold the certificates; secondly, you get the amount needed to protect your capital and the interest already earned against inflation as measured by changes in the Retail Prices Index. The return is paid out at the end of the five years or on earlier encashment.

Tax treatment Tax-free.

How long you invest for Five years. You can get your money back earlier, but you'll get only the extra interest at the reduced rates which apply to the earlier years. If you cash in during the first year, you get no interest at all (except on reinvested certificates). At the end of five years, make sure you cash in the certificates or reinvest in a new issue, otherwise they usually revert to a lower rate of interest (still index-linked) or just index-linking.

Charges No explicit charges. National Savings' underlying costs are one factor influencing the interest rates offered.

Risk No capital risk. Because you are locked in at a fixed rate, you'll lose out if other interest rates rise, though what is relevant here is 'real' interest rates, that is, interest less the inflation rate. Risk rating: two.

More information Post offices, the Department for National Savings,★ occasional reviews of National Savings products in *Which?*,★ personal finance magazines and the personal finance pages of newspapers, summaries in *Moneyfacts*.★

How to invest Via post offices or deal direct with the Department for National Savings.★

FIRST option bonds

What they are Bonds paying a return which is guaranteed for one year at a time and giving you the option each year to reinvest for a further year at whatever new guaranteed rate is announced. Alone among the National Savings products, these bonds pay out a net-of-tax return, which makes them convenient for basic-rate taxpayers.

Minimum investment £1,000.

Maximum investment £250,000.

Type of return Interest, with fixed rates guaranteed for one year at a time. A higher rate is paid on holdings of £20,000 or more.

Tax treatment Taxable and, since April 1996, paid with lower-rate tax already deducted from the return. At the end of each tax year, you get a tax certificate showing how much tax has been deducted. Non-taxpayers can reclaim the tax (but would generally do better to consider alternative investments). Higher-rate taxpayers have extra tax to pay.

How long you invest for You can leave your money invested indefinitely. If you cash in on an anniversary, there is no notice period and you'll be paid within a couple of weeks. If you want your money back between anniversaries, you lose half the interest earned since the most recent anniversary date. If you cash in during the first year, you get no interest at all.

Charges No explicit charges. National Savings' underlying costs are one factor influencing the interest rates offered.

Risk No capital risk. Vulnerable to inflation. Being locked into fixed rates means you could lose out if other interest rates rise, but the fixed period is fairly short at just a year. Risk rating: two.

More information Post offices, the Department for National Savings,★ occasional reviews of National Savings products in *Which?*,★ personal finance magazines and the personal finance pages of newspapers, summaries in *Moneyfacts*.★

How to invest Deal direct with the Department for National Savings★; application forms are available at post offices.

National Savings income bonds

What they are Bonds which produce a monthly income. At present, you can hold the bonds indefinitely (they have a guaranteed lifetime of at least ten years from the time you buy them, but the government could redeem them after that if it decided to and gave six months' notice).

Minimum investment £2,000.

Maximum investment £250,000.

Type of return Interest, which is variable. A higher rate of interest is paid if you invest £25,000 or more. The interest is paid out each month and can be paid automatically into either your bank or building society account or a National Savings investment account.

Tax treatment Taxable, but paid gross, that is, without any tax deducted. This makes the bonds very convenient for non-taxpayers.

How long you invest for No set period, but if you cash in the bonds during the first year, the interest will be cut to just half; any interest already overpaid to you will then be deducted from the cash-in value. You have to give three months' notice of withdrawal.

Charges No explicit charges. National Savings' underlying costs are one factor influencing the interest rates offered.

Risk No capital risk. Vulnerable to inflation. Vulnerable to falling interest rates. Risk rating: three.

More information Post offices, the Department for National Savings,★ occasional reviews of National Savings products in *Which?*,★ personal finance magazines and the personal finance pages of newspapers, summaries in *Moneyfacts*.★

How to invest Deal direct with the Department for National Savings;★ application forms are available at post offices.

National Savings pensioners bonds

What they are Five-year bonds which produce a fixed monthly income and are available only to people aged 60 or more.

Minimum investment £500.

Maximum investment £50,000 in the current (Series 3) issue. This is in addition to holdings of the previous issue.

Type of return Interest, which is at a fixed rate guaranteed for five years from the time you invest. Interest is paid each month into either your bank or building society account or a National Savings investment account.

Tax treatment Taxable, but paid gross, that is, without any tax deducted. This makes the bonds very convenient for non-taxpayers.

How long you invest for The interest rate is fixed for five years at a time, though you can invest for longer. If you cash in a bond within two weeks after the fifth anniversary of making the investment (or any other subsequent five-year anniversary), you do not have to give any notice and you get your money back within a few days. If you cash in at any other time, you must give 60 days' notice, during which time no interest is paid on the amount you are withdrawing.

Charges No explicit charges. National Savings' underlying costs are one factor influencing the interest rates offered.

Risk No capital risk. Vulnerable to inflation. Being locked into fixed rates means you could lose out if other interest rates rise. Risk rating: three.

More information Post offices, the Department for National Savings,★ occasional reviews of National Savings products in *Which?*,★ personal finance magazines and the personal finance pages of newspapers, summaries in *Moneyfacts*.★

How to invest Deal direct with the Department for National Savings;★ application forms are available at post offices.

Capital bonds

What they are Bonds which produce a guaranteed return payable at the end of five years.

Minimum investment £100.

Maximum investment £250,000. This includes holdings of previous issues (except Issue A) as well as the current issue.

Type of return Interest, at fixed rates which rise each year and are guaranteed for five years from the time you invest. Interest is credited to the bond each year.

Tax treatment Taxable, but paid gross, that is, without any tax deducted, which is convenient for non-taxpayers. However, although interest is not paid until the end of five years, taxpayers are taxed on the interest each year as it is credited to the bond, so you need to make sure you have money available from elsewhere to meet the tax bill.

How long you invest for You should aim to invest for the full five years. If you cash in earlier, you receive the lower rates of interest which apply to the earlier years. And if you cash in during the first year, you get no interest at all.

Charges No explicit charges. National Savings' underlying costs are one factor influencing the interest rates offered.

Risk No capital risk. Vulnerable to inflation. Being locked into fixed rates means you could lose out if other interest rates rise. Risk rating: three.

More information Post offices, the Department for National Savings,★ occasional reviews of National Savings products in *Which?*,★ personal finance magazines and the personal finance pages of newspapers, summaries in *Moneyfacts*.★

How to invest Deal direct with the Department for National Savings;★ application forms are available at post offices.

Children's bonus bonds

What they are Bonds bought by adults (defined as anyone over 16) on behalf of children up to the age of 16. The bonds can run until the child reaches age 21, building up a tax-free lump sum. The return is fixed for five years at a time and reviewed on each five-year anniversary.

Minimum investment £25.

Maximum investment £1,000 in the current issue (Issue H). This is in addition to holdings of previous issues.

Type of return Interest, at fixed rates guaranteed for five years at a time, including a bonus payable on each five-year anniversary.

Tax treatment Tax-free. Bearing in mind that children's income can be treated as income of the parents (see Chapter 16), the tax-free status means that these bonds can be particularly useful as gifts from parents to their child.

How long you invest for Money can remain invested in the bonds until the child reaches age 21, when the bonds stop earning interest. They can be cashed in before then. If you cash in a bond within one week after a five-year anniversary, you do not have to give any notice, and the money is paid over to the child's parent or guardian within a few days. If you cash in at any other time, you must give one month's notice, and you will forfeit the five-year bonus. If you cash in during the first year, you get no interest at all.

Charges No explicit charges. National Savings' underlying costs are one factor influencing the interest rates offered.

Risk No capital risk. Vulnerable to inflation. Being locked into fixed rates means the child could lose out if other interest rates rise. Risk rating: three.

More information Post offices, the Department for National Savings,★ occasional reviews of National Savings products in *Which?*,★ personal finance magazines and the personal finance pages of newspapers, summaries in *Moneyfacts*.★

How to invest Via post offices or deal direct with the Department for National Savings.★

Tip

Because they offer a tax-free return, children's bonus bonds make a good gift for parents if they are worried that income from the child's investments would otherwise be taxed as the parents' income – see page 280.

Premium bonds

What they are Strictly, these are a gamble rather than an investment. You buy the bonds, and they are entered into a monthly prize draw where each bond stands a 1 in 19,000 chance of winning a prize ranging from £50 to £1 million. Unlike most other forms of gambling, though, you never lose your stake money.

Minimum investment £100.

Maximum investment £20,000.

Type of return The money invested in premium bonds is placed in a prize fund from which around 430,000 prizes are paid out each month (from June 1997 onwards). Prizes range from £50 to £1 million. Small prizes (£50 to £1,000) can be automatically reinvested to buy new bonds.

Tax treatment Prizes are tax-free.

How long you invest for Up to you. Bonds must be held for one complete calendar month before they are eligible for the prize draws. You can withdraw your money at any time, though this is done by post and takes a few days.

Charges No explicit charges. National Savings' costs are one factor influencing the return on the prize fund (and hence the overall pay-out in prizes).

Risk No risk to capital. Vulnerable to inflation. Return can range from nil to £1 million. Risk rating: three.

More information Post offices, the Department for National Savings,★ occasional reviews of National Savings products in *Which?*,★ personal finance magazines and personal finance pages of newspapers.

How to invest Via post offices or deal direct with the Department for National Savings.★

Summary of lower-risk investments

Investment	Minimum period for which you should aim to invest	Type of return	Risk rating
Bank and building society investments			
Current accounts	No set period	Variable, taxed*, if interest paid at all	1
Flexible mortgage account	Mortgage term or shorter	Tax-free interest	1
Instant access accounts	No set period	Variable, taxed*	1
Notice accounts	No set period	Variable, taxed*	2–3
Term accounts and bonds	The specified period, e.g. 1 or 2 years	Fixed or variable, taxed*	3

Investment	Minimum period for which you should aim to invest	Type of return	Risk rating
Monthly income accounts	Varies	Fixed or variable, taxed*	1–3
TESSAs	5 years	Variable (or occasionally fixed), tax-free	2–3
Children's accounts	Usually, no set period	Variable, taxed*	1

National Savings investments

Ordinary account	No set period	Variable, taxable	1
Investment account	No set period	Variable, taxable	2
National Savings certificates	5 years	Fixed, tax-free	3
Index-linked National Savings certificates	5 years	Fixed, inflation-proofed, tax-free	2
FIRST option bonds	1 year	Fixed, taxable	2
National Savings income bonds	At least a year	Variable, taxable	3
National Savings pensioners bonds	5 years	Fixed, taxable	3
Capital bonds	5 years	Fixed, taxable	3
Children's bonus bonds	5 years	Fixed, tax-free	3
Premium bonds	No set period	Tax-free prizes	3

* Non-taxpayers can arrange to receive income gross, that is, before deduction of tax.

Chapter 14

Medium-risk investments

People who would like to achieve their investment or savings targets over a period of, say, five years or more would be unwise to rely too heavily on the lower-risk products described in Chapter 13: the returns tend to lag behind those of other investments and might not even keep pace with inflation. But going after higher returns inevitably means accepting some extra degree of risk. Chapter 15 outlines those investments where the value of your capital is fairly exposed. This chapter concentrates on the middle ground – a mixture of investments where either your capital is not at risk, though it may be tied up for some time, and/or you may have to accept that the return on it is unpredictable, or where the risk to your capital is generally fairly low.

Investments from the government

British Government stocks ('gilts')

What they are Loans you make to the government in the form of bonds which usually have a fixed lifetime. You do not have to hold them for that set period because you can buy and sell them on the stock market. At the time of writing, there are around 60 different conventional British Government stocks (as well as index-linked stocks – see page 234). Stocks are often described in terms of their 'nominal' or 'par' value of £100. This is a convenient way of dividing the stocks into units, but if you bought a nominal £100 stock, for example, what you pay could be more or less than that amount. British Government stocks are also called 'gilt-edged securities', or 'gilts' for short, reflecting the very sound nature of these stocks because of the unlikelihood that the government would ever default on them.

Minimum investment No set amount, but dealing costs mean that buying small amounts (less than £1,000 or so) through a stockbroker is generally uneconomic. But dealing costs are much lower if you buy stock on the National Savings Stock Register (NSSR) – see below. The minimum unit for buying 'gilt strips' (see below) is £10,000.

Maximum investment None overall, but if you buy on the NSSR the most you can buy of any one stock in any one day is £25,000.

Type of return The return is made up of two parts: while you hold the stock, you are paid a fixed amount of interest every six months; when the stock is sold or comes to the end of its life, you make a capital gain or loss. Some stocks pay a very low amount of interest and are useful only for people who are mainly after capital gains. Other stocks pay a high level of interest and are particularly useful for people who need income immediately; it may even be worth reckoning on some capital loss (by buying the stock at more than its nominal value) if a high income is a major priority.

If you hold the stock until the end of its life (until it is 'redeemed'), you will get back a known amount of £100 for each nominal £100 of stock you hold. This means that you know from the time you buy exactly what return you will get overall if you hold the stock to redemption: that is, the return is fixed and guaranteed. Alternatively, you can sell the stock before redemption, in which case you cannot be certain in advance what capital gain or loss you stand to make. So the nature of the return depends on how you choose to use these stocks.

In late 1997, 'gilt strips' were introduced. A single gilt-edged stock provides a stream of income payments plus the capital payment at redemption. Some stock can now be split up ('stripped') into components, each producing one payment. For example, a gilt with two years until redemption would produce four interest payments and a redemption payment. This could be split into five strips, one for each payment. Each strip (which is in effect a 'zero coupon bond') is traded separately. Gilt strips provide a very flexible form of investment and can be used, for example, to design an income flow tailored to your needs.

From 6 April 1998, the income from all gilts is normally paid gross – that is, without any deduction of tax – which is especially convenient for non-taxpayers. But the income is taxable, unless you are a non-taxpayer. You can request to receive the income from gilts bought through a stockbroker net of tax, in which case you will receive interest after deduction of tax at the savings rate of 20 per cent. There is no further tax to pay for either a lower- or basic-rate taxpayer. Higher-rate taxpayers have extra to pay. Before 6 April 1998, this was the normal way for income from gilts brought through a stockbroker to be taxed. Under transitional rules, if you already hold gilts on that date, you will continue to receive the income net unless you request to switch to gross payments. Interest from gilts bought through the National Savings Stock Register always have been paid gross and will continue to be so; you do not have the option of net payments.

Capital gains on gilts are tax-free. This means that stocks paying low interest, whose return is likely to be largely in the form of capital gain, can be particularly attractive for higher-rate taxpayers and people who would normally pay tax on their gains.

How long you invest for If you want to hold stocks until redemption, there is a large range of redemption dates, from stocks just about to mature up to lifetimes of 20 years or more. But, of course, you can sell at any time before then on the stock market, and some stocks, called 'irredeemables', have no redemption date at all, so you *have* to sell to cash in your investment.

Traditionally, gilts are divided into three groups:

- shorts (five years or less to redemption),
- mediums (five to fifteen years), and
- longs (over fifteen years).

The groups tend to behave in different ways. As short-dated stocks get closer to their redemption date, their prices tend towards the nominal value at which they will be redeemed; other short-dated stocks tend to react to changes in general interest rates. Longer-dated stocks are influenced more by the inflation outlook and wider-ranging economic factors.

Charges If you deal through a stockbroker (or advisers, who if not themselves authorised to deal in stocks and shares would use a stockbroker), charges vary. The table on page 235 gives an idea of the commission that a traditional stockbroker might charge compared with NSSR charges. The latter tend to work out cheaper for small deals. There is also a 'spread' between the price paid by buyers and sellers, with buyers paying a little more than the quoted mid-market price and sellers getting a little less.

Risk This varies, depending on how you use the stocks. If you intend to hold them until redemption (or you invest in 'gilt strips'), you know exactly what will happen to your capital, and your total return is fixed – though you are not locked into this because you could change your mind and sell before redemption. If you are holding conventional gilts for their income, bear in mind that the income is vulnerable to inflation (though see the section below on index-linked gilts). You can also buy and sell gilts on a more speculative basis, though their price movements tend to be more modest than those of shares. Buying on the NSSR, you deal by post and so cannot be certain of the price at which your deal will be struck, which makes buying and selling in this way more risky than buying through a stockbroker. Risk rating: around four when held as medium- to long-term investments.

More information For a fuller discussion of gilts and how you can use them, see *Which? Way to Save and Invest*, published by Which? Books.★ The Bank of England★ publishes an excellent booklet explaining how gilts work and how to invest. Post offices and the Department for National Savings★ provide information about stocks on the NSSR. You cannot buy and sell gilt strips through the NSSR. For stockbrokers (including many high street banks and some building societies which run their own stockbroking arms), contact the Association of Private Client Investment Managers and Stockbrokers (APCIMS)★ for a free directory of its members. Quality daily newspapers carry full lists of gilts, including their prices and returns. Articles in *Which?*,★ personal finance magazines and the personal finance pages of newspapers are other good sources of information.

How to invest Deal direct with the Department for National Savings★ for stocks on the NSSR; otherwise, deal through a stockbroker. If you invest in new issues, do so via a stockbroker or by contacting the Bank of England★ for a prospectus or look for a prospectus printed in the press.

Index-linked British Government stocks ('index-linked gilts')

What they are Basically, these are much the same as conventional gilts (see above), but both the income and the amount you get back at redemption are increased in line with inflation (measured as changes in the Retail Prices Index, subject to an eight-month lag). Their stock market prices will *tend* to increase along with the rising redemption value, but are, of course, subject to other forces as well, such as returns available on other investments, confidence in the economy, and so on.

Minimum investment As for conventional gilts.

Maximum investment As for conventional gilts.

Type of return Income is inflation-proofed, which is useful for, say, retired people wanting an income to supplement their pensions. Your capital would be inflation-proofed too if you bought a stock when it was first issued and held it until redemption, but this link to inflation is weakened when you buy and sell on the stock market at prices which may be out of line with the indexation.

Tax treatment As for conventional gilts.

How long you invest for In November 1997 there were 12 index-linked gilts with redemption dates ranging from 1999–2030.

Charges As for conventional gilts.

Risk In the main, as for conventional gilts, with one important exception: income and to some extent capital are protected against inflation. Risk rating: around three to four when held as a medium- to long-term investment.

More information As for conventional gilts.

How to invest As for conventional gilts.

Local authority bonds and stocks

What they are Loans to local government. Some loans are in the form of fixed-term bonds which must be held to redemption. Others are stocks, similar to gilts, which can be bought and sold on the stock market.

Minimum investment For bonds, this varies from, say, £200 upwards. With stocks, there is no set minimum, but dealing costs would make less than, say, £1,000 uneconomic.

What you pay in commission when you buy and sell gilts

	Typical traditional stockbrokers' charges*	NSSR charges from March 1996
Commission levels	• 1% on first £7,000 • 0.45% on next £13,000. Minimum £17.50	• Deals up to £5,000: 0.7% with minimum £12.50 for purchases (no minimum for sales) • Deals over £5,000: £35 plus 0.375% of amount over £5,000
For example, commission on:		
Small deal (£250)	£17.50	£12.50 (£1.75 on sale)
Medium deal (£2,500)	£25.00	£17.50
Large deal (£10,000)	£83.50	£53.75

* The service from a traditional stockbroker generally includes advice as well as dealing. A number of brokers now charge less but usually restrict their service simply to dealing without advice – that is, they offer an 'execution-only' service.

Maximum investment None.

Type of return Fixed-term bonds give you fixed interest, which is usually paid every six months. Stocks are similar to gilts, paying you a fixed income plus a capital gain or loss, depending on the prices at which the stocks are bought and sold (or redeemed). The interest rate on local authority stocks tends to be higher than on gilts, reflecting the higher risk (see below).

Tax treatment Interest from both bonds and stocks is taxable and, since April 1996, paid with lower-rate income tax already deducted. Non-taxpayers can reclaim tax. Lower-rate and basic-rate taxpayers have no further tax to pay. Higher-rate taxpayers have extra to pay. Capital gains on stocks are tax-free.

How long you invest for Terms vary. Like gilts, stocks can be sold before redemption on the stock market. Bonds are typically for two to eight years, and you are locked in for the whole period as these cannot be traded and there is generally no way to get your money back early.

Charges None for bonds. Stockbroker's commission and a spread between buying and selling prices for stocks.

Risk Bonds: the only risk to your capital is that the local authority might default on the loan and be unable to repay it, but this risk is slight; vulnerable to inflation; the fixed term and return mean you could lose out if other interest rates rose. Stocks: similar to conventional gilts, except for possible problems buying and selling, since the market for these stocks is sometimes not very active; slight risk that the local authority might default. Risk rating for both: around five.

More information Bonds: direct from local authorities, summaries in *Moneyfacts*.* Stocks are listed in quality newspapers with details of their prices and returns.

How to invest Bonds: contact the relevant local authority. Stocks: deal via a stockbroker.

Investments from commercial organisations

Annuities

What they are Investments offered by insurance companies whereby you swap a lump sum for a regular income. You cannot get your original investment back as a lump sum, though you are treated as if part of each income payment is in fact a bit of your original capital coming back (see Tax Treatment, below). Annuities can be for life ('lifetime annuity') or for a set period of years ('temporary annuity'). Pensions from a personal pension plan are a type of lifetime annuity ('compulsory purchase annuity'). Non-pension annuities are called 'purchased annuities'.

Minimum investment Varies, but you would usually pay thousands of pounds for a lifetime annuity.

Maximum investment None.

Type of return Income, which can be fixed or can increase each year either by a fixed percentage or in line with prices – you decide on the type of return at the time you invest. You can also choose annuities which guarantee to pay out for a fixed period – for example, five or ten years – even if you die during that period. The return from lifetime annuities depends heavily on the average life expectancy for someone of your age, so rates are generally higher the older you are and are higher for men than for women.

Tax treatment With the exception of annuities used to provide a pension, part of each regular payment is deemed to be the return of part of your capital and is tax-free. The remaining part is income, which is usually paid with tax at the lower rate already deducted, but you may be able to arrange to have it paid gross if you are a non-taxpayer (if not, you can reclaim the tax). Lower-rate and basic-rate taxpayers have no further tax to pay. Higher-rate taxpayers must pay extra. The whole of the income from a pension annuity is taxable at your top rate of income tax and is generally paid with the correct amount of tax deducted using the PAYE system.

How long you invest for A lifetime annuity is literally for life: having made your decision to invest, you have no chance to reverse it. Temporary annuities are for set periods: for example, five years. You are committed to investing for the full period and cannot get your capital back as a lump sum.

Charges No explicit charges. The insurance company's costs are one factor determining the annuity rates on offer.

Risk No access to your capital as a lump sum once you have invested. Annuities with no built-in increases are vulnerable to inflation: you are locked in at whatever annuity rates apply at the time you invest, and you will lose out if annuity rates subsequently rise. Risk rating: around four for annuities paying a fixed income; around three for annuities which provide some protection against inflation.

More information Example annuity rates are listed in a wide range of personal finance magazines, some newspapers and in *Moneyfacts Life & Pensions*.* A number of fax services* also give up-to-date rates. A few IFAs,* such as the Annuity Bureau* and Annuity Direct,* specialise in finding the best annuities for clients.

How to invest Either contact the insurer offering your chosen annuity or use one of the independent financial advisers which specialise in annuities.

Warning

The annuity rate at the time you invest determines the income you will get for the rest of your life in the case of a lifetime annuity or for the whole term in the case of a temporary annuity. Therefore, it is important to avoid investing at times when annuity rates are low. If you're not sure whether the timing is right, get advice.

Insurance company income and growth bonds

What they are Investments based on either single-premium insurance policies and/or annuities which give you a fixed income or fixed rate of growth over a set period and then return your original investment at the end of the period.

Minimum investment Varies from £1,000 upwards.

Maximum investment None.

Type of return You get either fixed income from income bonds or a fixed rate of growth from growth bonds (paid when the bond matures).

Tax treatment Depends on the underlying investments which make up the bond, but usually there is no basic-rate tax for you to pay. The insurance company has often already paid tax on the underlying investment, but this is the company's own tax bill, so non-taxpayers and lower-rate taxpayers cannot reclaim any tax, and higher-rate taxpayers may have to pay extra.

How long you invest for Depends on the fixed term of the bond, which is generally from one year to ten years. You cannot usually get your money back early.

Charges No explicit charges, although the insurance company's costs are one factor taken into account when setting the interest rate.

Risk No risk to capital. Vulnerable to inflation. Being locked into a fixed return, you will lose out if returns on other investments rise. Risk rating: around four.

More information Details of bonds available are included in many finance magazines, including *Money Management*★ and *Moneyfacts*.★ Regular summaries are also given in the personal finance sections of quality newspapers. For information about specific bonds, contact the insurer direct or use an independent financial adviser.

How to invest Either contact the insurer direct or invest through an independent financial adviser.★

Permanent income-bearing shares (PIBS)

What they are Loans to building societies in the form of stocks which have no redemption date at all and which are bought and sold on the stock market. (Holding PIBS often makes you a member of the building society. If the society converted to a bank or was taken over, you could be eligible for a cash or share windfall.)

Minimum investment Varies from £1,000 upwards.

Maximum investment None.

Type of return Fixed interest paid out twice a year, which makes PIBS popular investments with people seeking an immediate income. The rate of interest is higher than it is on gilts, reflecting the higher risk you take with PIBS (see below). Depending on the prices at which you buy and sell, you may make a capital gain or a capital loss.

Tax treatment Interest is taxable and, since April 1996, paid after deduction of income tax at the lower rate. Non-taxpayers can reclaim tax. Lower-rate and basic-rate taxpayers have no further tax to pay. Higher-rate taxpayers have extra tax to pay. Capital gains are tax-free.

How long you invest for No set period, but this is not a suitable home for money you might need back at a particular time or at short notice because prices may be low at that time.

Charges Stockbroker's commission and spread between the prices at which you buy and sell.

Risk Capital risk on three counts: prices can fall, the market in these stocks is not very active (so you might have problems selling – and buying), and there is a small risk that the building society might go out of business (though in the past the few societies that have run into difficulties have been absorbed into other societies rather than allowed to go bust). There is also a slight risk to income, because the building society is allowed to waive the interest if it is facing financial difficulty. The fixed income is vulnerable to inflation. Risk rating: around five.

More information Stockbrokers, summaries in *Moneyfacts*★ and the personal finance sections of some newspapers, occasional articles in personal finance magazines.

How to invest Via a stockbroker.

Corporate bonds

What they are These work in a similar way to gilts, except that they are loans to companies in the form of stocks which are bought and sold on the Stock Exchange (or other markets, such as the

Euromarket). There are various types of corporate bond: for example, those which are 'secured' either against the general assets of the company or against specific assets which can be seized and sold if the company defaults on the loan (in contrast to 'unsecured' loans, which are not backed by specific assets). There are also 'convertibles', which can be swapped for shares in the company at a set price at or before some specified date.

Minimum investment No set minimum, but dealing charges would make less than, say, £1,000 uneconomic.

Maximum investment None.

Type of return Usually, corporate bonds offer a fixed rate of interest, paid half-yearly. You also stand to make a capital gain or loss, depending on the prices at which the bonds are bought and sold, redeemed or converted.

Tax treatment Interest is taxable and, since April 1996, paid after deduction of income tax at the lower rate. Non-taxpayers can reclaim tax. Lower-rate and basic-rate taxpayers have no further tax to pay. Higher-rate taxpayers have extra to pay. Capital gains are generally tax-free.

How long you invest for Most bonds have a fixed lifetime, after which they are redeemed by the company. But of course you can sell on the stock market before then. This is not the home for money you might need back at short notice because prices could then be low.

Charges Stockbroker's commission: for example, one per cent on deals up to £5,000 or so, with a flat-rate minimum commission of £15–£20. There is also a spread between the prices paid by buyers and sellers.

Risk There is a risk to your capital because bond prices can fall. You also have the risk that the company might go out of business and be unable to repay the loan, in which case you would lose all your capital. This latter risk should be reasonably small if you invest in the bonds of a large, well-established company (though, as the collapse of Barings Bank showed, bondholders in even the most seemingly sound company can lose). The risk of default can be substantial if you pick new and/or struggling companies. Fixed incomes are vulnerable to inflation. Risk rating: from around five for the most sound ('blue chip') companies to ten for companies which are unproven or in difficulty.

More information Stockbrokers.

How to invest Via a stockbroker. If you invest in new issues, via a prospectus from the company's agents or printed in the press.

Preference shares

What they are Unlike loans to a company, buying shares gives you a stake in the ownership of a company. Ordinary shares are described on page 254, but preference shares are included here because they have various characteristics which are more akin to corporate bonds. Preference shares usually offer a fixed income, which is paid before any dividends to ordinary shareholders. Some preference shares have a redemption date, at which time they are bought back by the company, while others are irredeemable. In either case you can buy and sell them on the stock market. Convertible preference shares give you the right to switch to ordinary shares in the company at a set price at or before some specified date, which gives you the option to switch from a fixed to a variable income and participate in the generally more volatile movement of ordinary share prices.

Minimum investment No set minimum, but dealing charges would make investing less than, say, £1,000 uneconomic.

Maximum investment None.

Type of return Income is in the form of dividends, usually at a fixed rate and paid half-yearly. You also stand to make a capital gain or loss, depending on the prices at which the shares are bought and sold.

Tax treatment Income is taxable. The dividends are paid net of income tax at the lower rate. Non-taxpayers can reclaim the tax deducted. Both lower-rate and basic-rate taxpayers have no further tax to pay. Higher-rate taxpayers have further tax to pay. Capital gains are taxable, though you may have allowances to set against them (see page 34).

How long you invest for No set period, because you can sell at any time on the stock market. But this is not the home for money you might need back at a set time or at short notice, since share prices might then be low.

Charges Stockbroker's commission and spread between the prices which buyers pay and sellers receive.

Risk Capital risk because of fluctuating share prices. You also have the risk that the company might go out of business. If it did, preference shareholders are in line for a payout ahead of ordinary shareholders, but the company might not have enough assets to stretch even to the preference shareholders, in which case you would lose all your capital. This should be a small risk with large, well-established companies, but a major consideration with companies struggling to get established or going through a bad patch. Fixed incomes are vulnerable to inflation. Risk rating: around five for blue chip companies to ten for riskier ventures.

More information Stockbrokers, specialist magazines such as *Investors Chronicle*.★ Prices and so on are included in share listings in daily newspapers.

How to invest Via a stockbroker. If you invest in new issues of shares, via a prospectus from the company's agents or published in the press.

Pooled investments

Pooled investments are ready-made portfolios of particular types of assets, such as shares of a particular country, or a range of different assets, such as shares, gilts and property. They give you a way of spreading risks, investing relatively small sums and keeping down dealing costs. Against these advantages you must weigh the charges levied by the managers who run these investments and whether you are happy that the investment policy of the managers fits sufficiently well with your own investment aims.

With-profits life insurance

What it is This is one form of investment-type life insurance (and also pension plan) offered by insurers and by friendly societies (organisations which started life as mutual self-help organisations to help people cope financially with crises such as illness and death). Your premiums are invested by the insurer in gilts, shares, property, and so on to form a fund out of which it meets claims and the costs of running its business. But insurers tend to be prudent people and so, normally, the investments produce more than the amount needed to meet claims, costs, dividends to shareholders (if the insurer is set up as a company) and reserves. The excess is distributed to the with-profits policyholders as bonuses. The insurer's actuary advises on how much can be paid out in bonuses each year. Usually, some kind of smoothing is applied to avoid sharp variations in bonuses from year to year, so a with-profits policy tends to give you steady growth.

Minimum investment Varies, depending in part on the type of policy or plan you are looking at. But some regular-premium policies accept sums of less than £10 a month. Single-lump-sum premiums tend to start in hundreds of pounds.

Maximum investment Insurers may set their own maxima, in particular limiting the amount of life cover they are willing to give. Tax rules may also play a part: for example, friendly societies cannot accept more than £18 a month (£200 a year) into their tax-exempt plans (see below). There are also limits on what can be paid into a personal pension plan (see Chapter 11) – another insurance-based product which can be invested on a with-profits basis.

Type of return There are two types of bonuses: reversionary bonuses are added regularly, usually every year. Once added to the value of your policy, they cannot be taken away. A terminal bonus is paid when the policy matures or on death – but not if it is surrendered early. The terminal bonus can account for a large proportion – for example a half – of the total return.

Tax treatment The return you get counts as income. With a few exceptions, the insurer has to pay or allow for tax on the underlying investment fund. This is deemed to be equivalent to having had basic-rate income tax already paid when you get the bonuses, so basic-rate taxpayers do not have any tax to pay themselves. However, non-taxpayers cannot reclaim any of the tax deemed to have been paid. Higher-rate taxpayers do not have to pay any extra tax, provided the policy counts as a 'qualifying' one (this means that the policy meets certain rules and so qualifies for advantageous tax treatment; most regular-premium policies designed to last for at least ten years meet these rules). If the policy is not a qualifying one, there could be some higher-rate tax. Friendly societies can offer plans which are invested in a tax-free fund and whose proceeds are completely tax-free whatever your normal rate of tax.

Tip

The return from most investment-type life insurance is not tax-free because the insurer has had to account for tax on the underlying investments. But friendly society tax-exempt plans (of which 'baby bonds' are an example) are completely tax-free.

How long you invest for This depends on the type of policy or plan you have, because a whole range of them can be invested on a with-profits basis. The main ones are shown in the box below. In general, though, with-profits life policies are long-term investments, often designed to last at least ten years, which will give you a

---

Investment-type life insurance

Investment-type life insurance is usually invested on either a with-profits basis (see page 242) or a unit-linked basis (see page 262). Here, the variations common to both the with-profits and unit-linked routes are described. See also page 266.

Endowment policies These are designed to run for a specified length of time (the 'endowment period'), during which you pay regular premiums (usually monthly) and at the end of which the policy pays out a cash sum. The policy also pays out if you die during the policy term but, if it's life cover you need, term insurance is a cheaper option. In the past, endowment policies have been used widely as an all-purpose way of building up your savings: for example, as part of an endowment mortgage, to pay school fees, or to accumulate a nest egg for non-specific purposes. This made some sense, because premiums to most policies qualified for some tax relief, but that premium relief was abolished in 1984. Nowadays, personal equity plans are a more tax-efficient route for tackling medium- to long-term savings objectives.

Friendly society tax-exempt plans and 'baby bonds' These are usually endowment policies, but, unlike most life insurance plans, the return on the invested premiums is completely tax-free. This makes

---

very poor investment if you pull out early. Stopping a policy early crystallises charges (largely commission paid to advisers and salesmen) which would otherwise have been spread out over the lifetime of the policy. People are often taken by surprise by the fact that once those charges have been taken into account in arriving at the surrender value, their policy may have a very low value indeed.

Charges An administration fee is usually deducted from each premium. If you give up the policy early, there will usually be surrender penalties. Other charges are not explicit, but they are one of the factors taken into account when setting bonus levels.

Risk Provided you do not have to cash in your investment early, there is no capital risk. Because bonuses are linked to a broadly based investment fund, you stand a good chance of beating infla-

---

such plans very useful for all taxpayers, especially those who pay at the higher rate.

'Baby bonds' are simply versions of the tax-exempt plans aimed at children, and they are useful as gifts from parents who would otherwise be taxed on their child's income (see page 280). There is a snag: the government restricts the amount you can invest in these plans (in 1997–8 to just £18 a month or £200 a year). The low amount invested means that any set charges (as opposed to charges which vary with the amount invested or the return you get) can eat heavily into the value of the plan. Some friendly societies offer lump-sum versions of the plans whereby your money is invested in, say, an annuity (whose return is not tax-free – see page 236), which provides a steady stream of payments to meet the regular premiums for the tax-exempt plan.

Whole-of-life policies As the name suggests, these are designed to run for the whole of your life. Because the life cover element will inevitably have to pay out one day, such policies build up a cash value, which can be cashed in to provide an investment return. Whole-of-life plans, invested on a unit-linked rather than a with-profits basis, are used as **maximum protection plans** and **universal plans**, which package together life insurance, investment and often other types of insurance.

tion. But bonuses are unpredictable, especially the terminal bonus. You should be wary of simply assuming that past bonus levels will be maintained, or improved on, for the future: in recent times, some companies have cut even their reversionary bonuses. A useful indicator of an insurer's ability to keep up future bonus levels is some measure of their 'financial strength', which looks at factors such as the level of reserves, the nature of the assets held by the insurer, and so on – this is covered in the with-profits guide (see page 48). Risk rating: around four to five.

More information If you are interested in a particular insurer's or friendly society's products, the company must provide you with product details set out in a key features document; a with-profits guide, available on request, explaining how the company sets bonus levels; and an illustration if you request one. (See Chapter 3 for more about these documents.) *Money Management*★ and *Planned Savings*★ publish regular surveys of with-profits performance and financial strength. Standard & Poors★ also publishes surveys of the financial strength of the major life insurers. *Moneyfacts Life & Pensions*★ gives performance details and premiums for with-profits policies and a summary of insurers' bonus declarations. For more information about the different forms of investment-type life insurance which can be invested on a with-profits basis, see *Which? Way to Save and Invest*, published by Which? Books.★ For more about the taxation of life insurance, see *Which? Way to Save Tax*, also published by Which? Books.★

How to invest If, from your research, you have picked out a particular insurer's products, deal with the insurer direct if it allows this. Otherwise, use an independent financial adviser.★

Warning

With-profits life insurance policies are generally contracts designed to run for the long term. Their investment value builds up gradually. If you cash in the policy or stop paying premiums in the early years, your policy may be worth less than you have paid in premiums, and even worth nothing at all.

Gilt and fixed-income unit trusts

What they are Unit trusts are discussed more fully in Chapter 15. The gilt and fixed-income versions are professionally managed funds investing at least 80 per cent of the fund in British Government stocks and other investments offering a fixed income, such as corporate bonds and/or preference shares. You invest by buying units in the trust.

Minimum investment Varies from, say, £500 upwards as a lump sum and from £25 a month through a regular savings scheme run by the trust management company.

Maximum investment None.

Type of return Units earn income (called 'distributions'), which can either be paid out regularly or, if you hold what are called 'accumulation units', automatically reinvested in the fund. Gilt and fixed-income trusts are particularly useful for investors seeking a regular income immediately. It is important to note that, although the underlying investments produce fixed income, the income from the trust itself is variable, because of the changing mix of underlying investments. You also stand to make a capital gain or loss, depending on the prices at which you buy and sell your units.

Tax treatment Distributions are paid or credited with, since April 1996, income tax at the lower rate already deducted. You get a tax credit showing the amount of tax paid, which you use to reclaim tax if you are a non-taxpayer. Lower-rate and basic-rate taxpayers have no further tax to pay. Higher-rate taxpayers have extra to pay. Capital gains count as taxable, but you may have allowances you can set against them (see page 33). From April 1999, provided the bulk of the trust (taken to be 60 per cent or more of the marketable value of its investments) is invested in interest-bearing investments, such as corporate bonds or British Government stocks, this tax treatment continues unchanged. However, if the trust does not meet this condition – for example, if it has sizeable investments in preference shares – the changes affecting distributions from equity-based unit trusts (see page 255) will also affect this type of trust and, in particular, non-taxpayers will no longer be able to reclaim the tax credit.

How long you invest for No set period, but this is not the home for money you might need back at a set time or at short notice when unit prices could be low. Treat as a medium- to long-term investment.

Charges There is an annual management charge (around 1–1.5 per cent of the underlying fund) and a spread between the prices at which you buy ('offer price') and sell ('bid price') units. This spread incorporates what is called the 'initial charge' – often around 3–5 per cent of the amount invested – but the total you pay upfront is effectively the spread, which tends to be 1 or 2 per cent more.

Risk These trusts give you a stake in a spread of different fixed-interest investments, which is generally a lower-risk strategy than investing direct in just one or two such stocks. They are a particularly useful way of spreading risk if you want to invest in corporate bonds. Bear in mind that income is variable. Risk rating: four to five.

More information The Unit Trust Information Service run by the Association of Unit Trusts and Investment Funds (AUTIF).* Performance of trusts is published daily in quality newspapers and in specialist magazines, such as *Money Management*.* *Which?*,* personal finance magazines and the personal finance pages of newspapers all run regular articles about unit trusts. Having selected several trusts which interest you, contact the management companies for product details and illustrations (see Chapter 3 for more about these).

How to invest If, having done your initial research, you know which trust(s) you want to invest in, contact the management companies direct. Otherwise, deal through an independent financial adviser.*

Bond-based personal equity plans (bond-based PEPs)

What they are (PEPs themselves are discussed more fully in Chapter 15.) Since mid-1995, people have been able to use general PEPs to invest in corporate bonds and preference shares (but not gilts). Two types of bond-based PEP have emerged:

- those using the PEP to invest in fixed-interest unit trusts. Some trusts invest in a whole range of corporate bonds and shares; others specialise in, say, preference shares. Basically, from your point of view, this is simply investing in a unit trust (as described above) except that you gain certain tax advantages
- those investing in a single, newly issued corporate bond. The few which have been launched so far have offered a fixed return over a fixed period. The return is payable either as income or rolled up and paid out when the bond matures.

Open-ended investment companies ('OEICs')

Open-ended investment companies ('OEICs') are, from the investor's point of view, basically the same as unit trusts, though technically they are different. They are a cross between investment trusts (see page 269) and unit trusts. Like investment trusts, OEICs are companies which invest in funds – you invest by buying the OEIC's shares. Like unit trusts, though, the size of the fund varies with the number of investors involved, because shares are created and cancelled as investors come and go. This means that the price of OEIC shares behaves more like the price of units in a unit trust than shares in an investment trust, being directly related to the value of the underlying fund.

OEICs were developed largely as a way of widening the appeal of UK pooled investments. Foreign investors are unfamiliar with the trust status of unit trusts and feel more comfortable with corporate status. There is just one price at which shares in an OEIC are both bought and sold; this is in line with the way in which most Continental and US funds are priced. The price is based directly on the value of the investments in the fund, with charges shown separately. OEICs are taxed in the same way as unit trusts.

At the time of writing, OEICs are in their infancy, but newly created collective investment schemes are likely to adopt the OEIC model and unit trust managers may want to convert existing trusts to the new OEIC structure. The views of existing unit trust investors will have to be taken into account before this can happen, but in general their investment will be broadly unchanged.

Minimum investment For trust-based PEPs, the same as investing direct in the trust (see page 247); for single-bond PEPs, the minimum varies.

Maximum investment Inland Revenue rules set the most you can invest in this type of PEP at £6,000 in each tax year.

Type of return If it is a unit trust PEP, as for direct investment in the trust – see page 247. Most unit trust bond PEPs aim to provide a high income which is variable. For single-bond PEP, could be either fixed income or fixed growth.

Tax treatment At present, the return on investments held in a PEP is completely tax-free. This will continue to be the case from April 1999 onwards (assuming PEPs continue), provided the majority of the trust (taken to be 60 per cent or more of the marketable value of the investments) is invested in interest-bearing investments, such as corporate bonds. But if the trust does not meet this condition – for example if it has a sizeable investment in preference shares – it will be caught up in the changes applying to equity-based unit trusts (see page 272), which means that the PEP manager will no longer be able to reclaim the tax credit (then set at 10 per cent) on distributions from the trust.

How long you invest for For a unit trust PEP, no set period, but this is not the home for money you might need back at a particular time or at short notice, when unit prices might be low. For single-bond PEPs, there may be a fixed period, such as five years, during which you cannot get your money back at all.

Charges PEP managers may make extra charges (on top of those applying to the underlying investment), although in practice most unit trust managers do not: in fact, you may even get a discount on the initial charge, say, if you choose the PEP route. With single-bond PEPs, there are usually no charges.

Risk For unit trust PEPs, as for the underlying trust. Risk rating: four to five.

For single-bond PEPs, you run the risk that the company issuing the bond might default, in which case you would lose all your capital, but this risk should be slight with a blue chip company. You are also locked into a fixed-interest, fixed-term investment and could lose out if other interest rates rose. Risk rating: from around five for the most sound companies to ten for the those with no track record or experiencing difficulties.

More information For unit trust PEPs, as for unit trusts (see page 248). For single-bond PEPs, contact the issuers direct or through an independent financial adviser.

Warning

Although most bonds offer a fixed income, the income from most bond-based PEPs is variable.

How to invest For unit trust PEPs, as for unit trusts (see page 248). For single-bond PEPs, contact the issuers direct or through an independent financial adviser.★

Warning

Trust managers usually set their charges against income earned by the investments in the trust. With bond trusts, charges may instead be deducted from capital. This makes the income you get look higher, but be aware that your capital may be eroded – i.e. in effect you will be swapping part of your capital for an income now.

Guaranteed equity bonds

Another investment which is aimed at those people seeking medium levels of risk is the 'guaranteed equity bond'. These aim to combine the higher returns of investing in shares with a guarantee that, over a given period, you will either not lose any capital or that you will get at least a given minimum return: for example, you might be offered 133 per cent of the growth of the FT-SE 100 share index (one of the main measures of stock market performance). Although all the bonds share this common aim, they can be based on a variety of different underlying investments and you will need to refer to details of each of these to see how they are treated for tax purposes and what charges are involved:

- high-interest building society accounts (see pages 215–17)
- single-premium insurance bonds (see page 266)
- unit trusts (see page 266).

Don't be too impressed by the guarantees offered by these bonds. Points to watch are:

- does the guarantee relate simply to growth in share prices? Bear in mind that if you were investing direct in shares, you would usually get some dividend income as well
- can you cash in your investment early and, if so, what return will you get?

Summary of medium-risk investments

Investment	Minimum period for which you should aim to invest	Type of return	Risk rating
Investments from the government			
British Government stocks ('gilts')	a) Until redemption	a) Fixed income, taxed or taxable; fixed capital gain or loss, tax-free	4
	b) No set period	b) Fixed income, taxed or taxable; capital gain or loss, tax-free	4–5
Index-linked British Government stocks	a) Until redemption	a) Fixed income, inflation-proofed, taxed or taxable; capital gain or loss, ignoring the increases in line with inflation, is fixed at the time you invest, tax-free	3–4
	b) No set period	• Fixed income, inflation-proofed, taxed or taxable • Capital gain or loss, tax-free	4
Local authority bonds	Set period – usually 1–8 years	Fixed, taxed	5
Local authority stocks	As for British Government stocks	As for British Government stocks	5
Investments from commercial organisations			
Annuities	For life or for a set period	Fixed or with built-in increases, taxed	3 or 4
Insurance company income and growth bonds	Set period – usually 1–10 years	Fixed, taxed	4
Permanent income-bearing shares (PIBS)	No set period	Fixed, taxed	5
Corporate bonds	As for British Government stocks	Fixed income, taxed; capital gain or loss, tax-free	5–10, depending on quality of issuing company

Investment	Minimum period for which you should aim to invest	Type of return	Risk rating
Preference shares	No set period	Fixed income, taxed; capital gain or loss, taxable	5–10, depending on quality of issuing company

Pooled investments

Investment	Minimum period for which you should aim to invest	Type of return	Risk rating
With-profits life insurance	Set period, often 10 years or more	Bonuses, effectively taxed	4–5
With-profits friendly society tax-exempt plans	Set period, often 10 years or more	Bonuses, tax-free	4–5
Gilt and fixed-income unit trusts and oeics	No set period	Income, variable, taxed;capital gain or loss, taxable	4–5
Unit trust bond-based PEPs	No set period	Income, variable, tax-free; capital gain or loss, tax-free	4–5
Single-bond-based PEPs	Fixed period, e.g. 5 years	Income or growth, fixed, tax-free	5–10, depending on quality of issuing company

Chapter 15

Higher-risk investments

When it comes to any serious longer-term savings targets, you should consider investments whose returns are linked in some way to shares. This does not mean you have to buy shares in individual companies yourself (although this is one option, of course): a number of pooled investments give you cheaper and possibly more convenient access to a well-balanced portfolio. This chapter looks at the mainstream ways of investing in shares in the context of basic financial planning; it does not look at more esoteric investments, such as warrants, traded options, the Enterprise Investment Scheme, venture capital trusts, and so on. These may well have a place in your personal finances but, given their inherently higher risks, they should perhaps be viewed as fun investments rather than ways of achieving particular financial objectives. On that basis, they fall outside the scope of this book.

Direct investment in shares

Ordinary shares

What they are The shareholders of a company are its owners and share in the profits of the company. Your shares also give you the right to have a say in how the company is run (by exercising your voting rights at shareholder meetings) – but see pages 259–60.
Minimum investment No set minimum, but dealing charges mean that buying less than, say, £1,000–£1,500-worth of a company's shares at a time is usually uneconomic.
Maximum investment None.

Type of return This can come in two forms. An established company usually pays dividends every six months (with some companies, every three months) to its shareholders. The amount paid is variable, although most companies are reluctant to reduce or miss a dividend payment. Companies still establishing themselves or those facing difficulties might not pay any dividends at all. Shareholders might be quite happy to accept this, if they can see profits being ploughed back into the growth of the company, giving the promise of future rewards.

Because shares are traded on the Stock Exchange, you also stand to make a capital gain or loss if you sell your shares, depending on the prices at which you bought and sold them.

Tax treatment Dividends count as income for tax purposes. They are paid after deduction of tax at the lower rate, and you receive a tax credit along with the dividend cheque showing how much tax has been deducted. Both lower-rate and basic-rate taxpayers have no further tax to pay. Non-taxpayers can reclaim the tax. Higher-rate taxpayers have a further tax to pay. Capital gains on shares are taxable, though you can set your capital gains tax allowances against them (see page 34).

From April 1999, the taxation of dividends from shares held by individuals is due to change. The tax deducted will fall to 10 per cent. Lower- and basic-rate taxpayers will still have no further tax to pay. Higher-rate taxpayers will still have extra to pay, though the rate of extra tax will be adjusted so that overall they will have the same net income as they would have had before the change was made. However, non-taxpayers will lose out, because they will no longer be able to reclaim the tax credit.

How long you invest for No set period, but this is not the home for money you might need back at a set time or at short notice, when share prices might be low.

Charges For the purchase of newly issued shares, no charges. For other shares, stockbroker's commission; the table on page 259 gives an indication of the amount you might pay. Stamp duty of 0.5 per cent on purchases but not sales. Spread between the prices at which you buy and sell: say, 1.5 per cent for large, well-established companies, but a much higher percentage for small companies whose shares are not often traded. In addition, on a purchase or sale of £10,000 or more, you have to pay the PTM levy of £2, which helps fund the City's Panel on Takeovers and Mergers. Some brokers also make a separate 'compliance charge', which goes towards the cost of meeting the regulatory rules for the industry. Changes to the way in which share transactions are settled mean that you are likely to be encouraged to hold your shares in electronic form through your broker's 'nominee account'. Using a nominee account might be free or there could be charges: for example, on a regular basis or each time the broker hands over dividends. With nominee accounts, watch out too for extra charges if you want to receive company reports and accounts or to attend a company's AGM. As an alternative to using a nominee account, you could become a 'sponsored member' of Crest, in which case you directly hold your electronic shares. You must be sponsored by a broker who will usually make a charge. You do not have to hold shares electronically but, if you choose to hang on to paper share certificates, you will probably face higher charges when you sell or buy. Also, you will probably need to deal under a slower system than normal or else face fines if your money or certificates do not reach your broker in time. For more details see page 259.

Risk Capital risk, because the value of your shares can fall as well as rise. In addition, there is the risk that a company you invest in goes out of business, in which case you would lose all your capital. On the inflation front, shares offer a good chance of keeping abreast of, or bettering, inflation over the long term – but no guarantee of doing so. Income can vary. You can reduce risk by investing in shares of different companies from different sectors – see Chapter 12. Risk rating: from around seven for shares in a single, sound, well-established company to ten for a high-risk venture.

More information Share prices are listed in many daily newspapers, on teletext and on the Internet. ProShare★ is an independent organisation set up to promote direct investment in shares; it produces information packs, runs conferences, and so on. Among other perks, membership of ProShare gives you access to a telephone share information service. The *Financial Times*, *Investors Chronicle*★ and, to a lesser extent, the City pages of newspapers give reports and analysis of a wide range of individual companies. *Extel* and *McCarthy* cards are the standard source of basic company information; they are expensive, but larger public libraries might have them. A number of fairly costly, but comprehensive, company guides is available; these guides give you essential statistics about companies and summaries of stockbrokers' recommendations. Examples are *The Hambro Company Guide*★ and *The Estimate Directory*.★ Company reports and accounts can be obtained direct from companies, and the *Financial Times* and *Investors Chronicle*★ run a report and accounts service for readers. For a general introduction to investing in shares, see *The Which? Guide to Shares*, published by Which? Books.★ Numerous books have been written about how to analyse shares and how to make a million; if you cannot find what you want in your local bookshop, you could try *Which?*,★ *Investors Chronicle*★ and personal finance magazines, which run regular articles on finding a stockbroker. Consult a traditional stockbroker for advice on which shares to buy and sell or the timing of deals. If you are an Internet user, many useful sites can help you to keep track of company news and share prices and even give you a dealing channel. Some of the most useful are listed in the table on page 258.

How to invest To buy new issues, register with a broker offering a new-issue service or, in the case of privatisations, see details in the press. For other shares, buy and sell through a stockbroker. If you need advice, choose a traditional stockbroker. If not, a broker offering a dealing-only service will generally be cheaper.

Warning

Many small investors buy shares as new issues, attracted by the simplicity of the transaction and the fact that there are no charges. Privatisation issues, which were attractively priced at issue and have on the whole produced good profits, have fuelled this interest. However, companies try to launch their new issues when stock market conditions look set to raise the maximum possible money for the company. That is the worst time at which investors should buy. Waiting and buying 'second-hand' might be a better deal.

Useful Internet sites for shareowners

Internet address	Brief desription of site
http://www.londonstockex.co.uk	Official site of the London Stock Exchange. Description of its markets, publications, press releases etc.
http://www.ftse.co.uk	Home of FTSE International, which produces most of the share indices for the UK stock markets
http://www.ft.com	Home of the *Financial Times*. News, share information service, company briefings. Search facility enables you to track information and stories about particular companies
http://www.hemscott.co.uk	Company information specialist and publisher of *The Hambro Company Guide*, *The Hemmington Scott Guide* and *REFS*
http://www.esi.co.uk	Electronic Share Information Ltd (esi) provides a wide range of investment information, including share listings, charts etc. plus access to online share-dealing facilities
http://www.pcquote-europe.co.uk http://www.dbc.com	Share charts
http://www.economist.co.uk	Home of *The Economist*, the weekly journal covering economic, political and business news. A search facility enables you to track stories on specific topics
http://www.the-times.co.uk	Home of *The Times*. A search facility enables you to track stories on specific topics
http://www.news-review.co.uk	Summary of business and financial news from the UK weekend newspapers, including brokers' recommendations. A search facility enables you to track stories about specific companies

Source: *The Which? Guide to Shares*

Stockbrokers' commissions when you invest in shares

	Typical traditional stockbroker's service including advice	Example of a dealing-only service
Commission levels	• 1.5% on first £7,000 • 0.55% on next £8,000 • 0.5% on anything above £15,000. Minimum £20	1% Minimum £10
For example, commission on:		
Small deal (£250)	£ 20	£ 10
Medium deal (£2,500)	£ 37.50	£ 25
Large deal (£10,000)	£121.50	£100

Five-day trading, nominee accounts and all that

In order to compete with stock markets around the world, the London Stock Exchange has been speeding up the pace at which deals are completed. From June 1995, 'five-day trading' was introduced, meaning that payment takes place just five working days after shares are bought or sold. (This replaces ten-day trading, which itself replaced an earlier, rather more leisurely system of settling deals in bulk at the end of fortnightly account periods.)

Five-day trading is no problem for professional investors, but it is near impossible for small investors, who are generally reliant on the postal system to receive transfer documents and deliver share certificates or cheques within just five days. And, following the introduction in 1997 of Crest, the stock market electronic settlement system, the speed of settlement is due to increase further to just three days. Therefore, many brokers are encouraging their smaller clients to hold their shares through 'nominee accounts' and to open deposit accounts with the broker from which payments for deals can be made. With a nominee account, you cease to be the direct owner of your shares; instead, the broker owns the shares on your behalf. There are a number of potential drawbacks with this arrangement:

- as you are no longer the direct owner, you lose your automatic right to receive reports and accounts, to attend company meetings, to vote, and also the right to any share perks. Whether or not you can still exercise these rights depends on the services the broker offers as part of the nominee account
- you may have to pay an annual fee for the nominee account, and there may be extra charges for collecting dividends, passing on information about company meetings, and so on
- deposit accounts with brokers typically pay less interest than a comparable building society account
- the company holding the nominee account does not have to be authorised under the Financial Services Act (see Chapter 3). Make sure that your contract with the broker states that the broker (who must be authorised) accepts full responsibility for the nominee company – that way, you ensure that you have the protection of the financial services legislation.

You do not have to hold your shares through a nominee account. You can carry on dealing outside the five-day trading system, allowing longer for settling your deals. However, you may have to pay higher charges and/or accept a worse deal on share prices if you use the slower ten-day system. If you deal only occasionally, the slower system is likely to be best for you.

If you are a very active trader, consider the nominee route, but shop around for a service which suits you. Alternatively, consider becoming a 'sponsored member' of Crest. With this route, you have your own Crest account (in the same way that stockbrokers do), in which you hold your own shares electronically, which means they can be rapidly delivered when you sell them. For more details, see *The Which? Guide to Shares*, published by Which? Books.★

Single-company personal equity plans (PEPs)

What they are A PEP is not in itself an investment. It is a tax-efficient 'wrapper' which you can use to invest in shares and certain other investments. PEPs were originally introduced by the government to encourage direct investment in shares, but their scope has expanded over the years to encompass a much wider range of investments. You can have either or both of two types of PEP: a general PEP and a single-company PEP. In each tax year, you can invest up to £6,000 in a general PEP, which can be invested in shares and/or other investments – see page 271 for more about general PEPs. In addition, you can put up to £3,000 in a single-company PEP which, as the name suggests, holds the shares of just one company at a time, although you can switch from one company to another. The shares must be UK ordinary shares, similar European Union (EU) shares, shares issued under an approved employee savings-related share-option scheme or profit-sharing scheme, or 'paired shares' – that is, where shares in one company are bought and sold only in combination with the shares of another associated company.

Minimum investment As for direct investment in shares – see above. Note that you must invest cash, which is used to buy fresh shares; you cannot simply transfer shares you already own to a PEP (unless they are new-issue shares and you make the transfer within 42 days of issue or they are shares acquired under a profit-sharing scheme or share-option scheme at work, in which case you have 90 days within which to put them into a single-company PEP).

Maximum investment £3,000 in each tax year (in addition to £6,000 in a general PEP – see page 272).

Type of return As for direct investment in shares – see page 255. PEPs are not themselves investments; they are a tax-efficient 'wrapper' under which you invest.

Tax treatment The return from investments held in a PEP is completely tax-free. However, from April 1999, income from shares held in a PEP will become taxable, and your PEP manager will no longer be able to reclaim the tax already deducted from dividends (see page 255). From October 1999, capital gains will also become taxable. PEPs will by then have been superseded by the new Individual Savings Accounts (ISAs) – see page 122.

How long you invest for As for direct investment in shares – see page 255. The PEP rules do not require you to invest for any specified length of time.

Charges In addition to the charges associated with buying and selling shares, extra charges may be made to cover the costs of running the PEP. They vary, so you should shop around.

Risk As for direct investment in shares – see page 256. Bear in mind that you can hold the shares of only one company at a time in a single-company PEP. But you can use different tax years' PEPs to invest in different shares, building up a portfolio in that way. And, of course, your PEPs should be viewed in the context of the full range of investments that you hold – see the chart on page 275 about who should use PEPs.

More information The Association of Private Client Investment Managers and Stockbrokers (APCIMS)★ produces a free directory of members which includes details of those who offer a PEP service. *Which?*,★ personal finance magazines and the personal finance sections of newspapers run regular articles about PEPs, though discussion of single-company PEPs is often scant. One of the most comprehensive summaries of PEPs available is the *Chase de Vere PEP Guide*.★ See Inland Revenue leaflet IR89 *Personal equity plans*.

How to invest As for direct investment in shares – see page 257.

Warning

Investing directly in shares, you should ideally invest a minimum of around £15,000 to £20,000 in a dozen or more different companies to protect yourself adequately from risk and to avoid dealing charges eating too heavily into your profits. For many investors, pooled investments, such as unit and investment trusts, will be the better option.

Pooled investments

Unit-linked life insurance

What it is This is a form of investment-type life insurance (and also pension plan). The bulk of your premiums buys units in one or more funds investing in shares and/or other investments. The value of your policy depends directly on the value of these underlying fund(s), so if the prices of the shares in a share-based fund fall, so too will the value of your units. There is usually a very wide range of different investment funds to choose from, including:

- **deposit-based fund** (often called 'money fund', 'cash fund' or 'deposit administration') This invests in high-interest bank and building society accounts and/or money market funds. Like the underlying deposits, the value of these funds cannot fall, so a deposit-based fund is useful to switch into if you want to consolidate gains on a policy or you want to switch out of a falling stock market

- **unitised with-profits fund** This works in a similar way to traditional with-profits insurance, with bonus units being added to the plan, but the charges are explicit and the insurer usually reserves the right to adjust unit values downwards in exceptional investment conditions (although there may be a value below which the fund is guaranteed not to go)
- **fixed-interest fund** This invests in gilts, corporate bonds, and so on
- **property fund**, investing in, say, shopping centres and office blocks which provide rental income
- **managed fund**, investing in a wide range of assets which might include gilts, shares and property
- **share funds** – for example, those in the UK, Europe, the United States, Japan, or Australia, or shares in companies which are in the doldrums but expected to grow strongly in future
- **commodities and metals**.

Minimum investment Varies, depending on the type of policy – see the box on pages 245 and 266. But for regular-premium policies, payments start at under £10 a month. For single-premium policies, you might need a lump sum of at least £500, say.

Maximum investment As for with-profits policies – see page 243.

Type of return Your policy builds up a value according to the value of the underlying investment funds. How this value is used depends on the type of policy: for example, a maximum investment plan is designed to pay out a lump sum at the end of ten years, but a single-premium bond can be used to provide an income. The box on page 266 gives more detail.

Tax treatment As for with-profits policies – see page 243. In addition, special rules apply to single-premium bonds used to provide income. Each time you take any 'income' you are treated as cashing in part of the policy. Provided you cash in no more than a given limit, you can put off paying any tax due (which would be only higher-rate tax anyway) until the policy eventually comes to an end, and tax would be charged according to your tax status at that time. The limit on the amount you can cash in each year is one-twentieth of the premiums paid so far; any amount not used up in one year can be carried forward to future years.

How long you invest for This depends on the type of policy or plan – see the box on page 245. Many unit-linked life insurance products are designed to be long-term investments and will give you a very poor return if you pull out early. Stopping a policy early crystallises charges (largely commission paid to advisers and salespeople), which would otherwise have been spread out over the lifetime of the policy. As a result, the surrender value of your policy could be less than you have paid in premiums, or even nothing at all.

Tip and warning

If you are currently a higher-rate taxpayer, but expect to pay tax at a lower rate later on, a single-premium insurance bond can be a tax-efficient way of providing income because no tax is charged at the time you take out any income (provided this is below a certain limit). When the policy matures, only higher-rate tax is levied, so if you are a basic-rate or lower-rate taxpayer by then, there will be no tax at all to pay on the proceeds. But beware: if you are aged 65 or more when your single-premium insurance bond comes to an end and you qualify for age-related tax allowances (see page 35), you could lose some or all of the extra allowance. This means you could be paying effectively up to 34.5 per cent tax on the proceeds of the bond because you lose £1 of extra allowance for each £2 of 'excess' income.

Warning

Make sure you understand the nature of the unit-linked life insurance policy or plan you are investing in. If it is designed for the long term, you could get a very poor return if you pull out early.

Charges There are several charges to consider. First, there will be some form of policy or administration fee deducted from each premium; this will often be a flat-rate fee, so it can eat heavily into small payments. Next, you need to consider the 'unit allocation', which tells you what proportion of the remaining premiums will be used to buy units; this proportion might be low in the first year or two when the bulk of the costs (commissions, for example) are being paid by the insurer. Don't be too impressed by unit allocations of more than 100 per cent: this does not mean that more than you have paid in is being invested; the policy fee has already been deducted, so you are in effect getting a refund of part of the fee. Watch out for what are called 'capital units'; the distinctive feature of these is that they have a higher-than-usual annual management fee which persists for the lifetime of the policy. There is a spread between the offer price at which you are allocated units and the bid price at which you cash them in; typically, this is around five to six per cent. Finally, there is the annual management fee of around one per cent. Assessing the impact of this hotchpotch of charges would be a difficult task. Fortunately, nowadays the work is done for you, as insurers are required by law to tell you about the impact of charges on your investment (see Chapter 3). They must also tell you what happens if you cash in or stop your policy early, when surrender charges can heavily dent the value of your policy. If you switch between investment funds, the first switch or two might be free; you will be charged for subsequent switches (though the charge is usually fairly low).

Risk There is a risk to your capital because the value of the underlying investments can fall as well as rise. On the other hand, by investing in a fund you are spreading your risks and reducing the impact that any one company's share collapse could have on your overall investment. Your choice of fund affects risk: a UK managed fund (see page 263), for example, is far less likely to see sharp swings in value than a small companies or commodities fund. By investing in shares and similar investments, you stand a good chance of keeping pace with or beating inflation (but if you choose a deposit-based fund, this would not be the case). Risk rating: deposit-based funds, around three; other funds, from six upwards.

More information Price and performance details of insurance funds are included in quality daily newspapers and various personal finance magazines, such as *Money Management*,★ *Planned Savings*★ and *Moneyfacts Life & Pensions*,★ which publishes annual surveys of fund managers' performance. Articles in *Which?*★ and the personal finance pages of newspapers are also useful sources of information. For individual policies and plans, the insurer or friendly society will provide product details and illustrations (see Chapter 3).

How to invest If you are interested in a particular product, deal direct with the insurer or friendly society if they allow this. Otherwise, buy through an independent financial adviser.★

Unit-linked life insurance plans

The box on page 244–5 looks at the broad types of insurance policy which can be invested on either a with-profits or unit-linked basis. Here, two further plans, which are always set up as unit-linked insurance, are considered briefly.

Single-premium bonds

These are a form of whole-of-life insurance policy (see page 246) which provide minimal life cover and are intended to be used for investment purposes. There may be as many as 20 or so different funds to which you can link. You can invest in more than one fund simultaneously and switch between them at any time. The insurance company has to account for tax on both income and gains from the underlying investment funds, and you cannot reclaim any of that tax. This makes the bonds unattractive for basic-rate, lower-rate and non-taxpayers and anyone with unused capital gains tax allowances, who would do better generally to invest in unit and investment trusts. These bonds are therefore most suitable for higher-rate taxpayers and those who particularly want to switch funds regularly.

Maximum investment plans

These are ten-year endowment policies designed to build regular savings into a lump sum. Life cover is kept to a minimum, and you can choose from a wide range of investment funds. As with single-premium bonds, the tax treatment means that these plans are generally not suitable unless you are a higher-rate taxpayer or particularly need a cheap route for switching between different investment sectors.

Unit trusts

What they are These are professionally managed funds investing in shares and/or other stock market investments. They can invest in other assets too, such as property and futures and options (the last two let you speculate on which way the future prices of shares and other assets will move without actually holding the shares or assets themselves), though only a few do. The fund is divided up into units, and you invest by buying these units. The value of your holding depends on how the price of those units moves. Often, the unit trust management company operates a range of different trusts, for example:

- **UK general**, investing in shares of UK companies and aiming to produce a mixture of income and growth
- **UK growth**, again investing in UK companies, but specialising in shares expected to produce capital gains
- **UK income**, concentrating on shares with high dividend yields; the income can be reinvested rather than paid out
- **'index' or 'tracker' funds**, which mimic the movement of a particular stock market index, such as the FTSE 100, and which often have lower annual management fees because the underlying investments are less actively traded
- **gilt and fixed interest**, investing in British Government stocks (see page 230), corporate bonds (see page 239), preference shares (see page 241) and similar investments
- **convertibles**, investing in convertible corporate bonds (see page 240)
- **balanced**, investing in a mixture of shares and fixed interest
- **international funds**, investing in shares etc. from a wide range of stock markets around the world
- **smaller companies**
- **particular countries**, for example European countries or Japan
- **fund of funds**, investing in other unit trusts.

Minimum investment Varies, but could be as low as £25 a month if the management company runs a regular-savings scheme, and from, say, £250 as a lump sum.

Maximum investment None.

Type of return You can use most unit trusts to provide either growth or income, though some are better for one purpose than the other, and a few trusts can be used only for growth. Income is in the form of distributions, which are similar to dividends from shares. If you want to receive an income, choose 'distribution units'; if you do not, choose 'accumulation units', whose income is automatically used to buy you further units.

Tax treatment Distributions count as income for tax purposes. Distributions are paid after deduction of tax at the lower rate, and you receive a tax credit along with the distribution statement showing how much tax has been deducted. Both lower-rate and basic-rate taxpayers have no further tax to pay. Non-taxpayers can reclaim the tax. Higher-rate taxpayers have further tax to pay. Capital gains on units are taxable, though you may have allowances to set against them (see Chapter 2).

From April 1999, the taxation of distributions from unit trusts held by individuals is due to change. The tax deducted will fall to 10 per cent. Lower- and basic-rate taxpayers will still have no further tax to pay. Higher-rate taxpayers will still have extra to pay, though the rate of extra tax will be adjusted so that overall they will have the same net income as they would have had before the change was made. However, non-taxpayers will lose out, because they will no longer be able to reclaim the tax credit.

How long you invest for No set period, but this is not the home for money you might need back at a set time or in a hurry, as unit prices might be low when you come to sell.

Charges There is an annual management charge (usually around 1–1.5 per cent of the underlying fund) and a spread between the prices at which you buy ('offer price') and sell ('bid price') units. This spread incorporates what is called the 'initial charge' – commonly 5 per cent of the amount invested – but the total you pay up-front is effectively the spread, which tends to be 1 or 2 per cent more. A few trusts have reduced or scrapped their initial charge and make an 'exit charge' instead if you sell within, say, five years.

Risk There is a risk to your capital because the price of units can fall as well as rise. Your choice of trust affects this risk: a UK general trust, for example, is far less likely to see sharp swings in value than a smaller companies or futures and options trust. By investing in shares and similar investments, you stand a good chance of keeping pace with or beating inflation. Risk rating: from six upwards.

More information The Association of Unit Trusts and Investment Funds (AUTIF)* operates the Unit Trust Information

Service, which produces many useful leaflets explaining how unit trusts work, the types of trust available and how you can use them. The information service also publishes a directory of its members. Price and performance details of unit trusts are included in quality daily newspapers and various personal finance magazines, such as *Money Management*,★ *Planned Savings*★ and *Moneyfacts Life & Pensions*★ (which also covers unit trusts). Articles in *Which?*★ and the personal finance pages of newspapers are also useful sources of information. For individual trusts, the management company will provide product details and illustrations (see Chapter 3). If you are an Internet user, a useful site is that of Micropal,★ which produces performance statistics and risk ratings for unit trusts.

How to invest Contact the trust management company direct. Alternatively, deal through an independent financial adviser.★

Open-ended investment companies ('OEICs')

A new type of pooled investment came into being during 1997, similar to a unit trust – see page 249 for details.

Investment trusts

What they are Investment trusts are companies that are quoted on the stock market. Their business is managing funds invested in shares and other assets. You invest by buying the shares of the investment trust. There are different types of investment trust, specialising in different areas of investment, in much the same way as unit trusts. But there are some important differences between unit trusts and investment trusts:

- unit trusts are open-ended, meaning that when there are more people wanting to invest than to cash in, new units are created, expanding the size of the trust, and this new money is used to buy further investments in the fund. By contrast, investment trusts are closed-ended funds, because there is a finite pool of shares in the company. If more people want to buy than to sell, this drives up the share price. The unit price of a unit trust will, then, largely reflect the value of the underlying assets in the trust. But the underlying assets are only one factor influencing the share price of an investment trust

- investment trusts, but not unit trusts, can borrow money to invest. This has what is called a 'gearing effect', which magnifies gains on a successful investment but also magnifies losses on a poor one.

Minimum investment Varies from, say, £25 a month through a savings scheme run by the investment trust management company; savings schemes also accept *ad hoc* lump sums as small as, say, £250. Otherwise you buy through a stockbroker, and dealing charges would tend to make deals under £1,000 uneconomic.

Maximum investment None.

Type of return With some investment trusts, just one class of shares will automatically give you income (in the form of dividends) and growth (if the share price rises). But 'split capital trusts' give you a choice of shares. A split capital trust is set up for a fixed period. During that time, some of its shares (the 'income shares') receive all or most of the income from the trust; when the trust is wound up, the 'capital shares' receive all or most of the growth. There are some exotic variations on this theme: for example, zero dividend preference shares and capital indexed shares, both of which require some homework before you use them. Income shares can be useful for investors seeking a high income immediately, provided they are prepared to sacrifice capital growth.

Tax treatment As for direct investment in shares – see above. Capital shares in split capital trusts can be particularly useful for higher-rate taxpayers.

Charges As for direct investment in shares – see page 255 – if you buy through a stockbroker. The cost of investing is generally lower if you use a savings scheme run by many of the investment trust management companies (because they can then buy and sell in bulk and pass on cost savings to investors). There is a spread between the price at which you can buy shares and the price at which you can sell them. The management company's annual charge for its services is usually fairly low: for example around 0.5 per cent.

Risk There is a risk to your capital because share prices can fall as well as rise. A trust which has a high level of borrowing – that is, it is highly geared – will tend to have a more volatile share price than a less highly geared trust. Similarly, if the trust invests in inherently more risky companies – smaller companies or emerging markets, for instance – the share price can be expected to vary more widely and your risk will be greater. As with all share-based investments, you stand a good chance of keeping pace with or beating inflation. Risk rating: from seven upwards.

More information The Association of Investment Trust Companies (AITC)★ produces a number of useful explanatory booklets and a directory of investment trust companies. Price and performance details of investment trusts are included in quality daily newspapers and various personal finance magazines, such as *Money Management*.★ Articles in *Which?*★ and the personal finance pages of newspapers are also useful sources of information. See also *Investment Trusts*,★ published quarterly by Flaxdale Printers. Like all quoted companies, investment trusts must produce an annual report and accounts; you can get these direct from the trust management company or, for example, through the *Financial Times* service to readers. You can also get advice from stockbrokers offering a traditional dealing and advice service.

How to invest Through a stockbroker (see page 257) or, if there is one, through a savings scheme run by the investment trust management company: contact the company direct (details from the AITC★ directory).

Personal equity plans (PEPs)

What they are A PEP is not itself an investment, but it is a tax-efficient method of investing in a range of qualifying assets. There are two types of PEP: general PEPs and single-company PEPs. The latter are discussed on page 260; general PEPs are considered here. A general PEP can be invested in any of the following: UK ordinary shares, similar shares quoted on a recognised Stock Exchange in another European Union (EU) country, certain types of corporate bond and preference shares (see page 248 for bond-based PEPs) and qualifying unit and investment trusts. For a unit or investment trust to be 'qualifying', at least half of its portfolio must be invested in UK ordinary shares, comparable EU shares or eligible corporate bonds and preference shares. However, you can invest up to a quarter of your PEP in unit and investment trusts which invest in a wider range of shares and are 'non-qualifying'.

Minimum investment As for the underlying investments, that is, the shares, bonds or trusts.

Maximum investment Up to £6,000 in each tax year (in addition to £3,000 in a single-company PEP). The full amount can be used to invest in qualifying trusts, but only a quarter (£1,500) in non-qualifying trusts.

Type of return As for the underlying investments.

Tax treatment Income and gains from investments held in a PEP are both completely tax-free. However, from April 1999, income from shares held in a PEP will become taxable and your PEP manager will no longer be able to reclaim the tax already deducted from dividends (see page 255). From October 1999, capital gains will also become taxable. PEPs will by then have been superseded by the new Individual Savings Account (ISAs) – see page 122.

Charges Expect to incur the normal charges for the underlying investment, though check out whether there are any discounts for investing via a PEP. Charges for the PEP itself vary considerably, depending on the investments you choose and the PEP manager, which could be a unit or investment trust management company, a bank, a building society, a stockbroker, an independent financial adviser, a specialist PEP manager, and so on. Unit trust managers often make no extra charges at all (over and above the normal charges for the unit trust) if you use a PEP. By contrast, a PEP invested in your own selection of shares and managed by a stockbroker could be fairly costly.

Risk In general, as for the underlying investments. However, within your PEP you could build a mixed portfolio of trusts and shares, say, giving you a more tailored exposure to risk.

More information The directory of unit trust management companies published by the Association of Unit Trusts and Investment Funds (AUTIF)★ indicates those that offer PEPs. The directory of the Association of Investment Trust Companies (AITC)★ does the same for its members. Similarly, the directory of members of the Association of Private Client Investment Managers and Stockbrokers (APCIMS)★ includes details of those who offer a PEP service. *Which?*,★ personal finance magazines and the personal finance sections of newspapers run regular articles about PEPs – see, for example, *Money Management*★ and *Planned Savings*.★ For a listing of PEP details and performance, see *Moneyfacts Life & Pensions*★ (which also covers unit and investment trust PEPs). One of the most comprehensive summaries of PEPs available is the

Chase de Vere PEP Guide.★ See Inland Revenue leaflet IR89 *Personal equity plans.*
How to invest As for the underlying investments.

Summary of higher-risk investments

Investment	Minimum period for which you should aim to invest	Type of return	Risk rating
Direct investment in shares			
Ordinary shares – direct investment	No set period, but generally at least 5 years	Variable income and/or growth, taxable	7 and above
Single-company PEPs	No set period, but generally at least 5 years	Variable income and/or growth, tax-free	7 and above
Pooled investments			
Unit-linked life insurance – regular-premium plans	Usually at least 10 years	Growth, effectively taxed at equivalent of basic-rate income tax	Around 6 (around 3 for deposit-based funds)
Unit-linked life insurance – single-premium plans	Varies	Growth, but you can use partial withdrawals for income, effectively taxed at equivalent of basic-rate income tax	Around 6 (around 3 for deposit-based funds)
Unit-linked friendly society tax-exempt plans	Set period, often 10 years or more	Growth, tax-free	Around 6 (around 3 for deposit-based funds)
Unit trusts and OEICs	No set period, but generally at least 5 years	Income, taxed, growth, taxable; or just growth	6 and above

273

Investment	Minimum period for which you should aim to invest	Type of return	Risk rating
Investment trusts	No set period, but generally at least 5 years	Income, taxed, growth, taxable; or just growth; or just income	7 and above
Share-based PEPs	No set period, but generally at least 5 years	As for shares, unit and/or investment trusts, depending on underlying investments	6 and above

---

Tip

If you are interested in investing in unit and/or investment trusts, it usually makes sense to use your annual PEP allowance – see the chart opposite. If you are interested in investing in shares, you need to weigh PEP charges and any restrictions on the shares you can choose against the tax advantages.

Should you invest through a PEP?

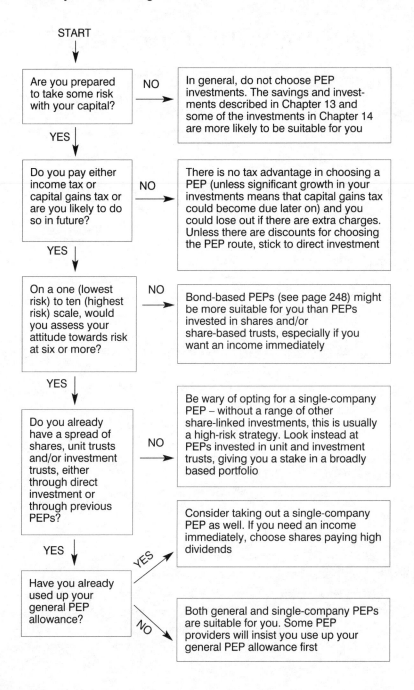

START

Are you prepared to take some risk with your capital?

NO → In general, do not choose PEP investments. The savings and investments described in Chapter 13 and some of the investments in Chapter 14 are more likely to be suitable for you

YES

Do you pay either income tax or capital gains tax or are you likely to do so in future?

NO → There is no tax advantage in choosing a PEP (unless significant growth in your investments means that capital gains tax could become due later on) and you could lose out if there are extra charges. Unless there are discounts for choosing the PEP route, stick to direct investment

YES

On a one (lowest risk) to ten (highest risk) scale, would you assess your attitude towards risk at six or more?

NO → Bond-based PEPs (see page 248) might be more suitable for you than PEPs invested in shares and/or share-based trusts, especially if you want an income immediately

YES

Do you already have a spread of shares, unit trusts and/or investment trusts, either through direct investment or through previous PEPs?

NO → Be wary of opting for a single-company PEP – without a range of other share-linked investments, this is usually a high-risk strategy. Look instead at PEPs invested in unit and investment trusts, giving you a stake in a broadly based portfolio

YES

Have you already used up your general PEP allowance?

YES → Consider taking out a single-company PEP as well. If you need an income immediately, choose shares paying high dividends

NO → Both general and single-company PEPs are suitable for you. Some PEP providers will insist you use up your general PEP allowance first

275

Chapter 16

Meeting your investment targets

The preceding chapters have described the array of savings and investment tools available, but which should you match to your own particular needs? Since targets are as varied and individual as people themselves, there is no simple answer. Chapter 12 looked at which investments you might use to meet broad investment and savings targets, such as growth or income either immediately or in the future. This chapter gives some guidance towards meeting a few of the most common specific financial targets.

An emergency fund

The most fundamental step in financial planning is ensuring that you have some cushion to fall back on in an emergency. This is not simply crisis management – mending a leaking roof, sudden car repairs, bailing out children stuck abroad penniless. It can also be an 'opportunist fund', letting you take advantage of special offers and events that arise unexpectedly.

Two decisions should be made about your emergency fund:

• How much do you need?
• Where should you keep it?

How much?

This depends crucially on your own circumstances, lifestyle, the type of emergencies you might have to cope with, and so on. If you are self-employed, for example, you might need quite a large buffer to cover short-term falls in receipts or a brief period of illness not covered by your permanent health insurance (see Chapter 5). Worse still, if your income would not be protected at all in the event of illness, you may be concerned to build up a sizeable emergency fund, though you should weigh up whether it would be better to divert some of those funds into appropriate insurance. If you have a large family, the probability of a crisis arising may be higher simply because, with more people involved, there's more risk of something going wrong. If you live in an older property, there may be a higher risk of unforeseen repairs being needed. You will have to examine your own situation and decide what size of emergency cushion feels right for you. Whatever you decide now should be reviewed periodically as your circumstances change: for example, if unemployment threatens, you may want to build up extra reserves, or as your children become independent, a smaller buffer may be enough. As a very rough guide, for most people an emergency fund of £1,000–£5,000 would probably be adequate.

Where to keep your fund

Conventional wisdom is that an emergency fund should be kept where you have instant access to it in times of need. Of course, you could meet that requirement by simply stuffing fivers under the mattress, but an emergency fund has other features too:

- It should be kept in a secure place. There should be no risk at all of losing the money put into your fund. At one level, this means that you shouldn't store it at home where it would be vulnerable to theft. At another, it means that you shouldn't invest it in assets whose value can rise and fall
- Ideally, the money should not be idle. It should be earning you some return.

The best place for an emergency fund is in some form of deposit account run either by a building society, bank or National Savings (see Chapter 13). Most people choose a building society. An instant access account is an obvious choice, and you might consider accounts which let you make withdrawals through cash machines so that you can cope with emergencies outside banking hours. The downside is that instant access accounts tend to offer the lowest rates of interest, especially on small deposits, so you cannot make your money work very hard.

In fact, if you have instant access to credit – for example, you have a high spending limit on your credit card which you usually do not fully use – you could consider putting at least part of your emergency fund in an account which requires some short period of notice (up to a month, say) if, in exchange, you will get a better rate of interest.

Tip

You do not need *instant* access to an emergency fund if you can rely on credit in an emergency. This may allow you to invest for a better return.

Similarly, although £1,000–£5,000 might be enough as an emergency fund, you might consider adding it to other lower-risk savings if this would give you a large enough lump sum: for example, to cross an interest rate threshold on a tiered account and so earn a better return.

If you have a mortgage, you might instead consider a flexible mortgage account as a possible home for your emergency fund – see page 213. The 'return' will generally be considerably higher than you could get on an instant access account and should also beat notice accounts.

The chart opposite summarises your choices for an emergency fund.

Investing for children

There are two main reasons for considering children's investments. The first is to help the child to understand how to value and use money; the second is to build up a nest egg for the child to use in later life. The chart on page 282 summarises the most useful options.

Learning about money

It's hard to beat a building society account for teaching children to handle money sensibly. Essential features are an accessible branch, a low minimum balance, instant access and tolerant counter staff

Choosing a home for your emergency fund

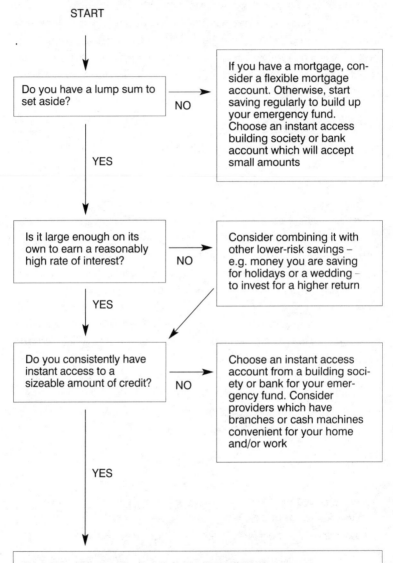

START

Do you have a lump sum to set aside?

NO → If you have a mortgage, consider a flexible mortgage account. Otherwise, start saving regularly to build up your emergency fund. Choose an instant access building society or bank account which will accept small amounts

YES ↓

Is it large enough on its own to earn a reasonably high rate of interest?

NO → Consider combining it with other lower-risk savings – e.g. money you are saving for holidays or a wedding – to invest for a higher return

YES ↓

Do you consistently have instant access to a sizeable amount of credit?

NO → Choose an instant access account from a building society or bank for your emergency fund. Consider providers which have branches or cash machines convenient for your home and/or work

YES ↓

Consider relying on the credit for an immediate response to an emergency. Pay off the credit by drawing on an emergency fund invested for higher interest, either in a notice account (with a notice period of up to one month) at a building society or bank or the National Savings investment account. You could also consider a building society postal account; these often pay higher interest but you pay in and withdraw only by post, which incurs some delay who don't mind counting a box full of change. Many societies have accounts especially aimed at children, often including free gifts, such as piggy-banks, magazines and birthday cards, but the interest offered is often pitifully low (though, if you are lucky, a small local society may offer better returns). For the child's own larger sums, such as birthday money, consider too a National Savings investment account.

Providing a nest egg

Parents' giving, or building up, relatively large sums for their off-spring (more than £2,000–£3,000, say) need to watch the tax rules. Even a child has a personal allowance to set against income tax – £4,045 in 1997–8. This means that most children are non-taxpayers (so make sure they receive income *gross*, that is, without tax deducted). A child can also make capital gains (over and above infla-tion) of up to £6,500 in 1997–8 tax-free. However, to prevent tax avoidance, if you give money or an asset to your own child, any income it produces counts as *your* income, not the child's, and is taxed at your top rate. This rule is waived if the total income pro-duced by gifts from a parent comes to no more than £100. This means that a child could receive up to £200 without problem if both parents made gifts. If the income exceeds that limit, then all of it (not just the excess) is taxed as your own. To avoid falling foul of these rules, choose investments for your child which produce a tax-free return or capital gains rather than income. Income produced by gifts from people other than parents counts as the child's own.

Tip

You may need to give the Inland Revenue proof that a gift to your child was not from you, so ask grandparents, godparents etc. to send a letter with money or investments they give your child.

To build up a nest egg to help a child in later years, longer-term investments offer the best prospect. As always, the particular choice of investment depends partly on the degree of risk you're willing to take. At the lowest end of the risk spectrum is the National Savings children's bonus bond (see page 226). As this offers a tax-free return, it is suitable as a gift from a parent.

A medium- to higher-risk product aimed specifically at children is the the so-called 'baby bond' (see page 246). These are variants of the tax-free insurance policies offered by friendly societies. They are useful for parents investing for children because there's no tax on the eventual payout. But what makes them special is that, unlike other insurance policies, there's also no tax on the fund in which the premiums are invested. Premiums are invested on either a with-profits or a unit-linked basis. Unit-linking is more risky than with-profits because investment values may have taken a tumble at the time your child wants to cash in. Over the long term, a unit-linked bond should tend to outperform a with-profits one.

In theory, the baby bonds' tax-free status should ensure very competitive returns, but charges have a big impact on the value of the bonds, because the government limits each person's investment in them to a very low maximum (see page 246). If you are comfortable with the risk of a share-based investment for your child, you could do better to look at unit trusts and investment trusts (see Chapter 15). Ideal for children's investments are the savings schemes run by many unit and investment trust managers. Some accept investments as low as £20 a month on a regular basis, and *ad hoc* lump sums from £200. Note that children under age 18 are not eligible for personal equity plans.

A popular gift for children is National Savings premium bonds (see page 227). Strictly speaking these are not investments, although if the holding is big enough and the child has average luck, the 'return' can compare well with building society rates and, of course, there's always that outside chance of making a million.

Paying for education

Large classes, mixed year groups, limited examination subjects, and no sixth form are frequently perceived as drawbacks of state schools which worry parents who want the best education for their children. With state funding for education uncertain, an increasing number of parents are considering private schools instead. According to a survey by MORI for the Independent Schools

Investing for children

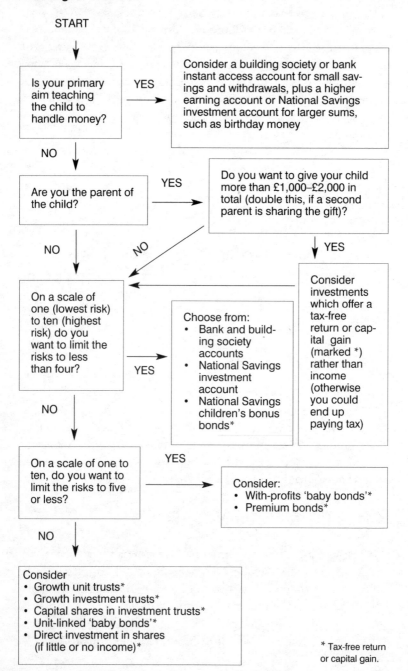

START

Is your primary aim teaching the child to handle money?

YES → Consider a building society or bank instant access account for small savings and withdrawals, plus a higher earning account or National Savings investment account for larger sums, such as birthday money

NO ↓

Are you the parent of the child?

YES → Do you want to give your child more than £1,000–£2,000 in total (double this, if a second parent is sharing the gift)?

NO ↓

NO → On a scale of one (lowest risk) to ten (highest risk) do you want to limit the risks to less than four?

YES ↓

Consider investments which offer a tax-free return or capital gain (marked *) rather than income (otherwise you could end up paying tax)

On a scale of one (lowest risk) to ten (highest risk) do you want to limit the risks to less than four?

YES → Choose from:
- Bank and building society accounts
- National Savings investment account
- National Savings children's bonus bonds*

NO ↓

On a scale of one to ten, do you want to limit the risks to five or less?

YES → Consider:
- With-profits 'baby bonds'*
- Premium bonds*

NO ↓

Consider
- Growth unit trusts*
- Growth investment trusts*
- Capital shares in investment trusts*
- Unit-linked 'baby bonds'*
- Direct investment in shares (if little or no income)*

* Tax-free return or capital gain.

Information Service (ISIS), the proportion of 'first-timers' – parents who didn't themselves go to a private school – has risen to over half of all parents choosing private schools for their children.

Sending your son or daughter to a private school is not an easy decision, with the cheapest charging around £1,000 a term for day pupils. Sending a child to the most prestigious boarding-schools can cost £13,000 a year for each child. There are basically three ways in which you can cope with school fees:

- borrow now, for example by extending your mortgage, and pay off the loan over a number of years. Bear in mind that a mortgage loan for this purpose does not qualify for tax relief on the interest, and that you could lose your home if you were unable to keep up the payments
- pay-as-you-go out of your current income or savings (maybe an inheritance). This could mean cutting other spending and/or taking on extra work. However, according to ISIS, over a quarter of pupils receive some contribution towards their fees through scholarships, bursaries or assisted places (means-tested help from the state). Some local authorities and charities can also help. Check with individual schools to find out what may be available
- plan ahead and start saving before your child gets to the entry age for the level of schooling you're interested in.

The last course offers several options for saving. If you have already chosen a particular school, contact the bursar to find out whether the school runs its own pre-payment scheme, which is often called a 'composition fee scheme'. Such a scheme has an advantage, because your savings are paid into a charitable trust where they build up tax-free until needed. But check what happens if you want to change your choice of school.

A few insurance companies used to operate educational trusts which also had tax-free status and didn't commit you to a particular school. But the tax perks were removed from these schemes from April 1997 onwards, so your choice is now limited to the standard range of investments for providing an income in the future. The methods described below are suitable not only for school fees but also if you want to build up a sum to help your child through university – an increasingly important task for parents as student grants are now frozen and tuition is no longer free.

Given the increase in school fees over the years, you are unlikely to build up an adequate sum using the lower-risk investments described in Chapter 13. But if you have only a few years until your child starts school, you would be unwise to choose higher-risk investments, so try to build up what you can using deposit-based investments. Even if there are fewer than five years to go until your child starts school, you might consider using a TESSA, which gives you the advantage of tax-free growth. Provided you take out only interest (not including the tax relief on it) during the five-year period, you will not lose the tax advantage.

Assuming you have a reasonable time to plan ahead (five years or more, say), you really should consider medium- and higher-risk investments. In the past, if you could save for at least ten years, advisers often promoted special school fee savings plans based on endowment insurance (see page 245). Two particular advantages are often cited:

- you pay in regular premiums – a useful discipline if you find it hard to save
- built-in life cover ensures that your child's schooling plans need not be upset if you were to die
- with-profits plans provide a middle course between deposit-based investments and higher-risk share-based investments, which is useful for people who want to limit their risks.

But unit and investment trusts provide a more flexible and cost-efficient alternative and, if you invest via a personal equity plan (see pages 248 and 271), you currently get a completely tax-free return. Admittedly, you do need more discipline to keep up a pattern of regular savings. And there is no built-in life cover, so you should take into account your commitment to paying school fees when assessing your overall life cover needs (see Chapter 4). If you prefer to avoid the risks of share-linked investments, bond-based trusts and PEPs are possible alternatives to with-profits policies. But there is no reason why you should use a single investment tool to build up the fund you need. Choosing a combination of, say, unit trust PEPs and with-profits insurance might give you a good mixture of savings discipline, risk and tax-efficiency.

In late 1997, the government announced its proposals for Individual Savings Accounts (ISAs), which will replace both PEPs

Providing for school fees

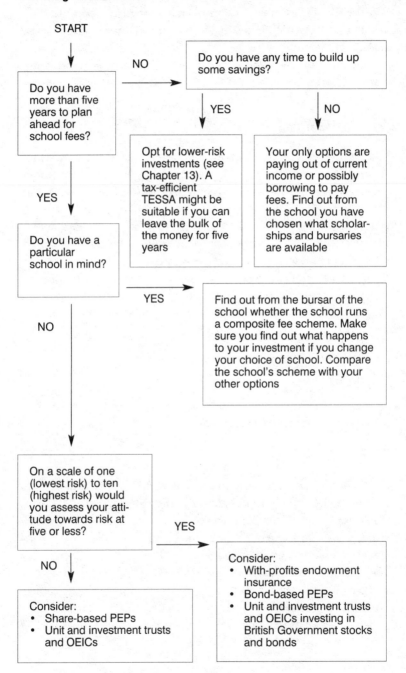

START

Do you have more than five years to plan ahead for school fees?

NO → Do you have any time to build up some savings?

YES → Opt for lower-risk investments (see Chapter 13). A tax-efficient TESSA might be suitable if you can leave the bulk of the money for five years

NO → Your only options are paying out of current income or possibly borrowing to pay fees. Find out from the school you have chosen what scholar-ships and bursaries are available

YES

Do you have a particular school in mind?

YES → Find out from the bursar of the school whether the school runs a composite fee scheme. Make sure you find out what happens to your investment if you change your choice of school. Compare the school's scheme with your other options

NO

On a scale of one (lowest risk) to ten (highest risk) would you assess your atti-tude towards risk at five or less?

YES → Consider:
• With-profits endowment insurance
• Bond-based PEPs
• Unit and investment trusts and OEICs investing in British Government stocks and bonds

NO

Consider:
• Share-based PEPs
• Unit and investment trusts and OEICs

and TESSAs from April 1999. Existing PEPs and TESSAs can be switched to ISAs, subject to an overall investment of £50,000. It seems that ISAs will be a suitable tax-efficient savings vehicle for school fees planning.

The chart on page 286 summarises the main ways of providing for school fees.

Boosting your retirement income

This is the holy grail of many pensioners and the target which seems most consistently to trigger cases of fraud and abuse among financial organisations. There is one basic lesson which you should never ignore: you cannot have an exceptionally high income without some risk to your capital. If you are offered a deal which promises high income from safe investments, be on your guard, take nothing at face value, ask questions, check documents and, ten to one, you'll find the deal is flawed. Don't touch it with a bargepole, and report the providers to the main financial regulator, the Financial Services Authority (FSA),* or to the police if you suspect a fraud.

Warning

Higher returns always go hand in hand with higher risks. If a deal looks too good to be true, it almost certainly is.

Chapter 12 examined the main ways in which you can produce an income by using a lump sum, and the chart on page 202 gives some guidance on choosing investments according to how much risk you are comfortable about taking. Understandably, many pensioners are very cautious about risk – after all, money lost at this stage of life cannot generally be replaced. However, if you stick exclusively with deposit-type investments, the value of your savings can be badly eroded by inflation as retirement progresses; ultimately, this means that the value of the income they produce will be a lot less too. You need to strike a balance between income, security and capital growth. No one, single investment will meet all these aims. Instead, you need to consider a portfolio of investments which will sustain your income over a long period, while giving you partial protection against the full array of risks.

The investments in your portfolio, and their mixture, is a matter of personal choice, but will probably include some from each of the lower-risk, medium-risk and higher-risk investments described in Chapters 13–15. So, for example, you might have a third of your money invested in monthly income building society accounts, a TESSA and National Savings pensioners bonds; a third in British Government stocks, bond-based PEPs and insurance company guaranteed growth bonds; and a third in a range of unit trusts. The balance of the portfolio should shift as investment conditions alter: for example, with less in unit trusts if the stock market seems likely to fall, more in deposits if interest rates are high. If inflation is a particular concern, index-linked National Savings certificates and index-linked British Government stocks would play a part in the portfolio too.

In addition to this general portfolio building, you could consider using a home income plan as described below.

Home income plans (HIPs)

How can you increase your income if you do not have a lump sum to spare? Many elderly people are 'cash poor, asset rich', having capital tied up, particularly in the home in which they live. A home income plan (HIP) lets you release some of that capital and convert it into income.

Broadly, HIPs work as follows: you take out an interest-only mortgage on your home – and under special tax rules, the interest qualifies for tax relief. You invest the loan for income, part of which is used to pay the mortgage interest, part to provide income. The loan is eventually repaid out of your estate after your death (or the death of both you and your husband, wife or partner), or out of the proceeds of selling the home if you move before then.

There are a number of variations on this theme, some of which gave HIPs a bad name in the late 1980s. The very worst combined two high-risk products: the mortgage allowed you to defer some or all of the interest, with the interest being added to the outstanding loan; the investment gave you an income which depended on the performance of the stock market. When property prices collapsed and the stock market dipped, many planholders were left with unmanageable debts and the fear of their homes being repossessed.

But there have always been perfectly sensible and sound versions of HIPs. In 1990 a group of companies formed Safe Home Income Plans (SHIP),★ a company to promote the safe versions of HIPs. These plans come in two forms:

- **mortgage-based plans** You take out an interest-only mortgage on your home (generally on up to 75 per cent of its value) and use the proceeds to buy an annuity which pays you a set income

---

Planning in practice

Fact-find: Jane is 68 and retired. She is a widow and lives in her own home. She has no mortgage. She receives a pension from the state and an employer's pension worth £7,000 a year. She has savings of £30,000 in a 90-day notice account at a building society, which currently pays 5.9 per cent interest.

Objective: Jane would like to boost her income, but is also worried that inflation will gradually eat into the value of her capital.

Solution: Jane puts £3,000 in a TESSA, which pays 7.5 per cent interest tax-free, and £3,000 into a National Savings pensioners income bond, which pays 7.5 per cent before tax. She also opens savings accounts: £4,000 goes into a 60-day notice account paying 6.5 per cent, and £2,000 into an instant access account that pays 5.8 per cent. Both accounts are run by post rather than through a building society branch, and, because of the lower running costs for postal accounts, they offer above-average interest rates. Jane considers buying an annuity, but is unsure whether she wants to hand over a lump sum for good. She decides to wait five years – income from annuities is higher for older people. For now, Jane plans to invest £6,000 in a bond-based PEP. She also puts £4,000 into gilts, which produces a yield of 9 per cent. Jane puts the remaining £8,000 into a high-yielding share-based unit trust to get a modest income and some capital growth. In future tax years, she

---

after the mortgage interest payments have been automatically deducted. Essential features making these plans safe are that the mortgage rate is *fixed*, the interest is paid as you go along (and *not* added to the outstanding loan), and the income is set and payable for life (so you're *not* relying on stock market performance)

- **reversion schemes** Instead of taking out a mortgage, you actually sell part or all of your home to the HIP company, but have the guaranteed right to carry on living in it, and use the proceeds to buy an annuity. The scheme offers some variations: the income you get could be fixed or, in the case of at least one provider, part or all of the income can depend on changes in property prices.

---

will be able to consider reinvesting this money through a tax-free PEP.   *Which?* April 1995

Fact-find: Richard is 25 and currently lives in a flat that's worth £50,000. He has no mortgage on his home – his parents bought it for him. His annual salary is £20,000. He has no savings and owes £2,000 on his credit card. He has just inherited £75,000.

Objective: To invest the £75,000. In around five years' time, he may want to buy a house.

Solution: Richard clears his £2,000 credit card debt. He can't join his employer's pension scheme until he is 30 and he has not paid anything into a personal plan yet. He puts £8,000 into a personal plan now, using up tax relief available from earlier years. Richard puts £10,000 into a 90-day notice account, £3,000 into a TESSA and £3,000 into an instant access account. Richard wants to have cash to buy a house in five years' time, so he decides to put £35,000 into gilts, which mature in 1999. He will probably reinvest the income in his TESSA and 90-day notice account. He decides to invest the rest of his money for growth over the long term. £6,000 goes into a unit trust PEP investing in leading UK shares. As Richard is looking for a long-term investment, he can take a slightly higher risk with some of his money: he puts £5,000 into an international growth investment trust and £3,000 into an investment trust which specialises in Latin American countries.

Which? April 1995

Tip

If you are interested in taking out a home income plan, consider providers who are members of SHIP (see above). Always take advice from your own solicitor before taking out the plan.

You usually need to be aged at least 65 or 70 to be eligible for a HIP; at younger ages, the annuity rates would simply be too low to make the scheme worth while. You'll need to own your own home outright – usually a freehold house or a long leasehold house or flat (though freehold flats in Scotland might also be accepted). For reversion schemes, your home generally needs to be worth at least £40,000.

Warning

Beware of taking out a HIP if you're getting income support, housing benefit or Council Tax benefit, as they are likely to be reduced.

Chapter 17

Passing your money on

An integral part of financial planning as you get older is deciding what you want to happen to your wealth when you have died, and then ensuring that your wishes will actually be put into practice. But even when you are younger, you should give thought to this, especially if you have a family dependent on you. There are two aspects to your planning:

- setting out your wishes formally in a will
- ensuring that your assets do not disappear in unnecessary tax bills.

Below, we look at what happens if you don't make a will and how to go about drawing one up. On page 299, we look at the tax aspects of inheritance. In its July 1997 Budget, the government announced that it would be reviewing the inheritance tax system – and also the capital gains tax system, which is important when you are considering making gifts during your lifetime. Some changes to both systems looked likely to be made in the March 1998 Budget, but at the time of writing the nature and scope of any changes were unknown.

What happens if you don't make a will?

Everything you leave when you die, less anything you owe, is called your 'estate'. A will sets out what is to happen to your estate. It is a legal document which, although it can be changed after your death (see page 300), will normally be followed. Only three adults out of every ten in Britain have made a will: see the table on page 293. Yet dying without one (called dying 'intestate') can cause unnecessary hardship for your survivors:

- delays in trying to find out whether or not you did in fact leave a will and in tracing your possessions
- delays in the formalities required before your estate can be distributed
- your next of kin will usually be appointed to sort out your estate, and he or she might not be the best person to do the job
- the law dictates who will inherit your estate and in what proportions. The rules do not recognise unmarried partners (although a partner may be able to make a claim on your estate; see opposite)
- the law may require legally binding trusts to be set up. These may be unnecessarily restrictive and expensive, especially where only small sums are involved
- there may be inheritance tax on the estate which could have been avoided.

Another very important reason for making a will is so that you can say who you want to look after your children if you have a young family.

Who gets what if there is no will?

Dying intestate means that the intestacy rules state who will inherit your estate. The charts on pages 294, 295 and 296 show the effects of the rules on those living in England and Wales. The rules are different in Scotland, as follows:

- **married, no children** Your husband or wife has 'prior rights' to the family home up to a value of £110,000, furniture and household effects up to £20,000 and a cash sum up to £50,000. He or she also has 'legal rights' to half the remaining 'moveable estate' (that is, excluding land and buildings). See below for the remaining estate
- **married, with children** Your husband or wife has prior rights to the family home up to £110,000, furniture and effects up to £20,000 and a cash sum up to £30,000, plus legal rights to one third of the remaining moveable estate. The children also have legal rights to one third of the moveable estate. See below for the remaining estate
- **children but no husband or wife** The children have legal rights to half the moveable estate. See opposite for the remaining estate

- **the remaining estate** Whatever remains after any prior and legal rights have been met passes to your survivors or relatives in the following order of priority: 1) any children or, if they have died, their children; 2) if there are no children but there are parents and/or brothers and sisters, half to the parents and half to the siblings; if a sibling has died, his or her place is taken by his or her children, if any; 3) if no parents, everything to the brothers and/or sisters; 4) if no brothers or sisters, parents take everything; 5) a surviving spouse; 6) uncles and aunts or, if they have died, their children; 7) grandparents; 8) brothers and/or sisters of grandparents or, if they have died, their children; 9) remoter ancestors. If you are survived by no family at all, the estate passes to the Crown.

Have you made a will?

Yes	– and I think it is up to date	31%
	– though it probably needs updating	7%
No	– I've intended to but not got around to it	23%
	– I've never even thought about it	22%
	– I think my husband/wife/children inherit automatically	6%
	– I've never really liked to think about it	5%
Don't know/other reason		6%

Source: Mintel 1995

Warning

If you do not make a will, your possessions will not necessarily be passed on in the way you would choose. This is a particular risk if you live with an unmarried partner.

Inheritance (Provision for Family and Dependants) Act 1975

Dying intestate can pose particular problems for an unmarried partner, because he or she has no automatic rights under the intestacy rules. But if the partner can show that he or she lived with you as

293

Who gets what if you die intestate and you are married with no children (England & Wales)

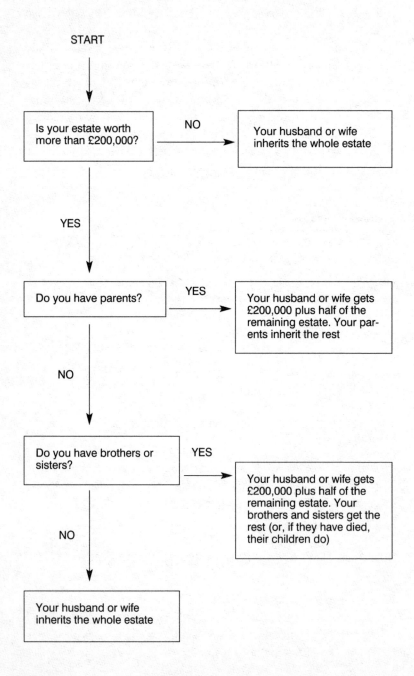

START

Is your estate worth more than £200,000? → NO → Your husband or wife inherits the whole estate

YES

Do you have parents? → YES → Your husband or wife gets £200,000 plus half of the remaining estate. Your parents inherit the rest

NO

Do you have brothers or sisters? → YES → Your husband or wife gets £200,000 plus half of the remaining estate. Your brothers and sisters get the rest (or, if they have died, their children do)

NO

Your husband or wife inherits the whole estate

**Who gets what if you die intestate and you have children
(England & Wales)**

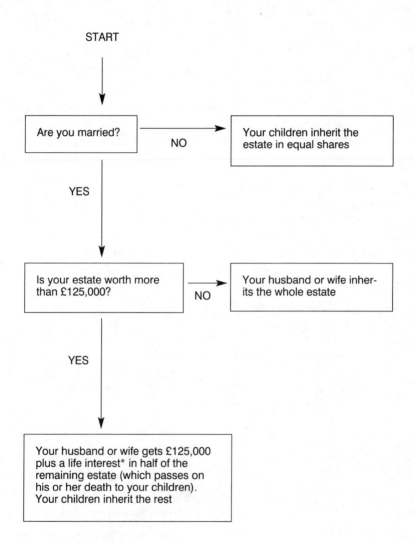

START

Are you married? — NO → Your children inherit the estate in equal shares

YES

Is your estate worth more than £125,000? — NO → Your husband or wife inherits the whole estate

YES

Your husband or wife gets £125,000 plus a life interest* in half of the remaining estate (which passes on his or her death to your children). Your children inherit the rest

---

* A life interest gives you the right to the income produced by an asset or to use the asset during your lifetime, but you do not own the asset itself.

Who gets what if you die intestate and you have no close family (England & Wales)

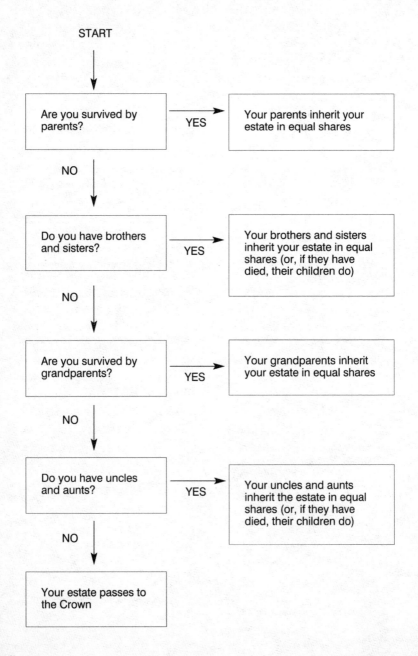

START

Are you survived by parents? — YES → Your parents inherit your estate in equal shares

NO ↓

Do you have brothers and sisters? — YES → Your brothers and sisters inherit your estate in equal shares (or, if they have died, their children do)

NO ↓

Are you survived by grandparents? — YES → Your grandparents inherit your estate in equal shares

NO ↓

Do you have uncles and aunts? — YES → Your uncles and aunts inherit the estate in equal shares (or, if they have died, their children do)

NO ↓

Your estate passes to the Crown

man or wife throughout the two years prior to your death, he or she can claim a share of your estate under this Act (which does not apply in Scotland, where the law, however, does recognise 'common law' husbands and wives). If your partner had not been with you for the two years, he or she may still have a claim on your estate by proving financial dependence on you. In either case, the claim must be made within six months of permission to distribute the estate being granted. It will then be considered by the courts. The whole procedure could take a long time, so it is much better that you make a will in the first place.

Similarly, if you write a will and use it to disinherit someone who is financially dependent on you, that person can (following your death) go to court and challenge the will. The court decides whether that person should have a share of your estate and how much this should be.

How to make a will

If your affairs are straightforward, you might consider making your own will using one of the d-i-y guides available: for example, *Make Your Will*, an action pack, published by Which? Books.★ But be warned – solicitors claim they make more money out of unravelling d-i-y wills than they ever do drawing up professionally prepared ones! It is essential that the will makes your intentions absolutely clear. According to *The Guinness Book of Records*, the shortest-ever UK will simply said 'All for mother'. However, the gentleman concerned meant his wife, not his own mother. The will was contested in court (though eventually accepted), which goes to show that you need to take care over the wording of even the simplest will. Do not choose the d-i-y route if any of the following applies to you:

- your permanent home is outside England or Wales
- you have young children by a former marriage
- you run your own business or farm
- you are leaving 'heritage property' for the public benefit
- you have been married more than once and your ex-partner is still alive
- you want to set up complicated trusts, for example for a disabled person

- you are involved with family trusts.

In any of these instances, go to a solicitor. For a straightforward will, the charge will be around £50 or so. You will pay more for a more complicated will. Will-writing services are often cheaper, but a survey by *Which?* found that overall they came out the worst when compared with solicitors, banks, building societies and insurance companies. Over a third of the wills drawn up by will-writing services were rated as poor, being overly reliant on standard formats and often failing to get the detail right. Some banks, building societies and insurance companies offer will preparation services, which came out consistently adequate in the *Which?* survey but often lacking in depth and so failing to cover all eventualities. Wills from this source can also work out expensive later on if you have to use the organisation as executor.

Make sure you keep your will up to date. Review it whenever your circumstances change and, in any case, every couple of years or so. The Mintel survey (the table on page 293) found that one in six people who have made a will admit that it is probably out of date. This can cause terrible problems, with the 'wrong' people inheriting, and distressing and costly battles between your survivors, especially if you have divorced and remarried. In England and Wales, a will is usually automatically invalid if you subsequently marry. If you divorce (but not if you merely separate), any bequests to your former husband or wife automatically lapse but are instead subject to the intestacy laws with all the problems that they can entail – see page 292 – although the rest of the will still stands. In Scotland, neither marriage nor divorce invalidates your will, although a new husband or wife can claim 'legal rights' from your estate (see page 292).

Warning

You can alter a will by adding a 'codicil' – a written amendment which must be signed and witnessed and should be kept with the will. But codicils can be lost, so unless the amendment is very slight it is better to draw up a fresh will when changes are needed.

Tax planning

Many people worry unnecessarily about tax taking a large slice of the inheritance they hope to leave to their families. In fact, under the regime in existence in 1997–8 only three to four deaths out of every hundred trigger an inheritance tax bill. There might not be any inheritance tax to pay on your estate at all, because:

- tax is payable only if the value of your estate plus any taxable or potentially taxable gifts made in the preceding seven years come to more than a set 'tax-free slice', which is £215,000 in 1997–8
- some bequests are tax-free and are deducted from the value of your estate for tax purposes. These include bequests to charity and to your husband or wife.

If it does look likely that there will be inheritance tax on your estate, you can take certain steps during your lifetime to reduce or avoid the tax bill on death. But always bear in mind that ultimately inheritance tax is a problem for your heirs, not you. Do not jeopardise your present financial security simply to save your heirs some tax on their inheritance in the future. In particular, consider what resources you might need if you require specialist care in your old age – see Chapter 7.

Inheritance tax tips

Use your tax-free slice If you are married, you may be tempted to leave everything tax-free to your husband or wife. But because bequests to children and other relatives or friends are *not* tax-free, there could be a hefty tax bill when your husband or wife then dies and everything passes to other members of the family.

If your husband or wife does not need all your money and assets, consider sharing them between your spouse and other family members, making sure that the bequests which are not tax-free fall within your available tax-free slice.

Make lifetime gifts Provided you can afford to make gifts during your lifetime, this is a good way to reduce the value of your estate, because many gifts are completely tax-free. Most other gifts between individuals count as potentially exempt transfers (PETs) and become taxable only if you die within seven years of making them (and, even then, only if the total of gifts made over the seven years up to the PET comes to more than the tax-free slice). Tax-free lifetime gifts include:

- gifts between husband and wife
- gifts to charities
- a regular pattern of gifts – for example, premiums for a life insurance policy – which count as normal spending out of your income
- any number of small gifts up to £250 per person
- wedding gifts up to certain limits
- up to £3,000 of any other gifts each year (or up to £6,000 if you did not use up the limit in the previous year).

Give away things whose value will rise The increase in value then benefits the person to whom you make the gift rather than swelling your estate.

Use life insurance You can pay the premiums (using one of the lifetime gift exemptions) on an insurance policy to benefit someone else. In this way, you can make an outright gift or you can ensure that the proceeds of the policy are available to pay an expected inheritance tax bill. Seven-year decreasing term insurance can be used to cover the potential tax bill on a PET.

More complex schemes If you have a large estate, you might be attracted to schemes which use loans, trusts and businesses to reduce the value of your estate. These can become complicated and, if not carefully set up, can fall foul of the tax rules, which disallow artificial methods of avoiding tax. Get professional advice.

Altering a will after death If all the beneficiaries of your will agree, they have two years following your death within which they can alter the bequests made under the will by drawing up a 'deed of variation'. This could be done to reduce or eliminate an onerous tax bill.

More information

To find out more about wills, see *Make Your Will* and *Wills and Probate*, both published by Which? Books.★ For a more detailed look at making gifts and bequests and the tax position, see *The Which? Guide to Giving and Inheriting* and *Which? Way to Save Tax*, also both

published by Which? Books.★ For anything beyond the simplest
will or tax-saving scheme, get professional advice from a solicitor or
accountant. See Inland Revenue leaflets IHT1 *Inheritance tax*, IHT2
Inheritance tax on lifetime gifts, IHT3 *An introduction to inheritance tax*
and IHT8 *Alterations to an inheritance following a death*, all available
from the Inland Revenue Capital Taxes Office.★ See also IR152
Trusts. An Introduction, available from your usual tax office or local
Inland Revenue Offices.★

Planning in practice

Henry Brown has three children, all under the age of 18. He will leave almost everything to his wife, Margaret, but if she dies at the same time or before him, he wants his children to inherit. Henry makes his wife an executor of his will, since she is the person who stands to gain most from the will. He also appoints as executor his friend Gordon Saunders, who will be guardian of his children if both he and his wife die. He appoints another friend as a 'reserve' executor. Apart from two small bequests, there are legacies for the executors as a reward for their efforts. Henry specifies that the residue should go to his wife, but that if she dies before him or within 30 days of him, it will be left for his children. If the children are under 18, the executors will act as trustees.

Make Your Own Will, An Action Pack from Which?

Sam dies and leaves his whole estate of £200,000 to his wife, Harriet. Since this is a tax-free gift, there is no inheritance tax to pay. When Harriet dies, her free estate is valued at £300,000 and is left completely to their only child, Phyllis. There is IHT to pay on the estate calculated as follows:

Value of free estate	£300,000
less tax-free slice	£215,000
	£85,000
Tax on £85,000 @ 40%	£34,000

However, suppose instead that Sam had left £100,000 to Phyllis (on which no IHT would be payable because it would be covered by the tax-free slice) and the remaining £100,000 to Harriet. On Harriet's death, her estate would have been valued at £200,000. Giving this to Phyllis would have been completely covered by Harriet's tax-free slice, so no IHT would be payable. Straightforward planning to make use of Sam's tax-free slice would save £34,000 in tax.

The Which? Guide to Giving and Inheriting

Appendix I

Targets and priorities

Work through this checklist. Column 1 aims to help you identify your personal targets. Columns 2 and 3 prompt you to look at your progress so far towards achieving each target. Where work remains to be done, Column 4 invites you to say what priority you give to each target; to do this, count how many targets you have identified, then try to put them in rank order: for example, if you have seven targets, give the most important target a score of one, the next most important a score of two, and so on. In Column 5, commit yourself to a date when you will review the target: this might, for example, coincide with the date on which you receive a statement for the product involved.

1 Nature of target	2 Are you already working towards this target?	3 Do you need to take additional steps to meet this target?	4 What priority do you give this target?	5 When do you next intend to review this target?
Things to consider				
Your specific targets				
Protecting your family • Would your survivors need income? How much? • Would your survivors need capital? How much?				
Protecting your income • Do you have cover through your job? Is the cover adequate? • Do you have savings to fall back on? Are they enough? • Do you need to take out insurance? How much?				

1 Nature of target	2 Are you already working towards this target?	3 Do you need to take additional steps to meet this target?	4 What priority do you give this target?	5 When do you next intend to review this target?
Things to consider				
Your specific targets				
Buying a home • Could you save money by switching your mortgage? Which type of mortgage do you want? Can you pay off part of your mortgage early?				
Care in old age • Are you happy to rely on the state?				
Treatment if you are ill • Are you happy to rely on the NHS? Could a delay waiting for treatment damage your finances?				

1 Nature of target	Your specific targets	2 Are you already working towards this target?	3 Do you need to take additional steps to meet this target?	4 What priority do you give this target?	5 When do you next intend to review this target?
Things to consider					
Investment targets List your targets – e.g. planning for school fees, saving for a holiday etc. – and consider the following questions for each one:					
• Do you want to invest for a lump sum? Over what period? How much can you invest?					
• Do you want to invest for an immediate income? How much can you invest?					
• Do you want to invest for an income later on? Over what period? How much can you invest?					

1 Nature of target	2	3	4	5
Things to consider	Your specific targets	Are you already working towards this target?	Do you need to take additional steps to meet this target?	What priority do you give this target?	When do you next intend to review this target?

Passing your money on
- Have you made a will? Is your will up to date?

- Is there a risk that you might have to pay inheritance tax? Can you take steps now to reduce the possible tax?

- Do you want to take out life insurance to cover a potential tax bill?

OTHER

Resources Calculators

To establish what scope you have for meeting your targets, you need to assess what income you have at this point in time and how that income is already committed. This indicates whether you have a surplus you can use or a shortfall which needs to be tackled. Similarly, you need to consider what assets you have, what debts you have, how assets are already committed to your financial targets, how well they are committed and whether you would do better to reallocate them. Bear in mind that if you alter the way your assets are used, this may affect the income you receive. You can use these Calculators to help you do that.

Income Calculator

Monthly income and expenditure		Yourself	Your spouse/ partner
Income (gross)			
Earnings from job	a		
Profits from business	b		
Income from investments	c		
Pensions	d		
State benefits	e		
Other income	f		
Gross income (a + b + c + d + e + f)	A		
less National Insurance	g		

Monthly income and expenditure		Yourself	Your spouse/ partner
less income tax	h		
Net income (A – g – h)	**B**		
Expenditure			
Mortgage/rent	i		
Council tax	j		
Gas/water/electricity	k		
Telephone	l		
Food, drink and household items	m		
Cost of running car	n		
House insurance	o		
Life insurance	p		
Other insurance	q		
TV licence	r		
Clothes	s		
Credit card bill	t		
Other loan repayments	u		
Child-related costs: school fees, riding lessons, hobbies etc.	v		
Miscellaneous spending money	w		
Pension contributions	x		
Regular saving	y		
Other	z		
Total spending (i + j + k + l + m + n + o + p + q + r + s + t + u + v + w + x + y + z)	**C**		
Surplus or deficit (B – C)			

Asset Calculator

Assets and liabilities	Yourself		Your spouse/ partner	
	Value (£'00)	Target (from Appendix I) if applicable to which asset is committed	Value (£'00)	Target (from Appendix I) if applicable to which asset is committed
Your assets				
Your home	aa			
Contents of home and personal belongings	bb			
Your car(s)	cc			
Other property	dd			
Other valuables	ee			
Cash in bank/building society	ff			
National Savings investments	gg			
British Government stocks	hh			
Corporate bonds etc.	ii			
Other stocks	jj			
Shares (except investment trusts)	kk			
Unit trusts	ll			
Investment trusts	mm			
Investment-type life insurance	nn			
Other investments	oo			
Total assets (aa + bb + cc + dd + ee + ff + gg + hh + ii + jj + kk + ll + mm + nn + oo)	E			

Assets and liabilities	Yourself		Your spouse/ partner	
	Value (£'00)	Target (from Appendix I) if applicable to which asset is committed	Value (£'00)	Target (from Appendix I) if applicable to which asset is committed
Your liabilities				
Mortgage	pp			
Outstanding credit card debts	qq			
Other loans	rr			
Other liabilities (e.g. tax owed)	ss			
Total liabilities (pp + qq + rr + ss)	F			
Net assets (E – F)				

Glossary

Accident insurance A type of insurance which pays out a lump sum if you suffer certain specified injuries, such as loss of a limb or loss of sight.

Accrual rate The rate at which a future pension builds up in a scheme where the pension is based on a formula linked to your pay. Usually expressed as a fraction of final pay: for example, sixtieths or eightieths.

Activity of daily living (ADL) A basic function in everyday life, such as keeping yourself clean, using the lavatory, feeding yourself, being reasonably mobile within your own home, and so on. Particularly important in the context of long-term care insurance (see below), where the number of activities of daily living you can manage is used as a test for whether you have a claim.

Additional voluntary contributions (AVCs) Contributions you choose to make to boost your pension and/or other benefits from a particular employer's pension scheme (see below).

ADL Abbreviation for activity of daily living (see above).

Annuity A regular income – monthly, for example – payable for life (lifetime annuity) or for a set period (temporary annuity), which you get in exchange for a lump sum. Once the annuity has been bought, you cannot get your original capital back as a lump sum, and you are locked into the income agreed at the outset: this might be a fixed income or, say, one increasing by a given amount each year.

Annuity deferral Until 1995 the only way to take a pension from a personal pension plan (see below) was to convert the fund you had built up into an annuity. Now, there is a further option: you can put off buying an annuity – up to age 75, if you choose – and in the meantime take an income direct from the fund.

Appropriate personal pension plan A personal pension plan (see below) which is used to contract out (see below) of the State Earnings-Related Pension Scheme (SERPS; see below).

Asset Something of value which you own, such as an investment, personal possession, and so on.

Authorised In the context of the Financial Services Act 1986, all investment businesses operating in the UK must be 'authorised' by being a member of a regulating body set up under the Act, unless the business is specifically exempted from this requirement.

AVCs Abbreviation for additional voluntary contributions (see above).

Basic-rate taxpayer Someone whose top rate of income tax is the basic rate (23 per cent in 1997–8).

'Best advice' rule Under the Financial Services Act 1986, anyone selling or advising about investments must give customers and prospective customers 'best advice', meaning that only investments which are suitable, given the customers' personal details and circumstances, are to be recommended.

Blue chip Describes a company which is considered to be very sound. An investment in such a company is likely to produce solid, if unexciting returns. (The description derives from the game of poker where blue chips have the highest value.) Not all blue chip companies live up to their name, as 1970s' shareholders in Rolls-Royce and bondholders in Barings Bank can testify.

British Government stocks (Also called 'gilts' and 'gilt-edged stock') Loans to central government which can be traded on the stock market. You receive regular interest and may make a capital gain or loss depending on the prices at which you buy and sell the stocks.

The Budget The government's announcement each year of its taxation plans for the forthcoming tax year (starting on the following 6 April). Under the Conservative government, the Budget was moved to November each year and included spending plans too. From 1998, the Labour government has reverted to March Budgets with a broad pre-Budget announcement the previous November.

Building society accounts Deposit-based investments with institutions which have traditionally been 'mutual' organisations – that is, owned by their members and having no shareholders to take a slice of any profits. Building societies can now become companies if enough members support the move.

Cancellation period A 'cooling-off' period, usually 14 days in the case of investments, during which you can change your mind about an investment you have just made and have your money back instead. Cancellation periods apply only to some investments and are not available if you buy 'off-the-page' (see below) in response to an advertisement or as an execution-only customer (see below).

Capital A vague term, given various meanings, including: the total resources you have, the amount you have available to invest, or the amount you originally invest.

Capital gains tax A tax on the profit or gain which you make from selling (or otherwise disposing of) an asset for more than its value at the time you bought (or otherwise acquired) it. Various allowances can be set against the profit before tax is worked out, so in practice many people escape the tax.

Capital Taxes Office Part of the Inland Revenue★ which deals with inheritance tax (see below).

Capped-rate mortgage A mortgage (see below) whose interest rate is variable – that is, it can be altered by the lender and tends to move in line with interest rates in the economy as a whole – except that it is guaranteed not to rise above a given level. The guarantee operates for a given time-period, after which the interest rate becomes fully variable.

CGT Abbreviation for capital gains tax (see above).

Chargeable gains For capital gains tax purposes (see above), a gain or profit which is potentially liable to capital gains tax but which might be reduced or eliminated once allowances are taken into account.

Codicil A legal addition to a will. Like the original will, it must be formally signed and witnessed.

Cold call An unexpected visit or telephone call from a salesperson or adviser, with whom you do not have any existing arrangements. Special rules govern the salesperson's or adviser's behaviour in order to protect you as a customer.

Commission Payment to a salesperson or adviser by the company whose products have been sold, generally based on the value of the sale.

Commission bias The unethical practice of salespeople and advisers recommending products primarily because of the commission they will earn rather than because the products are the most suitable for the customer.

Commission refund The return to the customer of part or all of the commission which a financial adviser or other intermediary has received on the sale of an investment or insurance product. The refund could take several forms: a reduction in fees otherwise payable to the intermediary, a cash sum, or enhanced benefits from the investment or insurance policy.

Company pension scheme Alternative name for an employer's pension scheme (see below).

Company representative A salesperson who can advise on and sell the products of only the one company that employs him or her. A company representative does not give independent advice about the market as a whole.

Compulsory purchase annuity A lifetime annuity (see above) bought with the fund built up in a personal pension plan (see below) or employer's pension scheme (see below). The whole of the income – that is, the pension – it produces is taxable.

Contracting out Giving up part of your State Earnings-Related Pension Scheme (see below) and getting instead a pension and other benefits from an employer's pension scheme (see below) or a personal pension plan (see below).

Convertible term insurance Term insurance (see below) which carries an option (for which you pay extra) to swap instead to an investment-type policy (see below).

'Cooling-off' period See cancellation period.

Corporate bond Loan to a company which can be traded on the stock market. You receive regular interest and may make a capital gain or loss depending on the prices at which you buy and sell the stocks. There are many variations on the theme: for example 'convertible bonds' give you the option to swap the bonds at a given future date(s) for ordinary shares in the company.

Credit insurance (also called 'payment protection insurance') Insurance bought at the time you take out a loan, or related to the amount outstanding on a credit card, which will cover the monthly cost of the debt for a limited period – for example, a year – if you cannot work because of illness or unemployment.

Crest Electronic settlement system, introduced in 1997 by the London Stock Exchange, under which paper share certificates are no longer needed. Instead ownership of shares can be logged electronically in a Crest account – in a similar way to the crediting of funds to a bank account.

Critical illness insurance Type of insurance (usually based on a whole-of-life policy; see below) which will pay out a lump sum if you are diagnosed with or suffer any of a specified list of life-threatening conditions, for example a heart attack or cancer.

Decreasing term insurance Type of term insurance (see below) which pays out a lump sum if you die within the term, but the size of the payout falls as the term progresses.

Deed of variation A legal document which alters the terms of a person's will after that person has died: for example, to change the people who inherit or the amounts that they inherit. To make such an alteration, all the beneficiaries under the original will must agree to the change.

Deferred annuity An annuity whose income does not start to be paid until some specified time after you invest your lump sum.

Deposit-based investment An investment where the original capital you invest cannot fall in value (though its buying power can be eroded by inflation) and earns interest which either accumulates or is paid out as income.

Deposit Protection Scheme★ A scheme set up under the Banking Act 1987 to compensate customers of banks which fail. It guarantees the return of 90 per cent of the first £20,000 of the amount you have invested with the bank.

Discounted-rate mortgage A mortgage (see below) whose interest rate is kept at a set percentage below the standard variable mortgage rate for an initial period. If this represents a genuine discount, such mortgages can be worth while. But, with some, the difference between the normal and discounted rates of interest is added to the outstanding loan, dramatically increasing the overall cost of the mortgage.

Discretionary service Type of service offered by a financial adviser, stockbroker or other intermediary whereby you hand over the bulk of the investment decisions to them.

Dividends Income you may receive as a shareholder in a company.

Emergency fund Money you set aside in some reasonably accessible form (such as building society accounts), which can be drawn upon in the event of some unforeseen need for funds.

Employer's pension scheme A scheme through which you can build up a retirement pension and other benefits run by the employer for whom you work. The employer must pay at least part of the cost; in a 'non-contributory' scheme, the employer foots the whole bill.

Endowment mortgage A mortgage (see below) of a given term (usually 25 years) coupled to an endowment policy (see below) of the same term. During the life of the mortgage, you pay only interest on the loan, plus premiums for the endowment policy; the endowment policy builds up a cash value which is used, at the end of the term, to repay the capital.

Endowment policy An investment-type insurance policy which runs for a given term, usually at least ten years. It builds up a cash value, generally on either a with-profits (see below) or unit-linked (see below) basis, which is paid out at the end of the term. If you die during the term, it also pays out, but the amount generally starts at a relatively low level.

Estate Everything you own less everything you owe.

Execution-only customer A customer who has made his or her own investment decision and simply wants a salesperson or adviser to carry out his or her instructions without giving any financial advice. Execution-only customers are not protected by the 'know your customer' (see below) and 'best advice' (see above) rules.

Executive pension plan A type of employer's pension scheme (see above) offered by insurance companies and taken out to cover one or just a handful of senior employees.

Fact-find Detailed investigation which a salesperson or adviser must normally carry out in order to establish a potential customer's personal and financial circumstances. The information is written down and the customer is required to indicate, by his or her signature, that the details are correct.

Family income benefit policy Type of term insurance (see below) which, if you die during the term, pays out a series of tax-free lump sums to your survivor(s) over the remaining term, as if the sums were an income.

Fee-based adviser An independent financial adviser (see below) who does not rely on commission but instead charges customers a fee, usually based on the time spent on their affairs. Any commission received is either set off against the fee or used to enhance the benefits of the investment being bought.

Final pay scheme Type of employer's pension scheme (see above), where your pension and certain other benefits depend on the amount of your pay at or near the time of retirement, the number of years you have been in the scheme and the accrual rate (see above).

Financial adviser A person or firm offering advice about investments, insurance, and so on. For investments covered by the Financial Services Act 1986, there are just two types of adviser: those who sell the products of a single company – company representatives (see above) and tied agents (see below) – and those who base their advice on all the products available on the market – independent financial advisers (see below).

Financial Services Act 1986 An Act of Parliament which introduced a detailed scheme of regulation for investment business and came into effect from April 1988. A new Financial Services Act is expected in late 1998.

Financial Services Authority (FSA)★ New 'super-regulator' which replaced the Securities and Investments Board (SIB) in October 1997 and is due to take over the regulatory responsibilities for virtually all forms of investments – including deposits – which are sold to the general public.

Five-day trading A system of settling deals to buy and sell shares on the London Stock Exchange introduced from June 1995 onwards. People buying shares are required to make payment within five working days. People selling shares must produce share certificates within the same time. Five-day trading – due to reduce to three days in 1998 – is voluntary; you can choose to deal under a slower system but you may have to pay extra.

Fixed-rate mortgage A mortgage whose interest rate is set at a particular level and does not vary during an initial set period. At the end of the period, the rate reverts, usually to the normal variable rate for that lender.

Flexible mortgage account A mortgage and current account combined. You overpay your mortgage by paying your whole salary into the mortgage account – and draw on the surplus as required using a debit card, chequebook, and so on. Any surplus left in the mortgage account (that is, your savings) effectively earns the mortgage rate – a relatively high and tax-free return.

Flexible whole-of-life insurance A whole-of-life insurance policy (see below) invested on a unit-linked basis (see below) which can be used for insurance and/or investment purposes. Not only can you choose and vary the balance between the insurance and investment elements but usually you have scope to add a wide range of insurance options to the policy.

Free-standing AVCs Contributions you choose to make to an additional voluntary contributions pension plan which is independent of your employer's pension scheme (see above), while a member of the employer's scheme. The proceeds of the FSAVC plan can be used only to boost benefits from the employer's scheme (up to the maximum amounts permitted by Inland Revenue rules).

Friendly society Similar to an insurance company, but friendly societies are allowed to offer some savings plans which are completely tax-free.

Futures A contract whereby you agree to buy or sell shares (or some other assets or goods) at a set price at a set future date. You do not necessarily take up or actually sell the shares or goods, because you can sell the futures contract. The price of the futures contract is just a fraction of the value of the underlying shares or goods, so gains or losses on the shares or goods can be very large relative to the amount you invest. This means that futures give you the potential of very high returns, but equally they are high risk because you could lose much more than your original investment.

Gilts Another name for British Government stocks (see above).

Gilt Strip Investment formed by dividing a conventional gilt, so that each interest payment and the redemption value too become separate investments which can be independently bought and sold.

Give-As-You-Earn Name commonly given to payroll-giving to charity – a scheme under which a donation is automatically deducted by your employer from each pay-packet and handed over to one or more charities of your choice. You get tax relief at your top rate on the donations.

Group permanent health insurance Insurance which employers can buy to pay replacement income to employees who are unable to work because of sickness or disability.

Health insurance Blanket term for a wide range of insurances related to health, including insurances to pay for private treatment, to replace your income if you are sick and to pay for care in old age.

Higher-rate taxpayer Someone whose top rate of income tax is the higher rate (40 per cent in 1997–8).

Home income plan Scheme to provide extra income if you are aged 65 or more. You take out a mortgage (see below) on your home and use the loan to buy an annuity (see above). Part of the income from the annuity is used to pay interest on the mortgage. The loan is repaid from the proceeds of eventually selling the property when you no longer need it.

Home Responsibilities Protection (HRP) Scheme to protect your entitlement to a state basic pension (see below) during periods when you are caring for someone at home, such as children or an elderly relative.

Home reversion scheme Scheme to provide extra capital or income if you are aged 65 or more. You sell part of your home, but retain the right to live in it until you die (or both you and your husband or wife have died, if it is a joint scheme). The amount raised can either be kept as a lump sum or be used to buy an annuity (see above).

Hospital cash plan Type of insurance which pays out a medley of cash sums in specified circumstances: for example, if you have to go into hospital, if you need dental treatment, if you become pregnant, if you visit a chiropractor, and so on.

HRP Abbreviation for Home Responsibilities Protection (see above).

Hybrid scheme Type of employer's pension scheme (see above) which works out pension and other benefits on both a final pay basis (see above) and a money purchase basis (see below), paying you whichever is the greater.

ICS Abbreviation for the Investors Compensation Scheme (see below).

IFA Abbreviation for independent financial adviser (see below).

Illustration An example showing the proceeds you might get from an investment-type life insurance policy or pension plan, based on standardised growth rates and on the actual charges which apply to that company's policy or plan.

IMRO Abbreviation for the Investment Managers Regulatory Organisation (see below).

Incapacity benefit An income from the state to which you might be entitled if you are unable to work because of either sickness or disability.

Income support An income from the state to which you might be entitled if your income from other sources comes to less than you are deemed to need to live on and you do not have much in the way of savings.

Income tax Tax levied on most regular payments you receive, such as earnings, pensions, income from investments, and so on.

Increasable term insurance Term insurance (see below) where the amount of cover (and the premium) can be increased either at certain times or at given events, such as the birth of a child. The extra you pay assumes that your state of health is still the same as it was when you originally took out the policy even if, in fact, it has deteriorated.

Increasing term insurance Term insurance (see below) where the amount of cover, and the premium, automatically increase during the term either by a set percentage each year or in line with prices. The extra you pay assumes that your state of health is still the same as it was when you originally took out the policy even if, in fact, it has deteriorated.

Independent financial adviser (IFA)★ An investment adviser who must consider the full range of products and companies in a market when giving you advice.

Individual Savings Account (ISA) New investment due to replace PEPs and TESSAs from 1999 onwards. If proposals are adopted unchanged, you will be able to invest in shares, unit trusts, cash and National Savings. There will be no income tax or capital gains tax on income and gains made by investments held in the ISA. Dividends from shares will be tax-free for the first five years.

Inflation Sustained increases in price or earnings levels, commonly measured by changes in the Retail Prices Index (price inflation) or the index of National Average Earnings (earnings inflation).

Inheritance tax Tax on your estate (see above) when you die and on some gifts made during your lifetime if those gifts come to more than a given sum.

Inland Revenue★ Government department dealing with the assessment and collection of tax on income, profits, gains and inheritance.

Insurance broker A person or firm advising on and arranging insurance, and often investments too, for customers. Those who use the title 'broker' must belong to the Insurance Brokers Registration Council (IBRC),★ a regulatory body which requires minimum standards and conduct from its members. For investment business, the IBRC is a Recognised Professional Body★ (see below) under the Financial Services Act 1986.

Interest-only mortgage A mortgage (see below) on which you pay only interest during the term of the loan. The amount borrowed is repaid at the end of the term usually out of the proceeds of an investment which has been building up over the term.

Internet An electronic network, linking participating computers across the world and giving you access via a computer and a telephone line to a wide range of information and services.

Intestacy Dying without having made a will. The law dictates how your estate (see above) will be distributed to your survivors.

Investment Managers Regulatory Organisation (IMRO)★ A Self-Regulating Organisation★ under the Financial Services Act 1986, responsible for businesses running investment funds: insurance companies, unit trusts (see below) and investment trusts (see below), for example.

Investment trust A company, quoted on the Stock Exchange, whose business is running a fund investing in, for example, the shares of other companies or British Government stocks and bonds. You invest indirectly in the fund by buying the shares of the investment trust.

Investment-type life insurance Life insurance policies which build up cash sums payable either at the end of a specified term or on surrender. Such policies also pay out in the event of the policyholder's death, but are a relatively expensive way of buying life cover.

Investors Compensation Scheme (ICS)★ A scheme set up under the Financial Services Act 1986 to pay compensation to investors who are eligible to claim against an authorised investment business which has ceased trading: for example, because they have lost money through a firm's fraud or negligence.

Irredeemable Describes investments, particularly bonds, which have an unlimited lifetime, in contrast to redeemable investments where your capital is repaid at some specified date.

ISA Abbreviation for Individual Savings Account (see above).

Joint life, first death policy A joint life insurance policy (see below) which pays out when one of the people covered dies. This type of life insurance is useful as a way of paying off a mortgage if either of a couple dies.

Joint life, last survivor policy A joint life insurance policy (see below) which pays out only when both of the people covered has died. This type of life insurance can be useful as a way of covering possible inheritance tax bills when a husband and wife have both died (bearing in mind that there is no tax on what they leave to each other).

Joint life policy A life insurance policy which covers two people's lives – often husband and wife – paying out when either one or both has died.

Key features document Written information about a life insurance policy or pension plan which must be given to an investor either before, or soon after, he or she signs the contract.

'Know your customer' rule The requirement that an investment business finds out *all* the details about a prospective customer's circumstances and investment objectives as might reasonably be expected to be needed if suitable advice is to be given.

Lifetime annuity Investment where you exchange a lump sum for a regular income which is paid for the rest of your life. You cannot get your original investment back as a lump sum.

Long-term care plan Insurance designed to contribute towards the cost of living in a nursing or residential home, or of being cared for in your own home, if you become unable to look after yourself. Some plans are insurance-based and pay out if you are unable to carry out a given number of activities of daily living (see above). Others are investment-based and provide an income in return for a lump sum: for example, from the sale of your home.

Low-cost endowment mortgage An interest-only mortgage (see above) linked to an endowment policy (see above) whose proceeds are not guaranteed to be enough to repay the mortgage at the end of the term but are expected to be sufficient, given certain assumptions about investment returns.

Lower earnings limit Minimum level of earnings, set each year, to determine the point at which National Insurance (see below) starts to be paid on earnings and used in calculating your entitlement to various state benefits.

Lower-rate taxpayer Someone whose top rate of income tax is the lower rate (20 per cent in 1997–8).

Major medical expenses insurance Type of health insurance (see above) which pays out a lump sum if you undergo specified surgery. The lump sum is pitched to be broad enough to cover the cost of private treatment, but you can in fact use the payout in any way you wish.

Maximum protection plan Type of flexible whole-of-life insurance (see below) used to provide high levels of life cover, especially in the early years of the policy.

MME Abbreviation for major medical expenses insurance (see above).

Money purchase scheme Type of employer's pension scheme (see above) where a specific slice of the pension fund is assigned to you. The size of the pension you get depends on the amount contributed to the scheme, how the invested contributions grow and annuity rates at the time you retire.

Mortgage Any loan secured against the value of your home. If you do not keep up the required interest payments and capital repayments (if applicable), the lender can take possession of your home in order to recover the amount owed.

Mortgage payment protection insurance Insurance, usually bought at the time you take out a mortgage (see above), which will cover the mortgage payments for a limited period – for example, one or two years – if you cannot work because of illness or unemployment.

Mortgage protection insurance Life insurance to pay off your mortgage (see above) if you were to die during the mortgage term.

Mutual organisation An organisation owned by its members, who therefore benefit from any profits made by the organisation (as opposed to an incorporated body, which is owned by its shareholders who generally expect to receive a share of profits in the form of dividends).

National Insurance Basically, a tax on earnings from employment (and profits from self-employment), but payment of enough contributions of the appropriate type entitles you to receive certain state benefits, such as a state basic pension (see below) or incapacity benefit (see above).

National Savings★ Deposit-based investments issued by the government.

Nominee account An arrangement, for example run by a stockbroker, whereby shares or other assets which you buy are not held directly by you but are held in the name of a nominee or trustee company. Shares held in a personal equity plan (see below) are held in nominee accounts. Such accounts are also becoming more widespread since the introduction of five-day trading (see above) and Crest (see above).

Non-taxpayer Someone whose tax allowances and any other deductions exceed the amount of his or her income which would otherwise be taxable.

Occupational Pensions Advisory Service (OPAS)★ A scheme, funded by the government, to help resolve misunderstandings and disputes between pension schemes and their members or pension plan providers and their planholders. If this system of advice and conciliation fails, the dispute can be referred to the Pensions Ombudsman.★

Off-the-page advertisement An advertisement which incorporates an application form and invites you to invest directly in response to the advertisement.

OPAS Abbreviation for the Occupational Pensions Advisory Service (see above).

Open-ended investment company (OEIC) Investment similar to a unit trust, but you buy shares in the OEIC. Shares are bought and sold at a single price and charges are shown separately.

Options A contract which lets you speculate about future price movements of shares (or other assets) by giving you the option to buy or sell the shares at a set price on or before a given date. You do not have to buy or sell the shares (called 'exercising the option'). You can simply let the option expire without taking any action. Alternatively, if it is a 'traded option', you can sell it on the stock market. Unlike futures (see above), where you can lose more than you invest, the most you can lose with an option is the amount of your original investment.

Ordinary shares Usually the largest class of shares (see below) issued by a company. Ordinary shareholders have no special rights to receive dividends but, in a well-established company, dividends are usually paid twice a year.

Payment protection insurance See credit insurance.

Pension A regular income, usually paid for life.

Pension-linked term insurance Term insurance (see below) taken out under the rules applying to either personal pension plans (see below) or retirement annuity contracts (see below). There is a limit on the amount you can pay in premiums, but you can claim tax relief at your highest rate on what you pay.

Pension mortgage A personal pension plan (see below) taken out simultaneously with a mortgage of a given term. During the life of the mortgage, you pay only interest on the loan. The idea is that the loan itself should be repaid out of the tax-free lump sum produced by the pension plan once you start to take the pension. The tax treatment of pensions makes this a very tax-efficient type of mortgage.

Pensions Registry★ A body set up by the government to keep a register of all occupational and personal pension schemes in order to help people trace pensions they have lost track of: for example, because a former employer has changed hands.

Pension transfer Moving your pension rights from one pension scheme or plan to another. In most cases this alters the package of benefits, so it is important carefully to compare what is on offer under each arrangement.

PEP Abbreviation for personal equity plan (see below).

PEP mortgage A mortgage (see above) of a given term (usually 25 years) linked to a personal equity plan (see below). During the life of the mortgage, you pay only interest on the loan. Simultaneously, you pay regularly into a PEP which you hope will build up a large enough fund to repay the capital at the end of the mortgage term.

Permanent health insurance (PHI) Insurance which replaces part of your income if you are unable to work because of illness or disability. 'Permanent' in the rather confusing name for this insurance refers to the fact that once an insurance company has accepted you for this type of insurance, it cannot turn you down, or load your premium, in subsequent years just because you claim against the policy. (Premium increases for other reasons are allowed but will apply to all, or a whole group of, policyholders and not just an individual.)

Permanent income-bearing shares (PIBS) Bonds issued by building societies which can be traded on the stock market. They pay interest at regular intervals. They have no redemption date, so the only way to get your capital back is to sell the bonds on the stock market, and this may result in a capital gain or a capital loss.

Personal equity plan (PEP) Tax-efficient scheme for investing in shares (see below), unit trusts (see below), investment trusts (see above) and corporate bonds (see above).

Personal Investment Authority (PIA)★ The Self-Regulating Organisation★ responsible for policing most investment businesses which deal with the general public: for example, insurance companies, unit trust companies and financial advisers.

Personal pension plan Money-purchase pension arrangement run by an insurance company, friendly society (see above), unit trust (see below), building society (see above) or bank. It aims to provide you with a pension at retirement and possibly other benefits. Unlike an employer's pension scheme (see above), a personal pension plan need not be connected with a specific job.

PET Abbreviation for potentially exempt transfer (see below).

PHI Abbreviation for permanent health insurance (see above).

PIA Abbreviation for Personal Investment Authority (see above).

PIBS Abbreviation for permanent income-bearing shares (see above).

PMI Abbreviation for private medical insurance (see below).

Policyholders' Protection Scheme A scheme set up under the Policyholders' Protection Act 1975 to compensate people who lose money on insurance policies (or personal pension plans offered by insurance companies), if their insurance company goes out of business. Compensation is limited to 90 per cent of reasonable benefits.

Positive licensing The process of granting a licence enabling someone to undertake some activity but only if they first meet given criteria: for example, they are fit and proper, have adequate resources, reach a minimum level of competence, and so on.

Potentially exempt transfer (PET) In the context of inheritance tax, a lifetime gift which is tax-free provided the person making the gift survives for seven years; otherwise, there might be a tax bill at the time the giver dies.

Pre-existing condition In the context of health insurance, a health problem which you have at the time you apply for insurance.

Preference shares Shares (see below) in a company which carry the right to receive dividends (if they are paid) ahead of any dividends paid to ordinary shareholders (see above). With 'cumulative' preference shares, any dividends failed to be paid must be carried forward and paid in arrears before ordinary shareholders receive anything. Similarly, if the company goes out of business, the preference shareholders receive their share of any assets before the ordinary shareholders (but after creditors, including corporate bondholders; see above).

Premium In the context of insurance, the amount you pay for cover or contribute to investment-type insurance.

Pre-paid funeral plan An arrangement offered by some firms of funeral directors whereby you pay either a lump sum immediately or a series of payments over, say, five years to buy a specified funeral package. The firm invests the money to ensure that enough funds will be available at the time of your death to pay for the chosen funeral. Despite this element, these plans do not count as investments under the Financial Services Act 1986 and are largely unregulated.

Private medical insurance (PMI) Insurance to pay part or all of the cost of private treatment if you need to go into hospital, provided your condition is one of those covered by the policy.

Professional indemnity insurance Insurance, which independent financial advisers (see above) are required to take out, to pay to customers if those customers lose money because of fraud or negligence on the part of the investment firm and the firm itself has insufficient assets to pay the compensation.

PTM levy Small additional charge made on large purchases or sales of shares. It is used to fund the Panel on Takeovers and Mergers (PTM), an unofficial watchdog which aims to ensure fair play for all shareholders when companies are being taken over or merging.

Purchased life annuity An annuity (see above) which you choose to buy (as opposed to an annuity which must be bought under the terms of a pension arrangement).

Recognised Professional Bodies (RPBs)★ Certain professional bodies, covering lawyers, accountants and actuaries, which are allowed to regulate the investment business of their members instead of those members having to join a Self-Regulating Organisation★ (see below).

Redeemable Describes investments, particularly bonds, where your original investment is repaid at some specified future date (or at some date yet to be announced within a specified time period).

Renewable term insurance Term insurance (see below) which guarantees that you can take out a further term insurance policy at the end of the original term. The further policy will be based on your health at the time you took out the original policy, even if it has worsened in the meantime.

Repayment mortgage A mortgage (see above), during the term of which you gradually pay off both the interest and the capital. Monthly payments are set at a level which ensures that you owe nothing by the end of the mortgage term.

Retirement annuity contract Type of personal pension plan (see above) on offer before 1 July 1988. People taking out contracts before that date can continue to contribute towards them; otherwise, these contracts have been superseded by personal pension plans.

RPB Abbreviation for Recognised Professional Body (see above).

Securities and Futures Authority (SFA)★ The Self-Regulating Organisation★ responsible for investment businesses dealing with marketable investments, such as shares (see below), corporate bonds (see above), options (see above) and futures (see above).

Securities and Investments Board (SIB)★ The self-regulating body, until October 1997, at the top of the structure created by the Financial Services Act 1986. It was responsible for the activities of the Self-Regulating Organisations★ (see below) and broad regulatory policy. It also itself authorised a few investment businesses. In October 1997 all its functions were transferred to the new Financial Services Authority (FSA)★ – see above.

Self-Regulating Organisations (SROs)★ Set up under the Financial Services Act 1986, these are the bodies directly responsible for policing investment businesses. It is a criminal offence for an investment business to operate without being a member of an SRO, a Recognised Professional Body★ (see above) or the Financial Services Authority (see above). The FSA is due to take over the roles of the SROs by 1999.

SERPS Abbreviation for State Earnings-Related Pension Scheme (see below).

SFA Abbreviation for the Securities and Futures Authority (see above).

Shares Shares represent slices in the ownership of a company. Depending on the type of shares, you may have the right to vote on decisions about the running of the company and you may receive a regular share of the profits in the form of dividends. By trading shares, you also stand to make a capital gain or loss, depending on the prices at which you buy and sell.

SIB Abbreviation for the Securities and Investments Board (see above).

Sickness and accident insurance A combination of two types of insurance: accident insurance pays out a lump sum if you suffer certain specified injuries, such as loss of a limb or loss of sight; sickness insurance pays a weekly cash sum for a maximum period – for example, two years – if you are unable to work because of short-term illness. Unlike permanent health insurance (see above), sickness insurance policies last just one year and there is no guarantee that you will be accepted for cover in subsequent years if, for example, you have a record of frequent claims.

Single-premium life insurance bond An investment-type life insurance, usually unit-linked (see below), which can be used either to build up a lump sum or to provide a regular 'income'. The latter option can be attractive for higher-rate taxpayers (see above), because tax rules allow you to take a limited sum from the bond each year while putting off any tax until the bond is finally cashed in (by which time you might no longer be a higher-rate taxpayer).

Six-week waiting plan In the context of private medical insurance (see above), a policy which will cover the cost of private treatment if the waiting list for NHS treatment is longer than six weeks.

Small self-administered pension scheme Type of employer's pension scheme (see above) sometimes set up by small companies.

Social Fund Part of the Department of Social Security★ benefits structure. The Social Fund can make grants and loans – for example, to buy essential equipment, such as a cooker – to people eligible for income support (see above) and certain other state benefits. However, there is an annual cash limit on the total fund, so there is no guarantee that even the most needy requests can be met.

Spread Term used to describe the difference between the prices at which you can buy and sell investments such as shares, unit trusts and bonds.

SRO Abbreviation for Self-Regulating Organisation (see above).

SSP Abbreviation for Statutory Sick Pay (see below).

Stakeholder pension New type of pension plan due to be introduced by the government. At the time of writing, no details had been decided, but the pensions are intended to be low cost and flexible.

State basic pension Flat-rate pension from the state, to which you are entitled if you (or, in some cases, your husband) pay enough National Insurance contributions (see above) of the right type over your working life (see below).

State Earnings-Related Pension Scheme (SERPS) Paid on top of the state basic pension (see above), employees can build up an entitlement to SERPS by paying National Insurance contributions (see above) on part of their earnings. Introduced in 1978, this part of the state pension has been progressively reduced. Many people are 'contracted out' (see above) of the SERPS pension and instead build up a pension through an employer's pension scheme (see above) or personal pension plan (see above).

State graduated pension An old state earnings-related pension scheme which ran from 1961 to 1975. Pensions under this scheme are very small.

Statutory Sick Pay A minimum income which must, by law, be paid to you by your employer if you are unable to work because of short-term illness and you earn more than the lower earnings limit (see above).

Stockbroker Someone who buys and sells shares and other stock market investments on your behalf. The stockbroker acts as your agent, carrying out your instructions, and in return you pay him or her commission either at a flat rate or as a percentage of the value of the deal.

Surrender value The amount of cash you will receive if you stop an investment-type insurance policy early. The impact of charges often means that payouts in the early years are less than you have paid in premiums, or even nothing at all.

Taxable gain For capital gains tax purposes (see above), the gain or profit which remains after all allowances have been taken into account, on which tax is due.

Taxable income Loosely used to mean income which you get without any tax having been deducted and which will be taxed unless you have unused allowances or other deductions to set against it. More technically, taxable income is the income which remains to be taxed after allowances and other deductions have been taken into account.

Tax-Exempt Special Savings Account (TESSA) Deposit-based investments, designed to run for five years, offered by banks and building societies (see above). Provided certain rules are met, the interest earned is completely tax-free.

Tax year Runs from 6 April in one year to 5 April in the following year.

Term insurance Type of life insurance which pays out a cash sum (or series of cash sums in the case of a family income benefit policy; see above) if you die within a specified period of time (the 'term'). If you survive the term, the policy pays out nothing.

TESSA Abbreviation for Tax-Exempt Special Savings Account (see above).

Tied agent In the context of the Financial Services Act 1986, a person or firm which advises on and sells the products of a single life insurance company or unit trust group.

The Treasury A government department responsible, among other things, for the operation of the Financial Services Act 1986.

Underwrite The process of setting an insurance premium, taking into account all the known facts – about your health, job, hobbies, and so on – which are thought to affect the risk of the policy having to pay out.

Unit-linked Describes an investment-type insurance or pension plan whose return depends directly upon the performance of an underlying fund of investments, such as shares (see above) or gilts (see above).

Unit trust A fund of investments in which you invest by buying units. The price of the units varies in line with the value of the investments in the fund.

Variable rate mortgage A mortgage (see above) whose interest rate is not fixed and tends to go up and down in line with interest rates in the economy as a whole.

Waiver of premium An option (for which you usually pay extra) with a regular-premium insurance policy, under which the company pays the premiums for you for a maximum period – for example, one or two years – if you are unable to work because of illness.

Whole-of-life insurance A type of life insurance which, rather than running for a fixed term, provides cover until you die whenever that will be. Because the policy will inevitably pay out at some time, it builds up a cash value and so can be used for investment purposes.

With-profits Describes an investment-type insurance or pension plan whose return is in the form of bonuses which depend on profits made by the insurer. Many factors influence the level of bonuses, including the return the insurer gets on investing premiums, cost levels, claims experience, whether there are shareholders who receive part of the profits, and the extent to which the company tries to smooth bonus levels from one year to the next.

With-profits guide Written information about the factors influencing an insurer's bonus levels for with-profits insurance and pensions which must be provided, if you ask for it, before, or soon after, a person takes out such a policy or plan.

Working life For the purpose of state basic pension entitlements (see above), working life is defined officially as the tax years from the one in which you reach the age of 16 to the last complete tax year before you reach the state pension age.

Zero coupon bond A fixed-interest investment such as corporate bond (see above) or gilt strip (see above), which offers you only the prospect of capital gain at some given date and no income.

Addresses

Association of British Insurers (ABI)
51 Gresham Street
London EC2V 7HQ
Tel: 0171-600 3333
Fax: 0171-696 8996
Web site: http://www.abi.org.uk

Association of Chartered Certified Accountants
29 Lincoln's Inn Fields
London WC2A 3EE
Tel: 0171-242 6855 (*general enquiries*)
    0171-396 5900 (*members*)
Fax: 0171-831 8054 (*general enquiries*)
    0171-396 5959 (*members*)
Email: services.enquiries@acca.co.uk
Web site: http://www.acca.co.uk

Association of Consulting Actuaries
1 Wardrobe Place
London EC4V 5AH
Tel: 0171-248 3163
Fax: 0171-236 1889
Web site: http://www.aca.org.uk

Association of Investment Trust Companies (AITC)
Durrant House, 8–13 Chiswell Street
London EC1Y 4YY
Tel: 0171-431 5222
Fax: 0171-282 5556
Web site: http://www.iii.co.uk/aitc

Association of Private Client Investment Managers and Stockbrokers (APCIMS)
112 Middlesex Street
London E1 7HY
(*written enquiries only*)
Web site: http://www.apcims.org

Association of Unit Trusts and Investment Funds (AUTIF)
65 Kingsway
London WC2B 6TD
Tel: 0181-207 1361 (*unit trust information service, 8am to 11pm daily*)
Fax: 0171-831 9975

Bank of England
Threadneedle Street
London EC2R 8AH
Tel: 0171-601 4878 (*public enquiries*)
Fax: 0171-601 5771
Web site:
http://www.bankofengland.co.uk

For prospectuses for new issues of British Government stocks:
Bank of England
Registrar's Department
Southgate House, Southgate Street
Gloucester GL1 1WW
Tel: (01452) 398000
Fax: (01452) 398020

Banking Ombudsman
70 Gray's Inn Road
London WC1X 8NB

Tel: (0345) 660902
Fax: 0171-405 5052
Web site:
http://www.interrid.co.uk/obo

Benefits Agency
See Department of Social Security

Building Societies Commission
Victory House, 30–34 Kingsway
London WC2B 6ES
Tel: 0171-663 5000
Fax: 0171-663 5060

Building Societies Ombudsman
35–37 Grosvenor Gardens
London SW1X 7AW
Tel: 0171-931 0044
Fax: 0171-931 8485

Chartered Institute of Arbitrators
24 Angel Gate, City Road
London EC1V 2RS
Tel: 0171-837 4483
Fax: 0171-837 4185
Email:
71411.2735@compuserve.com
Web site: http://www.arbitrators.org

Citizens Advice Bureau (CAB)
For your local branch, look in the telephone directory under 'Citizens Advice
Bureau' or check the advertisements in
your local newspaper

**The Complaints Bureau and
Arbitration Scheme (SFA)**
Cottons Centre, Cottons Lane
London SE1 2QB
Tel: 0171-378 9000
Fax: 0171-403 7569
Web site: http://www.sfa.org.uk

Council of Mortgage Lenders (CML)
3 Savile Row, London W1X 1AF
Tel: 0171-437 0655
    0171-440 2255 (recorded consumer
information line)
Fax: 0171-734 6416

Department for National Savings
See National Savings

**Department of Social Security
(DSS)/Benefits Agency**
For your local office, look in the telephone
directory under 'Social Security,
Department of' or 'Benefits Agency'

DSS Leaflets
From your local DSS office, some post
offices, some public libraries, or from:
BA Storage and Distribution Centre
Manchester Road, Heywood
Lancashire OL10 2PZ

**Department of Trade and Industry
(Insurance Directorate)**
1 Victoria Street
London SW1H 0ET
Tel: 0171-215 0200
Fax: 0171-215 0196

Deposit Protection Scheme
19 Old Jewry
London EC2R 8HA
Tel: 0171-601 3050
Fax: 0171-601 3019

Fax services
If you have access to a fax machine you
can obtain financial information by faxing
the number given and pressing 'Start' at
the prompt. Calls are charged at premium
rate. The number of pages is shown for
guidance only and may change.

Moneyfacts – selected fax services
(50p a minute at all times)
Residential mortgages selection
(7 pages)
(0336) 400239
Savings selection (8 pages)
(0336) 400238
Guaranteed income bonds (4 pages)
(0336) 400240
National Savings (3 pages)
(0336) 400241
Term insurance premiums (6 pages)
(0336) 400853

Purchased life annuities (5 pages)
(0336) 400235
Compulsory purchase annuities
(5 pages)
(0336) 400236
Low-cost share-dealing services
(6 pages)
(0336) 400245
Unit trusts (4 pages)
(0336) 400855

Financial Adviser – selected fax
services (around £1.50 a minute)
Top five fixed-rate mortgages
(0897) 439411
Top five discount mortgages
(0897) 439412
Top five standard variable-rate
mortgages
(0897) 439413
Top five capped mortgages
(0897) 439414
Top five cashback mortgages
(0897) 439415
Top five first-time buyer mortgages
(0897) 439417
Compulsory purchase annuities for
men
(0897) 439401
Compulsory purchase annuities for
women
(0897) 439402
Compulsory purchase annuities for
joint lives
(0897) 439403
Purchased life annuities for men
(0897) 439404
Purchased life annuities for women
(0897) 439405
Purchased life annuities for joint
lives
(0897) 439406

Investment trusts – *UK and Europe*
(0891) 437071

Office for National Statistics, Retail Prices
Index
(0336) 416037

Financial Services Authority (FSA)
Gavrelle House
2–14 Bunhill Row
London EC1Y 8RA
Tel: 0171-638 1240
    0171-929 3652 (*FSA Register*
    enquiries)
Fax: 0171-382 5900
Web site: http://www.fsa.gov.uk

FSA Enquiries Unit
Tel: (0845) 6061234

Friendly Societies Commission
Victory House
30–34 Kingsway
London WC2B 6ES
Tel: 0171-663 5000
Fax: 0171-663 5060

Funeral Ombudsman Scheme
26–28 Bedford Row
London WC1R 4HL
Tel: 0171-430 1112
Fax: 0171-430 1012

Funeral Planning Council (FPC)
Melville House, 70 Drymen Road
Bearsden, Glasgow G61 2RP
Tel: 0141-942 5855
Fax: 0141-942 2323

IFA Promotion
17–19 Emery Road
Brislington
Bristol BS4 5PF
For a list of independent financial advisers
in your area
Tel: 0117-971 1177
Fax: 0117-972 4509

IFAs specialising in annuities

The Annuity Bureau
Enterprise House
59–65 Upper Ground
London SE1 9PQ
Tel: 0171-620 4090
Fax: 0171-261 1888
Email: peter@annuity-bureau.co.uk

Annuity Direct
27 Paul Street
London EC2A 4JU
Tel: 0171-588 9393
Fax: 0171-684 5001

Incorporated Society of Valuers and Auctioneers (ISVA)
3 Cadogan Gate
London SW1X 0AS
Tel: 0171-235 2282
Fax: 0171-235 4390
Email: hq@isva.co.uk
Web site: http://www.isva.co.uk

Inland Revenue tax offices and enquiry centres
For your local office, look in the telephone directory under 'Inland Revenue'
Web site: http://www.open.gov.uk

Inland Revenue Capital Taxes Office

England and Wales
Ferrers House
PO Box 38
Castle Meadow Road
Nottingham NG2 1BB
Tel: 0115-974 2400
Fax: 0115-974 2432

Scotland
Mulberry House
16 Picardy Place
Edinburgh EH1 3NF
Tel: 0131-556 8511
Fax: 0131-557 2886

Northern Ireland
Dorchester House
52–58 Great Victoria Street
Belfast BT2 7QL
Tel: (01232) 315556
Fax: (01232) 331001

Institute of Actuaries
Staple Inn Hall
High Holborn
London WC1V 7QJ
Tel: 0171-242 0106

Fax: 0171-405 2482
Email: institute@actuaries.org.uk
Web site: http://actuaries.org.uk

Institute of Chartered Accountants in England and Wales
PO Box 433
Chartered Accountants' Hall
Moorgate Place
London EC2P 2BJ
Tel: 0171-920 8100
Fax: 0171-920 0547
Web site: http://www.icaew.co.uk

Institute of Chartered Accountants in Ireland
Chartered Accountants' House
87–89 Pembroke Road
Dublin 4
Republic of Ireland
Tel: (00 353) 1 668 0400
Web site: http://www.icai.ie

Institute of Chartered Accountants of Scotland
27 Queen Street
Edinburgh EH2 1LA
Tel: 0131-225 5673
Fax: 0131-225 3813
Web site: http://www.icas.org.uk

Insurance Brokers Registration Council (IBRC)
63 St Mary Axe
London EC3A 8NB
Tel: 0171-621 1061
Fax: 0171-621 0840

Insurance Ombudsman Bureau
Citygate One
135 Park Street
London SE1 9EA
Tel: 0171-928 7600
Fax: 0171-902 8197

Investment Managers Regulatory Organisation (IMRO)
Lloyd's Chambers
1 Portsoken Street
London E1 8BT

Tel: 0171-390 5000
Fax: 0171-680 0550
Web site: http://www.imro.co.uk

Investment Ombudsman
6 Frederick's Place
London EC2R 8BT
Tel: 0171-796 3065
Fax: 0171-726 0574

**Investors Compensation Scheme
(ICS)**
Gavrelle House
2–14 Bunhill Row
London EC1Y 8RA
Tel: 0171-628 8820
Fax: 0171-382 5901

The Law Society
113 Chancery Lane
London WC2A 1PL
Tel: 0171-242 1222
Call for relevant fax number
Web site:
http://www.lawsociety.org.uk

The Law Society of Northern Ireland
Law Society House
98 Victoria Street
Belfast BT1 3JZ
Tel: (01232) 231614
Fax: (01232) 232606

The Law Society of Scotland
Law Society Hall
26 Drumsheugh Gardens
Edinburgh EH3 7YR
Tel: 0131-226 7411
Fax: 0171-225 2934
Email: lawscot@lawscot.org.uk

Micropal
Web site: http://www.micropal.com

**Money Management National Register
of Independent Fee-based Advisers**
c/o Matrix Data Ltd
FREEPOST 22 (SW1565)
London W1E 7EZ
Tel: 0117-976 9444

Mortgage Code Arbitration Scheme
Chartered Institute of Arbitrators
24 Angel Gate, City Road
London EC1V 2RS
Tel: 0171-837 4483
Fax: 0171-837 4185
Email:
71411.2735@compuserve.com
Web site: http://www.arbitrators.org

National Association of Estate Agents
Arbon House, 21 Jury Street
Warwick CV34 4EH
Tel: (01926) 496800
Fax: (01926) 400953
Email: nea@dial.pipex.com
Web site:
http://www.propertylive.co.uk

**National Association of Pre-paid
Funeral Plans (NAPFP)**
618 Warwick Road
Solihull
West Midlands B91 1AA
Tel: 0121-711 1343
Fax: 0121-711 1351

National Debtline
Birmingham Settlement
318 Summer Lane
Birmingham B19 3RL
Tel: 0121-359 8501

National Savings
Sales Information Unit
FREEPOST BJ881
Lytham St Anne's
Lancashire FT0 1BR
Tel: (0645) 645000 (*calls charged at
local rate*)

Interest rates:
London 0171-605 9483
Blackpool (01253) 723714
Glasgow 0141-632 2766

**Occupational Pensions Advisory
Service (OPAS)**
11 Belgrave Road
London SW1V 1RB

Tel: 0171-233 8080
Fax: 0171-233 8016
Email: cd83@iclnet.co.uk.opas

**Occupational Pensions Regulatory
Authority (OPRA)**
Invicta House
Trafalgar Place
Brighton
East Sussex BN1 4DW
Tel: (01273) 627600
Fax: (01273) 627688
Email: helpdesk@opra.co.uk
Web site: http://www.opra.co.uk

**Ombudsman for Corporate Estate
Agents**
Beckett House
4 Bridge Street
Salisbury
Wiltshire SP1 2LX
Tel: (01722) 333306
Fax: (01722) 332296

Pensions Ombudsman
*You must first let OPAS try to resolve the
problem*
11 Belgrave Road
London SW1V 1RB
Tel: 0171-834 9144
Fax: 0171-821 0065

Pensions Schemes Registry
Occupational Pensions Regulatory
Authority
PO Box 1NN
Newcastle upon Tyne
Tyne and Wear NE99 1NN
Tel: 0191-225 6393
Fax: 0191-225 6390 (*A–JE by scheme
name*)
0191-225 6391 (*JF–Z by scheme
name*)
Web site: http://www.opra.co.uk

**Personal Insurance Arbitration
Service (PIAS)**
Chartered Institute of Arbitrators
24 Angel Gate, City Road
London EC1V 2RS

Tel: 0171-837 4483
Fax: 0171-837 4185
Email:
71411.2735@compuserve.com

Personal Investment Authority (PIA)
1 Canada Square
Canary Wharf
London E14 5AZ
Tel: 0171-538 8860
Fax: 0171-418 9300

**Personal Investment Authority (PIA)
Ombudsman**
Hertsmere House
Hertsmere Road
London E14 4AB
Tel: 0171-216 0016
Fax: 0171-895 8579

ProShare UK Ltd
13–14 Basinghall Street
London EC2V 5BQ
Tel: 0171-600 0984
Fax: 0171-600 0947
Web site:
http://www.proshare.org.uk

**Recognised Professional Bodies
(RPBs)**
See separate entries for:
    **Association of Chartered Certified
    Accountants**
    Institute of Actuaries
    the three **Institutes of Chartered
    Accountants**
    **Insurance Brokers Registration
    Council**
    the three **Law Societies**

Registry of Friendly Societies
Victory House
30–34 Kingsway
London WC2B 6ES
Tel: 0171-663 5000
Fax: 0171-663 5060

**Royal Institute of Chartered
Surveyors (RICS)**
12 Great George Street

Parliament Square
London SW1P 3AD
Tel: 0171-222 7000
Fax: 0171-222 9430
Web site: http://www.rics.org.uk

Safe Home Income Plans (SHIP)
The following companies are members of
SHIP

Allchurches Life Assurance Ltd
EIG Group plc
Beaufort House, Brunswick Road
Gloucester GL1 1JZ
Tel: (01452) 526265
Fax: (01452) 423557

Carlyle Life Assurance Company Ltd
21 Windsor Place
Cardiff CF1 3BY
Tel: (01222) 371725
Fax: (01222) 664440

Hinton & Wild (Home Plans) Ltd
(founder Cecil Hinton is secretary of
SHIP)
374–378 Ewell Road
Surbiton
Surrey KT6 7BB
Tel: 0181-390 8166
Fax: 0181-399 3461

Home & Capital Trust Ltd
31 Goldington Road
Bedford MK40 3LH
Tel: (01234) 340511
Fax: (01234) 271547
Email:
sales@homeandcapital.demon.co.uk
Web site:
http://www.homeandcapital.co.uk

Stalwart Assurance Company Ltd
Stalwart House
Station Road
Dorking Business Park
Surrey RH4 1HL
Tel: (0800) 378921
Fax: (01306) 808717

Securities and Futures Authority
(SFA)
Cottons Centre, Cottons Lane
London SE1 2QB
Tel: 0171-378 9000
Fax: 0171-403 7569
Web site: http://www.sfa.gov.uk

Self-Regulating Organisations
(SROs)
See separate entries for:
   Investment Managers Regulatory
   Organisation (IMRO)
   Personal Investment Authority
   (PIA)
   Securities and Futures Authority
   (FSA)

Society of Pension Consultants
St Bartholomew House
92 Fleet Street
London EC4Y 1DH
(*written enquiries only*)

PUBLICATIONS
Inclusion in this list of publications in no
way constitutes an endorsement by
Consumers' Association or Which?, except
in relation to its own publications

Chase de Vere PEP Guide
Chase de Vere Investments plc
FREEPOST
Bristol BS38 7JX
Tel: (0800) 526092

The Estimate Directory
Edinburgh Financial Publishing
3rd Floor, 124–125 Princes Street
Edinburgh EH2 4BD
Tel: 0131-473 7070
Fax: 0131-473 7080
Email: a.white@efp.com

The Hambro Company Guide
Hemmington Scott Publishing
City Innovation Centre
26–31 Whiskin Street
London EC1R 0BP
Tel: 0171-278 7769

Fax: 0171-278 9808
Web site: http://www.hemscott.co.uk

Investment Trusts
Subscriptions
PO Box 222, Woking
GU21 1FQ
Tel: (01483) 733894
*(published by Flaxdale Printers Ltd;
also available from newsagents)*

Investors Chronicle
Subscriptions/back issues
FT Finance
PO Box 387
Haywards Heath
West Sussex RH16 3GS
Tel: (01444) 445520
Fax: (01444) 445599

Moneyfacts
Subscriptions Department
Laundry Loke
North Walsham
Norfolk NR28 0BD
Tel: (01692) 500765
Fax: (01692) 500865
Email: mfacts@dircon.co.uk

Money Management
Subscriptions/back issues
FT Finance
PO Box 387
Haywards Heath
West Sussex RH16 3GS
Tel: (01444) 445520
Fax: (01444) 445599

Money Observer
Subscription enquiries:
Tel: 0181-289 7960

Moneywise
Reader's Digest
11 Westferry Circus
Canary Wharf

London E14 4HE
Tel: (01858) 435366 *(subscriptions)*
Fax: (01858) 432164
Web site:
http://www.Moneywise.co.uk

Pensions Management
Subscriptions/back issues
FT Finance
PO Box 387
Haywards Heath
West Sussex RH16 3GS
Tel: (01444) 445520
Fax: (01444) 445599

Planned Savings
33–39 Bowling Green Lane
London EC1R 0DA
Tel: 0171-505 8000
Fax: 0171-505 8186

**Standard & Poors UK Life Financial
Strength Digest**
Garden House
18 Finsbury Circus
London EC2M 7BP
Tel: 0171-826 3581
Fax: 0171-826 3590

What Mortgage
Charterhouse Communications
Group Ltd
3rd Floor, 4–8 Tabernacle Street
London EC2A 4LU
Tel: 0171-638 1916
Fax: 0171-638 3128
Email: chartcom@dircon.co.uk

Which? and Which? Books
FREEPOST
PO Box 44
Hertford X, SG14 1YB
Tel: (0800) 252100
Fax: (0800) 533053
Web site: http://www.which.net/

Index